MAKING INDIA GREAT AGAIN: LEARNING FROM OUR HISTORY

Making India Great Again: Learning from our History

MEETA AND RAJIVLOCHAN

MANOHAR
2026

First published 2020, 2021

Reprinted 2022, 2023, 2025, 2026

This edition is for sale in India, Sri Lanka, Nepal, Bangladesh, Afghanistan, Pakistan and Bhutan

ISBN 978-93-90035-20-5

Published by
Ajay Kumar Jain *for*
Manohar Publishers & Distributors
4753/23 Ansari Road, Daryaganj
New Delhi 110 002

Typeset by
Kohli Print
Delhi 110 051

Printed at
Replika Press Pvt. Ltd.

To our parents,
Rama and Awadh Bihari Sharma,
Chitra and Surender Kumar Jain,
who lived through the early years of independence
and constantly talked of their vision of India
of the future

Contents

List of Figures

List of Tables

Acknowledgements

This book was written because students were asking too many questions that could not be answered in brief or by reference to existing books.

The students at the Department of History, Panjab University, especially from the course on the History of Trade and Industry and the students at the Institute of Social Science Education and Research at PU, deserve special thanks for their questions and inquisitveness. We are grateful to the students from the University Business School at Panjab University who raised queries in history which did not have any answers in existing monographs. We are also grateful to the students of the e-Yantra Project run by Professor Kavi Arya at the Computer Science and Engineering Department, IIT-Bombay. They raised questions about history that could only be answered with some clarity by linking history with India's contemporary concerns. Professor Arya was kind enough to deliberate upon much of what is written here whenever we met up during our walks along the Marine Drive. We also benefited from the long interaction under the aegis of Chetana, with people from various walks of life, that Professor Arya organized. Interactions with students of the Punjab Engineering College, Chandigarh, through their NSS programme too helped shape the ideas that form the arguments of this book. Presentations at the Lal Bahadur Shastri National Academy of Administration to the Officer Trainees of the IAS and allied services helped fine tune many of the points made here.

Professor Ishan Sharma of the Department of Mechanical Engineering, IIT Kanpur, took out his valuable time to give incisive comments and suggestions.

Ravi Venkatesan, former Chairman, Microsoft India; Vishwanath Giriraj, Chairman, Maharashtra State Finance Commission; Kalpana Awasthi, Principal Secretary, Government of Uttar Pradesh; Dhaval Desai of the Observer Research Foundation; Sayli Udas Mankikar, Observer Research Foundation; Kaushik Chatterjee, Psychiatrist, Indian Navy, were kind enough to read parts and provide detailed comments. Vithal C. Nadkarni, formerly of the *Times of India*, Ravi Budhiraja, formerly of the IAS and Sudhir Srivastava, Chairman, Maharashtra Pollution Control Board, provided much moral support and feedback.

Ramachandran Nagaswamy, historian and Founder Director of the Tamil Nadu Archaeology Department and Prashant Kulkarni spent much time discussing numismatics with us and helped clarify many otherwise arcane matters.

Vikram Singh Bhati, Rajasthani Shodh Sansthan, Chopasani, Jodhpur provided especially useful comments on the literature of Marwar. Babai Nath, Technical Superintendent at Weavers Service Centre, Kolkata shared his knowledge of handloom weaving techniques, past and present, in Bengal.

Many others were extraordinarily generous with their time and insights. These included Vasant Shinde, Vice-Chancellor, Deccan College Post Graduate and Research Institute Pune; Jonathan Nitzan, Department of Political Science, York University, Toronto; Ujjayan Bhattacharya of Vidyasagar University, Midnapore, West Bengal; Farhat Hasan of Delhi University, Delhi; Praveen Kumar, Principal Scientist, Central Arid Zone Research Institute, Jodhpur; Ananya Vajpeyi of Centre for the Study of Developing Societies, Delhi and her circle of scholarly friends; Vinish Kathuria, SJM School of Management, IIT Bombay; O.P. Gupta, Controller General of Patents, Designs and Trademarks, Government of India; K.P. Sunny of the National Productivity Council.

Dr. Rajkumar, the then Librarian of A.C. Joshi Library, Panjab University, and his friendly and ever helpful staff ensured excellent library support as did the Librarian and staff of the Asiatic Library, Mumbai.

Ashvini Agarwal spent much time with us on matters of history. We have learnt a lot from him in our interactions spread over three decades. Paramjit Judge, read the various drafts and insisted on clarity of thought and expression.

Nikhil and Rashi Jain, Mudita Jain, Udit Vinayak and Abhay Vikram were, as usual, kind with their time and moral support as also in critiquing whatever we wrote.

Needless to say, we are fully responsible for any errors. Also, our respective employers do not necessarily share our views.

Introduction
What Prevents India from Becoming Rich Again

INDIA RICH BY DEFAULT AND NOT BY DESIGN

India has a past rich in natural resources, artisanal skills and entrepreneurship. Now that colonial rule is firmly and finally behind us, why do we find it so difficult to pick up the pieces? This remains a puzzle. One missing piece of the puzzle is lack of institutionalized state support to business ventures. Might a second piece be a certain inability to systematize information? After all, whether it is taxation, fighting battles or doing business and making money, it is a superior quality of information that would decide who might win and who finally loses. The Indian encounter with the English East India Company in the seventeenth and eighteenth centuries is important in that it shows both missing pieces. It was not superior technology nor a greater access to capital that gave the company decisive advantage over local rulers and merchants. Those advantages were generated by superior record keeping, a high quality of information for better decision-making and the knowledge that trading produces more profits when protected by the authority of the state. For India, poor information systems and absence of state support to business generated the conditions that led to colonialism. Both factors continue to be an Achilles heel for India even in the twenty first century.

For many centuries India had been rich by default and not by design. Richly blessed with a fertile soil, forests full of teakwood and ivory, diamonds and rubies, pepper that was known to the Romans as black gold to name only a few things; it exported products worth millions in the currency of the times. The artisans of India wove silk so fine it could pass through rings and ironmongers made the famous steel known to the world as 'Damascus steel'. Blessed in the riches that nature had provided, with some skills in working metal and weaving cloth, Indians lived an apparently happy enough life, content in a lifestyle that needed barely six months of toil to sustain it. It is not surprising then that Indians felt little need to increase their affluence or to wonder unduly about how other people got rich.

It was the fabled riches of India that drew the various East India companies to the country, to make their fortunes. Indians lived and did business with Europeans in these companies for one hundred and fifty years before the battle of Plassey. The European companies and their officials made plenty of money from the Indian experience. We welcomed these people as India had always welcomed foreigners and foreign traders. Still, the fortunes Indian businessmen made from the European encounter were short-term profits. So also were the profits made by Indian rulers. What we do not find is any realization on their part that the Europeans brought with them a substantially different perspective on the world of business.

Europeans did Business Differently, We Never Asked Why

The phenomenon that the companies represented—a state which was trying to enrich itself by promoting business, was a new kind of model. It did not have any precedent in India. Indian businessmen did tie up with rulers all the time but on a strictly individual basis. The state in India never made any consistent effort to help business in general as opposed to specific individuals. And it is difficult to find businessmen using coercion to promote the ends of trade. The occasional attempts that kings and princes made to drive down prices of what they bought, met with much hostility and little success. The European companies were different. Each company was based on a monopoly granted by their government. And the monopoly carried with it the right to raise armed troops. They did not need to be told that trading that was protected by arms produced more profits than trading that took peace to be the default.

Using coercion to make more profit was only one of the attributes the companies showed. An important skill the Europeans showed, was the ability to systematize information to manage their money better. In the process of systematization, they constantly set up protocols with which to work. They were very curious about how Indians lived and worked. Gathering information to improve the protocol, was a constant activity. The Directors of the English East India Company for instance, often commissioned special surveys about possible new products for which there could be a market. The English East India Company in that sense repeatedly displayed a keen sense of the importance of information. Much of the history of those times is reconstructed on the basis of the records they left behind.

No doubt the picture they left us is a biased one enforcing their world view. Be that as it may, information collated consistently over time, did generate significant insights that allowed them to improve profits. They made much smaller profits than Indian merchants, but they made those profits consistently. The Indian merchants on the other hand do not seem to have displayed an understanding of the connection between learning and earning. They showed plenty of enterprise, initiative and risk taking ability. But the failure to systematize information or to value learning reduced their ability to compete with the Europeans.

Collation of information in a scientific manner and use of the information to improve productivity can generally produce profits in most situations. But the ability to systematize and use that information or to see it as being of value, need not be universal. If the quality of life is already rather good, perhaps there might be little desire to improve it.

Certainly India was rich for centuries before the European companies set foot on the continent. But it is also possible that our riches were natural, not man-made. Could it be that we saw no need to systematize information to generate wealth? Why is it that Indians made little visible effort to learn about the other? For an answer to these questions, we propose to delve into India's past.

Extrapolating from Present to the Past, a Mistake

To use current ideas and practices to provide any answer to this and such questions, would be rather difficult. After all as L.P. Hartley once said 'the past is a foreign country; they do things differently there'. The kind of behaviour a king, warrior, farmer might have shown two hundred years ago, would be as alien to modern-day Indians as to modern-day Europeans, Africans and Americans. Indians for instance were used to carrying arms. For that they did not require permission from any government. Today when the state has made a monopoly of force real, we may find that strange. But not so our ancestors. When the English demilitarized India in the aftermath of the 1857 Mutiny, that action had tremendous psychological consequences. This is only one of the numerous instances in which our ancestors were very different from us.

Tribes of India were not a downtrodden, oppressed and exploited people. Till as recently as the early nineteenth century, there were large areas of the north-east where the Nagas and the Ahoms ruled. In central and eastern India, Gonds ruled over entire states as did the Bhils in western India. In this and in so many other attributes, we lead very different lives and think very differently from our ancestors.

To make any assumptions on the basis of our present behaviour and present ideas, can be very dangerous. Our effort throughout this book would be to look at history taking care to not let present-day presumptions colour it.

BECOMING RICH BY DESIGN

We begin by asking the question, what is it that obstructs India from becoming rich today? Over the last seventy odd years since Independence, different kinds of strategies have been tried but with little result. So much so that nowadays economists have begun to warn about India falling into the middle income trap from which there is no escape. No doubt much economic growth has happened in India in the past few decades but this has mostly been by default, not by conscious design. In 1950, the GDP of the United States of America was nearly fourteen times that of India; in 2017, the American economy is still nearly seven and a half times larger in size.[1] Today the Indian GDP is more or less the same size as that of the United Kingdom. The gap is narrowing, but slowly. We have certainly grown but other countries have grown faster. Surely poverty has gone down in India but per capita incomes remain low. With all the tremendous advantages of a young and energetic population, abundant natural resources and a democratic government, we still haven't found a winning design for growth. No wonder then it is said that the so-called Hindu rate of growth might have doubled from 3 to 7 per cent but there it remains. Is it that we are missing out on some key element?

India Grows but There's Scope to do Better

The colonial legacy is one of the usual bogeys. Still, as the largest functional democracy of the world, India has relatively stable political structures. With a vibrant services and industry sector, it would be imprudent to say that after seventy years, India still lags behind due to colonialism. Moreover, within Asia itself, we can see many countries that were devastated either by the European encounter or by the world wars and who have managed to recover pretty well. Take the case of China and Korea. Or of Japan. While Japan was never colonized, the Second World War devastated the country. Yet it was able to re-build itself after all the devastation and the suffering caused by Hiroshima and Nagasaki. China began at a lower base than India in 1950; yet China's GDP improved much more and today the size of its economy rivals that of USA with the US GDP only about 1.58 times that of China.[2] So we can safely discard the bogey of colonialism and of victimhood.

Another viewpoint could be that an interventionist state is needed, both to create equal opportunities and for more efficient resource allocation. This model has been tried for nearly forty years. In the euphoric years after 1947, India experimented with the centralized model of planning. It was believed that this model offered much greater scope for addressing the huge income and social inequalities in the country. But between 1950 and 1990 when the model was finally questioned and modified, annual growth rates remained low. And by 1991, the Indian government faced a serious balance of payments crisis. In the post-liberalization era, there has been some improvement in growth rates and the incidence of poverty. In the year 1990, going by the then international poverty line of roughly one dollar per day, more than half the Indian population, that is one in two persons or 420 million people were poor.[3] In 2018, 264.8 million people or one out of five people in India were poor according to the new international poverty line of 1.9 US dollars a day.[4] Numbers have improved but still, India just about beats Nigeria for being home to the largest number of poor in the world. There is certainly a case for doing much better.

Whichever way we look at it, India has lagged behind its growth potential. It has been argued that the restrictions on a free market are responsible for the lag.

After 1991, the set of ideas that restricted market competition was more or less confined to the dustbin of history. The cumbersome work of dismantling four decades of restrictions and regulation was begun. In an erudite volume, Jagdish Bhagwati and Arvind Panagariya have pointed out that dismantling of the regulatory structure has not gone on fast enough.[5] And that the state machinery in India continues to stifle innovation and to disincentivize any scaling up. The underlying assumption continues to be that the only thing that we need to do for wealth to increase, is to allow the market to operate and to set innovation free. Given less regulation, globalization and direct foreign investment will do the rest of the work.

Is a Free Market Enough?

An open market certainly means opportunities to create wealth. At the same time, surely there should be the ability to utilize those opportunities. Better technology, greater efficiencies, greater output per enterprise, higher productivity—it is such factors that would enable any country to make full use of a free market. What prevents us from achieving all these things?

THE LESSONS OF HISTORY

One kind of answer generated in the decades since liberalization has been that it is too much regulation combined with a lack of enterprise and of risk-taking ability among youth, that holds back the Indian economy. Yet, Indian history has been full of enterprising businessmen. That is also the case today.

Businessmen Need Reliable Legal Systems, Knowledge Archiving

When we go to history to look at the encounter between Indian and European merchants in the seventeenth and eighteenth centuries, we find that while Indian merchants showed plenty of entrepreneurship, it was lack of regulation, lack of legal systems and a certain inability to systematize information to improve efficiencies in Indian business or to manage money that was responsible for the rise of colonialism in the country. The existence of legal systems that work and of fair regulatory mechanisms are important resources for the average businessman. The rich and powerful might be able to get a trade dispute resolved quickly but things are difficult for the small time businessman. Denied such resources, small and medium enterprises depend on extended family and on trust to get things done. Where such state mechanisms are absent, the ability of the businessman to survive any crisis is rather low. Three hundred years ago, the situation was hardly different.

To make things even more difficult, Indian businessmen in the past do not seem to have developed any system for information archiving that might enable one person to learn from another. Each businessman might make the same mistake and learn the same lesson, in the same way. Where the competition is powerful as was the case with the English East India Company, the costs to be paid for mistakes can be very high. So how did we lose the plot?

Societies have Learning Curves too

There have been a few rich Indians throughout our history. Still the individual desire of large numbers of people in the country including businessmen and artisans, to make money, could not sustain India's wealth in the modern age. Making money consistently by large numbers of people, requires systematic effort. Learning from each other is not natural. It takes effort.

No doubt India had at one time, large numbers of skilled artisans. These artisans produced wondrous textiles, bronzeware and special steels among other things. Many books tell us how India clothed the world. Scientists today spend much effort in unpacking the secret of a special kind of steel called *wootz* that was special to India. These are only two among India's most well-known products.

The numbers of those who were skilled and those who were rich, kept on varying. Still, till the seventeenth century, India had a sufficiently large number of skilled people and riches for other countries to be drawn by the riches of the 'Orient'. It was in the period from the seventeenth to the twentieth century, that the numbers came down dramatically. More importantly, the ability of the few learned ones and the few rich ones was never transmitted down the line to improve the general average ability of the population. Nor was information systematically recorded. It is this process of recording and transmitting information that has been weak in India. The slowdown in the process of wealth generation in our country, became visible from the seventeenth century onwards. It was not that we became poor. Merely that other countries became richer; we got left behind.

The encounter between Indian and European merchants in the seventeenth and eighteenth centuries, is especially insightful with regard to Indian attitudes to information and to productivity. The European companies represented a new kind of sensibility. Each company represented a substantive information network. India had substantial businessmen and a historical tradition of centuries of business; yet they found it difficult to generate any sustained response to the challenge of the foreign companies. They could not adjust to a rapidly changing world.

That encounter gives us some insight into what might happen if an unregulated market and a non-existent legal system was accompanied by a certain reluctance to deal with a changing world.

The use of historical information to improve the quality of decision-making about the present, whatever the sector, is something we do not see in India. Yet, the availability of systematic sets of information does help to deal with a rapidly changing world.

Would Systematization of Information Help the Learning Curve

So the question that we ask in this book is, would the systematization of information to improve decision-making, help India to grow rich, rather than just a few Indians? A related question is, that might an inability to systematize information, have historical roots?

History shows that so long as we remain indifferent to using information to improve productivity and to improve decision-making, market openness would do little to help. Even the existence of liquidity in the market cannot help in the face of a reluctance to improve efficiencies. It is important to remember here that by the end of the sixteenth century, there already existed a merchant class in India who were engaged in a variety of businesses. They also had access to capital. They were engaged in trade not only overland within the country but also sent goods to various countries in Southeast Asia, Central Asia and West Asia. This is why the European companies were able to meet most of their needs for working capital locally. Rather the companies were always on the lookout for local merchants who could not only provide capital but who could help them access cloth weavers and other suppliers in the hinterland.

Indian merchants and shippers gave a tough fight to the East India companies. The internal correspondence of the companies refer all the time to the commercial acumen and competitiveness of the 'Gentoo' merchants. So with some capital to pursue their business objectives, with advanced accounting techniques, it would be important to see why the merchants eventually lost out to the East India Companies. To say that the companies were better organized militarily provides little insight. Even if this were true, nothing prevented the rulers and merchants of eighteenth-century India from improving military organisation. Again any such improvement normally comes from a desire to learn, to improve efficiencies.

Actually a brief look at English army organization shows that one thing which they were good at was, managing money and resources. They were able to pay their soldiers consistently and organize their supply lines. The military dominance of the English company came much after their economic success and effective money management had an important role to play in military dominance.

STATISTICS CAN BEAT GUNS OR HOW THE ENGLISH WON

We often forget that the English East India Company was not a major military force in India right up to the Battle of Plassey. At that point of time, they had only a small military, raised with the objective of protecting the properties of the Company. But they were able to win the loyalty of those men simply by paying better. That Indian rulers lost some battles to the company gives rise to a belief that better tactics, better weaponry, better organization won the day. We need to remember that Indian rulers cottoned on to all those techniques very fast. Before 1757, they won some battles and lost some. The Marathas had one of the most powerful armies in the world. What counted more was the Company's ability to manage money, to manage taxation much better so that they could depend on revenues to pay their soldiers.

Managing Money and Taxes Key to English Victory

It was in their taxation systems that Indian rulers were extremely weak. The Nawab of Bengal had access to one of the richer province in the country. But he was not able to make it yield enough revenue to manage his army. This was something the Company did very well. That Mir Jafar betrayed his master was not important. What was important was that the soldiers of the Bengal Army saw nothing wrong in betraying their master either. The Nawab had not cared to pay them in a regular manner or to earn their loyalty.

What happened to the armies of various Indian rajahs and nawabs against the English East India Company is an abject lesson in the criticality of financial management. Wondering English observers reported about the way in which Indian armies were continuously in arrears of pay for the rank and file. It was routine for troops to protest against non-payment of salary. An early-recorded instance of protest was penned down by William Henry Tone, an English East India Company official who served in the army of one of the Maratha rulers towards the end of the eighteenth century. He tells us that the Maratha cavalry was one of the most irregularly paid of all the troops. In those times, the cavalry was only paid a daily ration of flour; the cash salary came as and when the *silladar* (armour bearer), that is the man who had hired the troops, got his dues. The *silladar* in turn, had to pay out a sizeable cut to the state official who took the roll call. Tone says that 'upon this occasion it is always necessary that the Brahman who takes it should have a bribe. . . .' In order to recover arrears of pay, the troops resorted to the time-honoured tradition of *dharna*. *Dharna* essentially consisted of putting the debtor in confinement until such time as he paid up. It did not matter how high the social status of the debtor might be. 'Any person in the sircar's service has a right to demand his pay of the prince or his minister. . . .' No one would dream of interfering with this kind of *dharna* since it was in a common cause and nor could the soldier be accused of mutiny.[6]

Colonel Thomas Duer Broughton, commander of the Resident's escort at the camp of Daulat Rao Sindhia, the Maratha general, gives us a remarkable eyewitness account of life at an army camp in the early nineteenth century. Chronically bankrupt, Sindhia was used to being accosted in his camp by intemperate subordinates who had not been paid for months together. The attempts at resource mobilization included daily collection of a few paisa per merchant in the vicinity. Sindhia was liberal in giving advance receipts for future cash instalments to be paid to him by the Company. Broughton narrates an incident where two Khans who commanded important units in Sindhia's army, had not been paid for months. They then proceeded to do dharna against Sindhia himself with drawn swords. So Sindhia had two thousand rupees sent to them and promised to settle the rest. The Khans then returned to their tents only to be surrounded by guns and battalions. Sindhia had sent orders that they were to leave the camp and prepare to march next morning. He also promised to settle their bazaar debts of Rs. 3 lakh and send Rs. 20,000 besides. When the Khans refused and pitched tents outside the camp, they were harassed by creditors to the point that they had to sell off any spare dresses and arms and even killed rats for food, so says Broughton. So much so that Sindhia had to post two companies of soldiers to protect the Khans against their creditors. His minister tried to negotiate with the Khans to return; he even said that Sindhia was drunk when he asked them to leave the camp and that the promised arrears would be settled. Negotiations failed and the troops marched away. Needless to say, neither were the debts settled, nor any cash paid.[7]

Indian Rulers Never Paid the Soldier Regularly

The armies of the Marathas were some of the best in the country. The troops were brave and hardy, they hardly cared for caste distinctions and they were well equipped with military tactics. But their rulers never managed to set up taxation systems that would enable them to provide their soldiers with salaries on time.

The Indian soldier in a local army, had to organise his own horse, his own gear and even his own arms. These were costly assets. Often his greater anxiety was to preserve his equipment, rather than the battle fortunes of his regiment.

The English company in contrast, spent much time and effort on taking care of their *sipahis*, and especially the invalid ones. An entire section of the Company army administration was devoted to what they called the 'Invalid Establishment'. This establishment was to see to the affairs of all those who had served the company army for 10-12 years but were no longer able to serve due to age or infirmity. Further it took care of even those who had served a lesser amount of time but had suffered wounds in the service of the company. From 1788 onwards, it was company policy to allot lands to these invalid soldiers and to settle them in 'invalid thanahs' in company territory.[8] In addition to the land, they were also given some cash gratuity. From 1790 onwards, special provisions were made for company *sipahis* on foreign service, to remit money to their families.[9]

All this the English company was able to do by managing its

finances such as to pay its soldiers regularly. This ability of the English company to manage information, to manage money, to systematize taxation, is something that is difficult to find in the Indian landscape. The Mughal army might have offered more by way of spoils or even cash salary but there was no such provision for the retired life of the common soldier. The English company set-up systems whereby each commanding officer was to certify the years of service put in by the soldiers under his command. Only upon verification of his record of service, was the soldier admitted to the 'invalid establishment'.

One company employee, William Henry Sykes, worked out detailed mortality tables for soldiers in different age groups ranging from 21 to 52. He showed that mortality in the various age groups ranged from roughly 2.5 to 6 per cent. These figures he used to argue for the introduction of life insurance for the natives of India at low premiums.[10] Such statistical calculations enabled the English East India Company to put its pension establishment on a sound footing. Later such mortality tables became critical to the life insurance business.

If the English company was able to offer more regular pay to the Indian soldier, it was able to offer greater security to the average Indian businessmen. And for the rich businessmen who were their business rivals: the Company made it difficult for them to operate independently of the Company.

Whichever way we look at it, the economic predominance of the English East India Company preceded military predominance. So we should ask then with the existence of an unregulated market, with large numbers of Indian businessmen who were skilled, how was it that such a situation emerged in the first place. Also we shall see how the lack of state intervention and low taxation, did not help businessmen; it was a positive hindrance.

LOW RATES OF CUSTOM DUTIES

Low tariff structures are believed to distort the market the least. In such case, Mughal officialdom, whether by design, corruption or indifference to efficiencies in tax collection, maintained a minimalist tax regime. Customs duties were imposed at rates ranging from 2.5 to 5 per cent on imports of goods. The actual recovery of these duties depended entirely on local officials. The narratives of the English East India Company are full of complaints about the extortions of petty officialdom. But their own records show that they made all possible efforts to evade as much customs duty as they possibly could. It was they who generated much of the conflict over payment of duty that led eventually to the battle of Plassey.

English Company Cheats on Customs Duty

William Hedges, agent of the English East India Company and Governor of their affairs in Bengal, recorded in his diary in November 1683 that evasion of duty could help make Company trade prosperous. The first method listed was suppression of rivals of the Company. Evasion of duty was the second one. He writes that on a £600,000 investment, if they were to pay duty on inward of goods at 3.5 per cent and another 3.5 per cent on their return, that would amount to 7 per cent or £42,000. At the then rupee-pound exchange rate of Rs. 8, this would have meant paying Rs. 3.36 lakh as duty. Hedges writes that he would undertake to settle the matter in perpetuity for half that amount.[11] Some of the amount so saved must have been spent in greasing the hands of various Mughal officials from the Governor downwards. Still, the East India Company undoubtedly made a profit on all the skulduggery.

The English devote much space in their written records on their efforts to procure a single *firman* (royal order) from the Mughal emperor for a flat annual fee which would exempt them from paying these grievous 3.5 per cent duties. Mostly local officials cooperated with their efforts. In 1651, Shah Shuja, the Governor of Bengal, had issued a permit to the English company for trade free of all restrictions in Bengal, for an annual payment of Rs. 3,000.[12] The permit was renewed repeatedly by many Bengal governors. English company officials made consistent efforts to restrict cash outgo to this amount or lower if possible. Company officials also insisted that the permit issued in 1651 should be held valid for all times to come and against any tax of any description. They resented the Dutch who paid ten times as much as the English-roughly Rs. 30,000 to 40,000 customs duty annually. The English Company said that such compliance would encourage the Mughals to demand more.

Much of the fortifications the English company built was intended to protect itself against any prospective Mughal efforts to recover payment of taxes due. They came from a country which charged them at far higher rates. A study of the records of the East India Company for the period 1709-42 shows, that more than 20 per cent of the cost of operations of the company was spent in paying customs duties on goods imported from Asia to the English government. In any given year in this period, the company paid duties from £300,000 annually to upwards of £500,000.[13] The Mughals however were different.

The local Mughal officials displayed little concern on the matter. They even made a case for the English company, and wrote to the emperor on their behalf on occasion. In turn, the Mughal emperors seemed to pay little attention to the Company or to make much effort to stop the leakage of revenue. Even after winning the skirmish with the English East India Company in 1686, the Emperor Aurangzeb went back to square one. He merely restored the earlier exemptions on payment of a nominal annual fee.

Much the same story can be seen in the Gujarat region.

Officials Collude with Company as 'Protection Money'

So why then did Indian officialdom collude so blatantly with the Company to defraud the government? Bribe taking could be one reason. The other reason seems to be that Mughal nobility and officials invested considerable sums in trade, both domestic and foreign. Once the European companies arrived on the scene and practised militarized trading, Indian shipping suffered quite a bit. Indian merchants did not organize naval protection for themselves. Nor did the Mughals provide them with such protection. The cargo ships of even Mughal governors and princes were under threat.

In the circumstances, the local nobility seem to have figured that it was easier to come to terms with the East India companies and to use them for carrying freight. Perhaps in return for such assistance, they looked the other way when company officials repeatedly violated tax laws.

Not only did the English East India Company avoid paying duty on company imports, their own servants used the various directives granted in favour of the company, for their own private trade. Still, Mughal rulers continued to feel that the benefits of the overall bullion brought into the country by the European companies outweighed the need to tax them more rigorously. A statistical calculation would have shown that the companies could easily have afforded to pay more; indeed they expected to. Yet statistics, figures, calculations or any systematization of information seemed to be alien to the way in which Indian rulers conducted their business.

CRONYISM AND THE CONDUCT OF TRADE

With such large investments in trade, the Mughal nobility still made little effort to support local businessmen in general. They did hire individual merchants to manage their investments. But they never seemed to feel that any increase in the turnover of business in general would bring more profit to the exchequer. The inward flow of bullion was good; whether the local man got rich or the foreigner, seemed an irrelevant question.

To the question whether Indian merchants were given any special privileges over foreign merchants, available information hardly reveals any privileges. One of the main reasons that all the East India companies, English, French, Dutch and Portuguese, did so much business in India was that local rulers imposed no sanctions upon foreign merchants. Foreign merchants had brought in business for many hundreds of years, perhaps even thousands of years. As long as they respected local convention, they were welcomed with open arms.

In ports like Surat and Hugli, there were large numbers of foreign merchants. These merchants had started venturing into the interior in search of cheaper goods to buy. Foreign merchants were able on occasion to get exemption from the toll duties. Local merchants still had to pay those duties.

Indian Merchants End up Paying More Duty

Sometimes, domestic merchants did complain that tax exemption from transit duties to foreign merchants, would put the local merchants at a disadvantage. The Dutch company in Bengal repeatedly pressed for exemption from transit duties. Often the local officials agreed to such demands subject to some limitations. So in 1653, the *diwan* of the *subahdar* of Bengal, instructed the *faujdar* of Maksudabad (later Murshidabad) to allow the Dutch to take out 1,000 bales of raw silk, duty free from Kasimbazar. Later the Dutch managed to get the prince to withdraw even the limit of 1,000 bales. Such orders affected the revenues of the local government as it did the profits of the local merchants. So in 1661, Mir Jumla, the new *subahdar* encouraged the local merchants to complain to the emperor that such exemptions would make it difficult for them to compete. The merchants complained. When the complaint was referred to Mir Jumla, he supported the local merchants and the limit was re-imposed. At this point the Dutch managed to get some other local merchants to write a letter saying the exemptions did not affect them. As soon as they got the letter, the Dutch sent it to the emperor. Royal orders issued in 1662 allowed the Dutch company exemption from transit duties without any limit.[14]

Instance of tariff protection given to local producers, is not reported at all. A noted scholar has observed that so far as the Mughal emperors were concerned, any expansion in trade brought in more bullion into the country and also led to increase in custom duties which went directly to the emperor's coffers. Transit and toll duties on the other hand, went to the local government and this might explain the emperor's indifference to the various exemptions granted to the companies.[15]

More devoted votaries of free enterprise than the Mughal emperors in the seventeenth and eighteenth centuries, would be difficult to find. They even countenanced foreign companies in a market for goods like salt which was a royal monopoly. In the *subah* of Bihar, we find occasions where Portuguese merchants were awarded the revenue farming contract for the royal monopoly of salt in Bihar.

Similarly, in the saltpetre trade, we find the European companies competing for ever larger quantities of saltpetre. Saltpetre was useful for gunpowder and as ballast on ships. Many merchants, foreign and Indian, tried to use their influence with local officials to get better access to saltpetre. Mughal officials could be bribed for their favour; the only problem was that if your rival offered a larger bribe, the favour granted to you could be overturned.

Government Permits up for Sale

Indian merchants did whatever was possible to jack up prices for the companies. Two Sikh merchants in particular, Amirchand and Deepchand, had serious interests in saltpetre. In 1745, they paid Rs. 25,000 to Patna officialdom to force the European companies to buy saltpetre only from them.[16] The Dutch promptly paid more to get the decision reversed and Amirchand and Deepchand were told not to interfere in the trade. In 1747, Amirchand got into an agreement with the English Company to provide them saltpetre. Once again, the Dutch paid more to the Patna *durbar* asking them to prevent Amirchand from supplying the commodity. This time the *naib nazim* (Deputy Governor) even posted guards and horsemen over the saltpetre lands to prevent Amirchand from accessing the saltpetre.[17]

All these agreements, contracts and counter contracts were rather fluid. All parties routinely double crossed each other and shifted alliances. Sometimes the Dutch and the English companies made common cause to drive down prices quoted by the local merchants but often one company would go behind the other's back to contract for the saltpetre.

The ruler's actions never indicated that he considered the Indian merchants especially favoured or conversely that the Europeans were discriminated against. Rather when the Marathas raided Bengal, Alivardi Khan asked all the merchants including the

European companies to contribute to the war effort. After all, they made a profit out of the trade and should contribute to the general upkeep.

THE RISE OF COLONIALISM

Low tariffs, no protection to local traders, a complete lack of regulation—all these provided Indian businessmen with plenty of market opportunity for enterprise. No doubt the government extorted money off and on and bribery was a way of life but there was still much profit to be made.

So how is it that Indian businessmen gradually lost competitive advantage to the European companies? Consistently those businessmen did well who were willing to trade with the company on the terms dictated by the company. Business rivals who opposed the Company, gradually lost out in Surat, in Bengal, in Malabar and in the Madras region before 1757.

How is it that colonialism was victorious? In hindsight, it might seem as if the procession was inevitable but this was by no means the case. Nor was the conflict between the English East India Company and Indian rulers a foregone conclusion. Till the 1750s, there were some wins and some losses on either side. It was the Battle of Plassey that gave the English East India Company access to the resources of the state government. That access brought men, money and materials. And once the company could use Indian revenues and Indian soldiers to fight Indian rulers, they went from strength to strength.

In the European encounter, there were two qualities displayed by Indian merchants time and again which made a lot of difference to their ability to survive a conflict. One, there was a profound indifference to the resources of the state; matched by the indifference of the state to business concerns. The other, was a certain inability to recover their debts. Both lacunae increased the risks of business for the Indians and gave advantage to the Europeans. And after Plassey, the tide turned against Indian merchants and rulers.

Key to Colonialism: No State Support to Business

An absence of state support to business meant that Indian merchants did not enjoy a high quality of protection against looting and piracy on the high seas or even at home. A lack of protection put them at a severe disadvantage. A defining feature of the European companies was that they had internalized protection and they used military force to protect their ships on the seas. On land, they built fortifications wherever they could.

State intervention in markets can help businesses in many legitimate ways. By protecting the goods and worldly wealth of citizens for instance.

For merchants or individuals of high net worth, the value of such protection would be very high. Yet, a high quality of protection was the one feature unavailable to Indian merchants. On the high seas, there was no protection whatsoever since the Mughals were never a naval power to contend with. For protection on land, merchants had to make do with whatever the Mughals and other land-based powers took it upon themselves to provide.

The Europeans on the other hand, had no issues with armed trading and they brought to the Indian Ocean, the idea of the system of passes for trade. Initially it was the Portuguese East India Company that issued passes for safe passage. They insisted that a trading vessel pass through a port under Portuguese control so they could earn some money through duties. Soon it became common practise for other European companies to insist on passes too. Indian traders then had to spend money on getting the passes. It was not just individual traders but princes and influential nobles of the Mughal empire, who had to ask for passes too.

Akbar Negotiates with Portuguese for Free Passes for his Wife

Here we do not talk of the ordinary trader but the emperor himself. In the year 1576, the ladies of Akbar's household including his aunt Gulbadan Begum, his wife Salima Sultan Begum and others determined to proceed on the *haj* pilgrimage. Given the Portuguese intransigence about passes, Akbar was apprehensive of a slight. So he deputed a senior noble to Gujarat to see to the safe departure of the women. The noble's report was such that Akbar cautioned the ladies to postpone their departure by an year. The *firman* he issued says,

> There is likelihood that a party of the Portuguese, thinking of the money and assemblage (accompanying her) might obstruct the passage and so vexation and trouble may be caused to her. That would really be a vexation for us. It is (a matter of) protecting one's honour, a matter regarding one's good repute (sharifi). Let it not happen that an indecorous incident occurs, and that news spread throughout the world.[18]

But the ladies had made up their mind. They insisted. At this point Akbar gave in and his officials negotiated free passes from the Portuguese for the royal ships to proceed on the *haj* and also for exemption from any duty on the cargo they might bring back.[19]

For the other traders, it was the cost of the passes that concerned them much more than any slight to their honour. At about the same time, Mughal noble Bayazid Bazat, who wanted to proceed on the *haj*, was forced to pay 10,000 *mahmudis* (*c*. Rs. 4,200) to the Portuguese who had taken his son hostage.[20] This was a considerable sum in those days. These voyages normally combined religion with trade so some of the losses were offset against the profits made. But risks remained high.

And the Portuguese did not always keep to their word. In 1577, five ships returning from the *haj* which had picked up cargo from Jeddah, were detained by the Portuguese at Diu. These included one imperial ship, which carried a huge load of gold and silver. For its return, the Mughal governor at Gujarat practically had to plead with the Portuguese.[21] The ship was returned but there were other incidents as well. In 1613, the imperial ship *Rahimi*, was sent to Mocha by Maryam-uz-Zamani (mother of emperor Jahangir), with a Portuguese pass. The Portuguese captured the ship along with its cargo and 700 passengers and took it to Goa. A contemporary English account says that the ship carried a 100,000 pounds worth of goods.[22] Jahangir did retaliate by temporarily stopping the traffic through Surat, seizing the Portuguese town of Daman and closing the Jesuit church at Agra. But these were hit and miss methods. There was never any sustained response or policy.

The Portuguese behaviour was nothing new. Merely that they kept on escalating the conflict inherent in the situation between two great powers.

Mughal princes and nobles continued to suffer considerable losses due to the pass system and piracy in so far as their individual trading interests were concerned. An interesting fact that emerges from the capture of the ship of Maryam-uz-Zamani is that women of the royal family, had considerable trading interests. Other senior nobles also invested heavily in trade, often tying up with merchants to represent their interests. Given that the Mughals possessed no navy worth its name, these nobles needed the services provided by the European companies. Whether it was free passes for their ships or for carrying cargo at concessional rates, the Mughal nobility availed of the European companies' good offices. For a price of course.

Helpless Merchants, Helpless Emperor

Here was an interesting spectacle. The officials of one of the richest and most powerful empires of the world were willing to pay protection money to various piratical organizations rather than generate the protection for themselves. Either they believed that the emperor would not listen to them if informed that a navy was needed here or they believed that organizing a navy was a 'sunk cost' and not worth it.

Till today the relationship between a functioning legal system, a fair regulatory system, a reliable policing system and a flourishing economy, continues to seem invisible. Might it be that these are seen as sunk costs, of no particular value to anyone in the foreseeable future? Perhaps. The one person who suffers in the process is the businessman. It is he who has to pay through his nose for all such lacunae. Three hundred years ago, the Indian merchant suffered from all these lapses too. We do not know if he ever complained to his kings that he deserved better treatment and that he brought them real time income. The treasury of the kings suffered too but we have no evidence that they realized they were losing money.

We have seen that Mughal nobility and administration often turned a blind eye to tax evasion by the companies in return for their services in shipping and trade. But let us turn a bit to merchants who were not part of the administration and see how the lack of protection affected them. One case that stands out is that of the merchants of the city of Surat.

INDIFFERENCE TO THE RESOURCES OF THE STATE AND THE DECLINE OF THE MERCHANTS OF SURAT

Surat in those times, was one of the richest ports of the Mughal empire. The trade of Surat enriched not just the merchants but the emperor as well. A diary entry made by Joan Diodati of the Dutch East India Company in the year 1699, tells us that customs duties from this port amounted to Rs. 8.16 lakh in that year.[23] If we take the customs rate at 3.5 per cent, this means the port had an annual turnover of Rs. 2.33 crore. While a very large part of the Surat trade was with cities like Mocha and Muscat in the Gulf of Oman and Red Sea area, ships also went from Surat to the Malabar region, Coromandel coast, Southeast Asia.

Yet the Mughals did little to protect this port or its prized trade. The losses they suffered in shipping and the decline of royal protection eventually destroyed the status of Surat as the major port of the empire on the Western coast. What Surat lost, Bombay gained.

PIRACY HITS THE MERCHANTS OF SURAT

Merchants in this area had suffered the occasional act of piracy. Their response had been some hand wringing and much resignation. But with repeated acts of piracy against Surat shipping from 1684 onwards, the situation became far more threatening. One of the largest merchants to be so hit was Mulla Abdul Ghafur, the merchant prince of Surat. Then in 1692 the attacks escalated and four Surat ships were attacked at the mouth of the Red Sea by pirates. Two of the vessels had belonged to Mulla Abdul Ghafur; these had carried treasure amounting to Rs. 5 lakh. This was a very serious matter. Mulla Abdul Ghafur was no ordinary merchant.

This was a man originally from a humble background. Some even said that he had merely been a teacher at a mosque before he came to Surat. Yet he had risen up within a few decades to become one of the richest merchants in Surat.[24]

Itimad Khan, the Mughal governor of Surat was at a loss. Members of the Dutch council were also invited for a discussion on the future course of action once Mulla Abdul Ghafur complained about his losses. But the Dutch declared that they had no idea who the pirates might have been. Itimad Khan proposed that each of the three European companies should provide one warship and they would all go looking for the pirates along with the Mughal warships. The Dutch were most reluctant to get involved in something that did not concern them at all, and claimed that they did not have any authority to proceed like this without the say-so of the Council at Batavia.[25]

Knowing well that the Mughals were not interested in spending any money on strengthening their navy, the Dutch suggested that trading ships be armed instead. This the merchants were most reluctant to do. Their ships were so overloaded with cargo that operating guns was problematic; nor did the ship-owners provide enough trained gunners to the ships. Without any firm decision, they still decided to proceed in convoy for greater safety. But again next year, two of Mulla Abdul Ghafur's ships were attacked; one escaped but the other was looted and the merchant lost Rs. 2.5 lakh.[26]

To add fat to the fire, at about this time, an imperial ship, the Ganj-i-Sawai, was looted of some Rs. 16-18 lakh in 1695 by an English pirate Henry Every. Not content with loot, he also abducted some women who belonged to a noble family of Surat.

Protection Responsibilities Farmed Out to European Companies

Wringing of hands was no longer an option for the governor. It was decided then that the Dutch and the English would provide one or more ships each year to escort the Surat ships to Mocha. For these services, they would be paid fixed rates: Rs. 20,000 for a large ship and so on. Half the payment would be made by the royal treasury and the merchants would pay the rest. This arrangement worked for three years.[27]

At this point, a merchant Hasan Hamdani who had refused convoy, lost a ship to a pirate. Unmindful of the fact that it was he who had been at fault, he made a great to-do about the loss and brought pressure to bear on the Mughals for redressal. In January 1699, the Mughal court instructed the Governor of Surat to make the English, French and Dutch pay compensation to Hasan Hamdani. Not only this, the Europeans were also asked to pay compensation for such losses to pirates in future as well. If they failed to agree, they would be asked to leave the Mughal empire. The Indian Ocean was divided into three zones for this purpose: the Persian Gulf was assigned to the French, the Arab coast to the Dutch and the south-west coast of India and Indonesia to the English.[28] In short, the Mughals assigned the responsibilities of the government to the various East India companies. Perhaps they did so in the hope that the trading wealth of India was sufficient inducement for the companies to make this investment. This is what the governor reportedly said. If so, he and others like him were very wrong.

The Europeans were very clear that their own trading needed protection, for which they were willing to spend money. A Governor of Bombay said at one time, that without a naval force, the Company's Malabar settlements would be quickly overrun by the coastal kings. As he put it rhetorically, 'if no Naval Force no Trade, if no Fear no Friendship', the Company must judge whether the trade of the whole coast, Persia and Mokha was worth the expense of keeping a naval patrol.[29] But this did not mean that they were willing to bear the costs of protecting Asian merchants.

To demand protection in this way was an impossible kind of demand. Throughout the next year, Surat saw constant wrangling between the merchants and the European companies who did their utmost to resist any payout whatsoever. To their mind, it was the job of the Mughals to protect their people. They had little to do with the matter. To the extent that the Mughal emperor was a powerful force on land and had the potential to threaten their factories, they were obliged to listen to him somewhat. No more no less. For their part, they did their best to hire other agents to lobby for their case at the court. Plenty of monies exchanged hands. But they were unsuccessful. Mulla Abdul Ghafur was no helpless weakling. He ensured that a royal *firman* (directive) instructing that compensation be paid by the Dutch, was issued.[30]

As long as he lived, he was able to force the issue with the European companies. He even wrung some compensation out of them at one time. What he was unable to do and perhaps he never really tried to do, was to forge support for a permanent institutional mechanism that would protect the merchants. At one point of time, he was able to persuade all the merchants to threaten to suspend trading if no compensation was paid for damages of piracy by the Europeans. But this was as far as unity went. The merchants were not particularly united. Many of them were afraid of the power of Mulla Abdul Ghafur who it was said, was capable of getting the Governor of Surat changed. Nor did Ghafur help matters by telling the governor that it was his duty to help his co-religionists.[31] Such appeals were not calculated to appeal to the Hindu merchants of Surat who were far larger in number.

The governor for his part was caught between the Europeans and the indigenous merchants. Some of the time, he was quite happy to accept bribes from the various East India companies for ignoring the complaints of the merchants. But the one thing no stakeholder ever did do, whether merchants or Mughals, was to go out and hire professional soldiers for protection. They seemed not to see that only such a long-term measure would protect their money. The actions of the European East India Companies which had internalized protection, either seemed meaningless or irrelevant to the way that the people of Surat did their business.

So the main issue remained unresolved—that it was the job of the sovereign state of the Mughals to provide protection to the life and property of its citizens from acts of piracy. This the Mughal state refused to do. At most it hired the tribe led by the Sidi to police the western coast for an annual payment from the revenues of Surat. This duty the Sidi hardly ever performed; rather the tribe acted as a predator on more than one occasion.

Aurangzeb Worries about his Treasury, Indifferent to Merchants

We get an interesting insight into how the Mughal emperor Aurangzeb regarded the difficulties of the merchants. Contemporary reports indicate that he was well aware of the piracy practised by European traders on the high seas. He advised Prince Azam, *subahdar* of Gujarat that it was time to take strict action; enough leniency had been shown. The ships of the Surat merchants were being plundered for the last twenty years. In response, Mughal officials should reach out to the ruler of Muscat since he had a well equipped fleet for battle at sea. The *subahdar* of Multan was instructed to approach the ruler of Muscat and offer him a bribe for fighting the hat-wearers (Mughal term for Europeans). Aurangzeb never seems to have initiated any action from the side of the Mughals. He seemed far more concerned with whether the port officials of Surat had deposited the money recovered from the Europeans with the royal treasury. Nor was the idea of contacting the ruler of Muscat taken too seriously since it was never followed up. On the contrary, when Itibar Khan in Surat, enforced the indemnity bond that had been extracted from the European companies and forced them to compensate local merchants for the losses, Itibar Khan was superseded and a new official sent in his place.[32]

The idea that the Europeans brought in bullion and that any attempt to discipline them might result in their abandoning the trade seems to have weighed quite a bit on the emperor's mind. A serious concern with immediate returns as opposed to future profits can be rather counter-productive.

The narratives of the times also make it clear that the merchants of Surat never really made much of a sustained case for protection to the emperor. They were well aware of the potential danger from the new practice of armed trading that the East India companies had brought to the Indian Ocean. In the early seventeenth century, when the English East India Company first made efforts to begin trading at Surat, the Gujarati merchants, having heard something about the strong arm nature of their activities, opposed the

English strenuously. They did not want any concessions to be given to the English. In a letter of January 1618, Sir Thomas Roe reported that there had been some negotiation with the merchants of Surat in the presence of the Mughal nobles, Itmad-ul-daulah and Asaf Khan. To the English offer of carrying the cargo of the Surat merchants, the local merchants said if they were to accept such an offer, they would lose all freedom and the shipping of the country would decay. They were willing to accept the English offer of protecting their convoys, but they would not pay for any such protection or for the passes. Sir Thomas Roe apparently hoped to awe the Gujarati merchants into cooperating with the English trade and accepting the English convoy. The letter says that to Roe's offer of a pass (*cartraz*), Itmad-ud-daulah (father of Nur Jahan), said that he had never heard so noble an offer but the Indian merchants were firm that they would not use the English ships to send their freight because they would prefer to be master of their own ships.[33] Eventually, the English won their point—they got permission to trade and also agreed to issue the passes to merchants.

No Tax, No Protection

Still, the merchants were never able to persuade the Mughals of the rightness of their demand for protection. No doubt Roe and others would have greased many palms to get their permissions. But nothing stopped the merchants from doing a simple calculation. All they really needed to do was to calculate the following: first, the amount of revenue they brought to the Mughal state, second the value of a small surcharge on the trade for protection and agreeing to pay the surcharge. This was something they never did. Perhaps doing such paperwork would have involved putting the volumes of their trade on paper and they were unwilling to display that much transparency. Perhaps they feared the Mughals as much as the East India Company. Whatever the immediate reasons might have been, they paid a far heavier price in the long-term for their inability to trust each other and to work together.

Surely they had freedom from tax; but that freedom did not work in their favour but against them.

Once the Mughal state gradually collapsed, to the threats of foreign pirates, was added the terrors of dacoits and theft on internal trade routes as well. The raids of the Marathas in the 1720s were the last straw. By the middle of the eighteenth century, the commercial importance of Surat had become a thing of the past.

During the period that the Marathas raided Gujarat, the merchants of the cities of Gujarat including Ahmedabad, Cambay, Broach, Vadnagar and Surat among others, shelled out over Rs. 2 crore as ransom.[34] In modern terms, this would amount to several hundred crores. And yet they saw themselves as helpless merchants!

Protection of Property is Key to Business

The ability to act, to protect oneself and to generate an ecosystem that nurtures economic growth, is as much an attribute of the mind, as of the economy. Freedom to trade cannot in itself, generate any such ecosystem. For markets to work, trade requires that governments guarantee protection against armed aggression of any kind and safety of property. Failure to provide that kind of protection raises the risks of doing business. The high interest rates chronically faced by Indian businesses, have been a response to a high level of perceived risk.

In this particular episode then, Indian merchants and rulers both seemed to be completely unaware that the resources of the state should be used to support businesses, and that in return businesses can help fill the coffers of the state. There could hardly be a greater belief in the virtues of entrepreneurship.

Now we come to a second kind of quality that gave definite advantage to the English East India Company and conversely worked against Indian merchants. This was the ability of the Company to systematize information and to recover their debts much better.

TRUST AND HONOUR NO SUBSTITUTE FOR LAWS OF CONTRACT

Systematization of Information and Ability to Recover Debts

Managing money is critical to the success of any business. And debt recovery is key to money management. Given a lax to non-existent legal system, recovering debts was a serious problem for the Indian merchants. Mostly they functioned on the basis of social norms, convention and trust. Trust in business was important and those who lost credibility in the market would find it difficult to do business. But this is hardly a reliable means for getting contracts enforced. The Mughals mostly preferred to refer any disputes to the merchants themselves and their internal mechanisms for settlement. For trade limited to the region, this might have worked, but for those who did business across the country, contract enforcement was a serious problem. No doubt there was a convention that the successors of a merchant would honour their parental debts. But trust, convention and honour can go only so far. This could be one reason why Indian business fortunes while great on occasion, did not sustain themselves for very long. The cases where any family did great business beyond two generations, are rare indeed. While the ability to make profits is important to business success, the ability to avoid losses is perhaps even more important.

The Europeans were a different kettle of fish. They had moved to a stage where the written word and contract was far more important than trust. Use of the written word gave them competitive advantage in debt collection and money management. They simply collated information on different business processes assiduously: on buying goods, maintaining accounts, following up on debts. And a corporate style of functioning meant that everyone kept an eye on each other.

Good money management also meant that they were able to survive on small profits even when circumstances were adverse. The average rate of return on East India Company stock was roughly

8 per cent. Indian merchants in comparison were used to much higher rates of profit which could range anything upwards of 15 per cent. Perhaps this had to do with high interest rates and poor enforcement. It also had to do with poor ability to recover debts. In effect they ran much higher levels of risk than did the Europeans. In this respect, in any dispute over outstanding payments with the European companies, they often lost out.

The European companies had extensive money dealings with local merchants. When the English East India Company first arrived in India, it looked for big merchants who could be relied on to invest sufficient capital without going bankrupt and who would deliver on contracts agreed to. The Europeans had little knowledge of local conditions, producers and commercial practices. So the services of the Indian merchants were key to the trade. In addition, often when the European ships did not arrive on time with bullion with which to pay for the company investment, the companies depended on the merchants to supply capital for investment. As a precaution, the companies mostly chose to deal with the most substantial merchants who were more than capable of advancing such monies and taking such risks. Once they discovered that the local merchants had plenty of capital, that they were lending to the local nobility and that the tools of transaction were rather sophisticated, the European companies increasingly depended on local merchants for their financial needs.

They all employed Indian brokers for their procurement and trade connections. The Indian broker in the seventeenth century was not an employee of the East India Company but a merchant with substantial dealings independently of the company. Merchants from Bengal, the Coromandel and Malabar participated actively in trade. Trade was conducted with Southeast Asia, with Mocha and Jeddah to the west. And many of these merchants worked as brokers to the Company as yet another avenue to use for profits.

Indian brokers took advances from the company in return for a commitment to supply goods for export to Europe. The capital was used among other things, to give advances to weavers for making textiles according to the given specifications. Second, the brokers often lent money to the East India companies on interest, when there was a shortage of bullion. They also lent money to many of the European traders for their private trade. Third, the brokers also engaged to procure a variety of permissions and customs exemptions from the Mughal government. All these operations meant extensive money dealings. They also led to frequent disputes. Some of the disputes routinely turned acrimonious.

One major source of disputation was the quality of goods supplied which was specified in the written contract the companies insisted on. The written contract was the instrument used by the English Company to standardize the process of purchasing goods. Once the terms of the contract were settled, the success or failure of any task could be evaluated in terms of deviation from the terms of the contract. A precondition of their business was that the Indian brokers they used, should sign a contract with them.

The reason they insisted on a contract was that they hoped to do business with the merchants in the long term. The business model was this—that the Company provided an advance to the Indian merchant to arrange to supply goods to the Company of the quality as required by the Company. The goods were to be provided in a limited period of time. The reason for the time constraint was that the company ships were tied to a calendar. Every year the ships had to return to Europe by February-March with goods for sale. Each year the Company signed contracts with a variety of agents specifying the goods they required and the delivery period. In case the goods were not supplied in time the Company risked losing the season.

The contract provided that in case the goods were not of the same quality as the specifications, there would be a penalty levied. Also in case the advance was not settled within a month of the departure of the ships, there would be interest levied on the outstanding amount. And the quality of the goods led to a lot of disputes. Indian producers were not accustomed to making goods according to such standardized norms. The Europeans often complained that the weavers could not produce two identical pieces. Apart from this, the company often suspected that the weaver, who was an independent producer, not a wage labourer, sometimes sold the goods he had made, to another party for a higher price. No doubt the weaver often did do so.

Equally, the Indian brokers complained that the company unfairly tried to drive down the prices of goods by grading them as being of poorer quality than was justified. All these money dealings meant that the accounts of Indian brokers often led to serious disputes.

Then there was the matter of procuring receipts for bribes paid to the Mughals. That could not have been an easy matter. And the company was always looking for ways to reduce the outgo of funds. It was in the interest of company officials to understate costs.

No Records Meant High Business Costs

A prolonged dispute between the Parsi merchant Rustum Manock, a broker of the English company at Surat and the English East India Company's Bombay office, gives us some insight into very different ways of thinking of the two parties. The Company had asked Manock to procure trading concessions at Surat including exemptions from custom duty. Rustum was able to report success in this matter in 1701. Upon his return, he gave Nicholas Waite, the head of India operations, the receipt for the money paid to Aurangzeb's official Gazdaur Khan. The receipt was never returned to Rustum. He claimed to have spent Rs. 175,000 to 180,000 of his funds on this mission. Waite however reported to the directors that Rustum had overcharged the company by Rs. 138,888 and that a maximum of Rs. 40,000 could be allowed for such a mission.[35]

This particular dispute caused a lot of bad blood between the family of the Parsi merchant and the company, nor did it end with his death. Nowros, a descendant of Rustumji went all the way to England to argue his case before the Court of Directors on the outstanding debts of the Company. He won.[36] But travelling to England, spending many months in that country, all required the kind of capital and social contacts, that very few Indian merchants had access to. The average Indian businessman continued to suffer the disabilities imposed by a non-existent legal system and an inability to track and recover debts.

While Manock's successors learnt from his mistake, many other merchants throughout the country came a cropper over managing debt on money either lent to or spent for the company.

Conracts Loaded Against Indian Merchants

It did not help that the contracts signed with the Indian merchants were often heavily loaded in favour of the company. This was not so much a reflection of the market power of the company as a reflection of the Indian merchant's belief that paper contracts did not matter. Some of the contracts signed by the English East India Company with merchants in Balasore in the Bengal-Orissa area in the 1670s, stand out in this regard. These contracts provided that in return for a full advance from the company on the investments to be made, the Indian merchants would repay any arrears within a month of the departure of the ships for Europe. Failing this, the merchants were liable to pay penal interest of 1.5 per cent until such time as the arrears were settled. Failure to supply goods would mean that the merchants would forfeit their share in the investment. These contracts were extremely one-sided. The contracts had no termination clause and all the penalties were on the side of the merchants.[37] The companies believed that by signing the contract, the merchants were placing themselves under company 'protection'.

It does not seem as though the Indian merchants took any of this seriously. So far as they were concerned, the terms were negotiable. They signed the contracts because the English insisted on it and they brought a profitable trade. This did not mean that they saw any value in the terms of the contracts. The English did not see it like that at all. But for a long time, they were in no position to insist strongly on the terms of contract. Gradually as the English became stronger, they began to insist on enforcing the penalties which had always been written into the contracts.

It was at this point that the Indian merchants faced difficulties.

The Indian merchant could not easily appeal to an impartial Mughal court of law in case of any dispute with the company. Legal systems were weak.

Finding a relative free-for-all, the English company often resorted to strong arm methods to enforce their version of the contract. We find instances where the company factors imprisoned local merchants as a coercive tactic. Sometimes local officialdom intervened in favour of the merchants but most of the time, there was a payoff involved.

The one thing that the English company did differently was that they set up resources independently of the Indian merchants and rulers. In eastern India, very soon they set up the mayoral court at Calcutta for mercantile disputes. An independent legal system was a clear attribute of sovereignty. This attracted some protest by Indian merchants but there is little evidence that they pursued their objections too seriously.

In 1744, some Indian saltpetre merchants in Bihar including the Sikh Amirchand had got into a dispute with Humphrey Cole, the chief of the English factory in Patna over unpaid debts. Cole had borrowed a great deal of money from the merchants and they were afraid he would decamp without making payment. They appealed to the administration. At this point the *naib nazim* (Deputy Governor) sent one hundred and fifty horsemen to lay siege to the English factory. The siege was lifted when Cole's successor gave an undertaking taking responsibility for the debts and after making suitable payment to the *durbar*.[38]

Indian Legal System Dysfunctional

Humphrey Cole still filed a legal suit over the matter in the Mayor's court at Calcutta. This was an open breach of local convention by which the merchants set up their own mechanisms for dispute resolution. Khwaja Wajid, an Armenian merchant and the informal leader of the Patna merchants, wrote to the English company protesting the action of the company in this case.[39] But the Indian rulers never did do anything about it. Amirchand and Deepchand, despite all their links with the *durbar*, never did file a counter suit in the Patna *durbar*.

It is possible the Indian businessmen did not protest such discriminatory policies since they were making high profits and they could still beat the Dutch and the English. Making common cause with each other to press the government for redressal might have seemed too onerous. Pooling resources is not something we find in the Indian business climate.

And there is little doubt that the Indian merchants were making a lot of money.

Skills of Indian Businessmen

The above discussion should not be taken to mean that Indian businessmen were bad at business. Merely their ways of doing business were different. In earlier times, all these strategies had been very successful. Lack of support from the state, inability to recover debts, had mattered much less when the competition was less powerful.

The working atmosphere in India was rather congenial to the doing of business. Various businessmen of medieval India, whether from the house of Jagat Seth in Bengal, the family of Virji Vora or Bhimji Parak in western India, the Ali Rajas of Cannanore in the Malabar region or even the women of the royal Mughal family, to name very few; all pursued the making of money with considerable vigour. We find great wealth among business families as also the landowning nobility. There was considerable sophistication in financial markets. And money was made buying and selling the innumerable products of India. Superior textile products were only one among these. In the ledgers of the English East India Company, we find 91 different types of textile products, 41 types of other products including spices and fragrant woods that were exported to Europe. In contrast, there were only 12 goods that were imported from Europe and bullion formed the greatest part of those imports.

Business in India was fiercely competitive. The European companies that entered India soon found that out to their cost. In the first hundred and fifty years of doing business in India, the Europeans complained bitterly about the cut price methods of Indian businessmen. How were the Asians able to offer such low prices, they wondered. One reason why the Asian traders consistently undercut the Europeans was, so the Europeans claimed, in their ability to exist on rice-based diets on long voyages and a rather low maintenance lifestyle.[40]

No one had any doubts about the skills of the Indian traders. Indian businessmen have not seen fit to leave behind much by way of records of their thoughts and ideas. The picture that we get from European records is that of a skilled group of people, very focussed on the making of money, great at negotiation and able to make profitable deals.

Indians were Great Negotiators

In the middle of the eighteenth century, traveller John Henry Grose could write of the Hindu banias of Surat that,

I have before observed, that the Gentoos[41] were extremely numerous here; especially that tribe or caste of the Banyans,[42] who are constitutionally or professedly merchants. I have often read, often heard them re-presented as a tricking, artful set of people, full of low cunning, that made it difficult to deal with them: but this can, I think, only be understood, if it be at all true, of the petty, under-dealers among them: for those of them who are properly merchants, in the extensive sense of that word, are in general, the fairest, openest dealers in the world, and those of Surat were especially famous for the simplicity and frankness of their transactions. For example, on a ship's importing there, nothing more was to be done, than for the commander, or supracargoe, to bring his musters or samples on board together with his invoice; and the considerable merchants reporting to them, would immediately strike a bargain for the whole cargo, if the assortment suited them, with no other trouble than settling the percentage upon the items of the invoice. In this manner many a cargo from five to ten, twenty, thirty thousand pounds and upwards, has been sold in half an hour's time with very few words, and the amount paid down upon the nail, either in ready money or by barter, according as the vendor and purchaser agreed, with as much good faith, at least, as is ever observed among the European merchants of the most established character of probity. Then their readiness at running all the hazards of trade was even proverbial, in so much, that it has not been unjustly observed of them, that if their personal equalled their commercial courage, they would incontestably be the bravest people on earth. . . .[43]

He writes further of their coolness in the middle of an argument and that however impassioned you might become in the middle of a discussion, they would never lose their composure.

They calmly suffer you to evaporate your resentment without interrupting you, and waiting patiently till your fit of drunkenness is off, for they look on it in no other light, they return cooly to the same point, as if nothing had stirred them from it and if they depart from it, you may depend that it is not in the least out of any consideration for what you (have said to them in your fury), but purely for their own ends, and inconsequence of their own inward representations to themselves. In that they have, in this point, the same advantage over the Europeans, that a cool gamester has over a passionate one.[44]

The European companies, Dutch, French or English, found it difficult to meet their procurement targets. The letters exchanged between the servants of the English East India Company and headquarters in London, constantly direct employees to buy the goods at lower prices and to buy more of them. They were in an intensely competitive market. For many years the companies were merely small players. In the seventeenth century at least, in the Malabar area where some figures are available, the Portuguese, Dutch and English East India companies put together accounted for barely 10 to 12 per cent of the market for pepper. In Bengal, one scholar has estimated that they accounted for at the most, one-third of the market for textiles till early into the eighteenth century.[45]

Where they saw a profit in it, the Indian merchants also collaborated loosely with each other to negotiate for better prices with the company.

Khemchand and Chintaman Shah, major merchants in Balasore (Orissa) in eastern India, often worked together in the last quarter of the seventeenth century. Both merchants were brokers to the English company. They routinely formed cartels with the other merchants and ganged up on the English to secure better terms of trade. They were aware that a great weakness of the company was its need to procure goods on time for the ships' departure to Europe. Too much delay could mean the loss of an entire season. So they happily used whatever leverage they could. The company certainly did not like being dictated to; they did their best to encourage other brokers as competitors. When they found they had no better alternative, they tried to bribe local rulers to harass the brokers.

Company Tries to Use Local Government Against Traders

In Hugli, Mathuradas was the chief Indian agent. He was rich enough to dictate the terms of trade to the English company. Much of Mathuradas' power also came from support of the local *faujdar*. The English tried to win the favour of the Nawab of Bengal to counter Mathuradas. Once the English did succeed in getting a letter out of the Bengal Nawab warning Mathuradas to stop his ill-behaviour to the English, otherwise he would be expelled from Bengal. The Hugli *faujdar* was furious with the letter; he promptly wrote to the diwan saying that a person who brought Rs. 18,000 a year to the King's treasury, could hardly be turned out of the country.[46] The English had little choice other than to lump it. But over time, their position improved. With rise in economic power, their ability to harm business competitors also improved.

POOLING OF RISK

So when they were in a position of greater wealth and power to begin with, how did the Indian merchants eventually lose out to the English company? The English company had gradually systematized information over decades. The resulting insights enabled them to reduce costs of insurance, to reduce the cost of capital and to increase efficiencies.

The results of information collated over a long span of time can be rather counter intuitive. In the specific case of insurance, risk pooling is very counter intuitive. It makes sense to believe that if any individual were to insure his goods, he would incur a certain cost which would be a high percentage of the insured cost.

The insurance industry however, depends on risk pooling and on the fact that when large numbers of people purchase insurance, only a few ever need to encash it. As an aside, even today, much of the debate over health insurance schemes in India runs on the theme of the minimum cost that each insured person would incur and the need to cover those costs. Actually if every insured person fell ill, the insurance company would go out of business. Many years of experience and information shows that this never does happen. At any given point of time, only a few individuals fall ill. This is what makes it possible to achieve low premiums when large populations are insured. For individuals to insure themselves on a purely individual basis without any institutional backing, would be costly indeed. If everyone who insured his goods against fire, then proceeded to burn his goods to claim the money in any given year, the insurance company would collapse and rates would skyrocket. The larger the insurance pool, the lower the incidence of claims, the lower the cost of insuring oneself.

In India however, information of this kind was never systematized, and risk pooling was not practised. So individuals insured themselves at fantastic costs.

Company Pooled Risk; Indians Did Not

Here is one instance of how insurance worked in medieval India. Sir John Malcolm, writing in the early nineteenth century, writes in his memoirs about an incident from Indore in the Malwa region, in 1801. A few months before the city was attacked by the Sindhia army, a consignment of goods from Mirzapur worth Rs. 6 lakh which was to go to Gujarat, arrived in Indore. The place was already surrounded by Pindaris. No one was willing to insure the goods for further transmission. In those days it was common for firms to enter into agreements that not only insured the goods but also contracted for transport including payment of custom duty. At this point, Kewaljee of the firm Poornassa Maun Singh, agreed to insure the goods beyond the river Mhye for 4 per cent. The Dhar state had already refused protection but the reputation of the firm was so good that the merchants agreed to pay. Kewaljee then increased the body of two hundred armed men in his employ to six hundred. He also contracted with Kishnajee Maljee, the Indore Collector for three hundred horse and two guns. For this he paid Rs. 5,000. And so the convoy was safely conducted beyond the river. Malcolm says that one of the partners of the firm Seeta Chund, showed him the transaction accounts. These showed that the premium paid was Rs. 24,000, the cost was Rs. 14,000 and there was a clear profit of Rs. 10,000. He quotes Seeta Chund as follows: 'No insurer', he added, 'ever lived in Malwa, but my brother Kewaljee, who would have dared to undertake such an enterprise. But he had a "Burrah Chattee", a great Breast—"B'hot Burrah Chattee", a very great breast!'[47]

This was a daredevil way to do insurance, but it was costly. Twenty four thousand rupees on an investment of Rs. 6 lakh amounted to 4 per cent. Comparatively, in areas like insurance and the cost of capital, the English East India Company had learned to use institutional mechanisms to cut costs. The Indian merchants might have had better products; they may even have been more skilled, but their ability to pool resources was very limited. And they rarely seemed to use information to systematize their business operations. Surely their business operations were large. But large volumes of business need not provide protection against business risk.

By the mid-eighteenth century, we hardly find any rich merchants whose operations rivalled that of the English company. There were exceptions like the house of Jagat Seth in Bengal. While the Indians had largely moved out of shipping in the eighteenth century, they continued to do overseas trade by freighting their cargo on European vessels. Domestic trade also continued despite several fluctuations and political interruptions. The house of Jagat Seth had built up its banking business towards the last quarter of the seventeenth century and by the eighteenth century, it was perhaps the largest banking house in the country. In the 1750s, the entire paid-up capital of the English East India Company was

Rs. 2.55 crore at the estimated exchange rate in those times, while the entire wealth of the House of Jagat Seth in Bengal, that is one single banking house was estimated to be Rs. 14 crore.[48]

Still, this house actively connived to set up English rule in Bengal. The individual merchants of this house seemed to feel that collaborating with an unknown entity with different business methods, posed no threats. They displayed a relative indifference to the relation between power and profit.

Company Uses Market Intelligence to Get an Upper Hand

In the meantime, by the 1750s, the situation had changed in the favour of the English East India Company. Even before the Battle of Plassey changed things, the English had settled down, familiarized themselves with locals in Bengal. Most important of all, they had established local networks of their own, independently of Indian merchants. The company council was no longer in any mood to be dictated to by the Indian merchants. In Murshidabad in 1751, the accounts that the company drew up, reflecting dues of local merchants, were not acceptable to the latter. Sobharam Basak, one of the biggest merchants of Murshidabad, refused to sign the contract and simply said that 'he esteemed his contract of no validity and paid no regard to it'. Other Indian merchants refused too. In short, these terms and the penalties prescribed by the company, were not acceptable to the local merchants.[49] As it turned out, their refusal to agree to the English terms was like the neighbourhood provision stores telling Walmart, that they wanted six months of credit; fifteen days would not do.

At this point, the English dug in their heels. When the merchants would not relent, they changed their methods of doing business. They decided that since the system of advances gave too much power to the local merchants, they would now operate independently of the merchants and instead use their own agents to directly get in touch with the weavers. They were able to make their threat good. The situation changed irretrievably as it turned out for the Indian merchants. The system of *dadni* advances had gone for good.

TRUST VS. FORMAL LEGAL SYSTEMS

Few Indian businessmen seemed to consistently maintain information or market intelligence that would have improved capabilities. In contrast, when we look at how the English East India Company operated, we can see how they systematized information and used it in a rather counter intuitive fashion. Pooling of risk, using standard protocols to purchase goods, using written contracts extensively; none of this is intuitive. After all, so far as the small merchant is concerned, they know most people they do business with. With less known other parties, they prefer a spot contract and a cash transaction. That is a simpler method of operating. Also, quite cheap on the face of it. That was how the Indian merchant community seemed to conduct their business.

Trust played an important role in most such transactions. Nor was it the merchant alone who operated largely on trust. Rulers and even raiding parties invading a country were no different. We can see this in the manner in which the *hundi* system worked in India. The *hundi* was a kind of bill of exchange for a specified amount to be paid on sight (*darshani hundi*) or after a specified period from the date of the *hundi* had passed (*muddati hundi*). Such hundis were used extensively to transfer funds from one location to another or even to take loans. The *hundis* could be bought and sold at a discount which varied depending on the region where it was to be en-cashed. *Hundis* originating at Jaipur in the eighteenth century were encashed at rates ranging from 5-6 per cent at Agra, Delhi and Benares.[50] The system continued to be in operation till the establishment of scheduled banks in the late nineteenth century by the British government.

MARATHAS INSIST THAT *HUNDIS* BE OF A RELIABLE BANKER

In Rajasthan, rulers authorized bankers of repute to draw *hundis*. These were used to remit money collected in tax revenue, to the state treasury. Contemporary records indicate that when the Marathas raided Rajasthan and demanded tribute, a portion of the tribute was paid through *hundis* drawn on a known banking house. Sometimes the Marathas even insisted that the *hundi* be drawn only on specific bankers of high repute like Dhanesar Das![51]

While the state often did authorise specific bankers for drawing the *hundis*, for enforcement of these instruments in case of any legal dispute, the government left it to a panchayat of merchants. Bankers did approach the state on occasion for redressal where the borrowers refused to honour loans taken through *hundis* and in such cases, help was offered but the entire system was an informal one. The general understanding seemed to be that all such affairs were the internal matters of merchants in which the state had little role to play. It was an informal network that was being used.

No doubt there were many large merchants. We have seen many merchant princes of India in the history books. But they continued to conduct business using extensive kinship networks. Decision-making remained rather personalized. This was a risky way of doing business but it survived well so long as the state system in which they lived, remained neutral. The government might have offered no protection but it did not harm them either. Might it be that the limited role of the state in trade matters also meant that merchants could not really perceive any necessary connection between power and the ability to make a profit?

OF POWER AND PROFIT AND THE INVISIBLE STATE

Where mercantile disputes were concerned, merchants were free to settle these internally most of the time. Even where the kings tried coercive mechanisms to interfere in market forces, they needed the merchants too much to persist with such tactics. Many European observers point out that the Indian kings could not really dictate prices, however much they tried. Royal monopolies on a few commodities like salt were the one exception.

In the Malabar region, the Dutch East India Company tried to coerce the local kings into establishing a monopsony in the pepper market; they failed. In 1694, the Dutch East India Company had entered into contracts with the ruler in the Malabar that his subjects would supply them with pepper. But the company found it next to impossible to enforce those contracts at a price favourable to them. In practice, the company had to pay for the pepper according to what the market price was.

Julius Valenteijn Stein van Gollenesse, Governor-in-charge of the Dutch establishment in Malabar from 1735 to 1743, writes in his memoir when he was leaving the coast:

> One point I must notice which is of great importance in the Company's service, viz. that although the kings and princes exercise great authority over their subjects, affairs are so regulated by the laws of Cheruman Perumal that their rule can in no way be called despotic; subjects obey their king ungrudgingly as long as he remains within the limits of the law; even if a chief were to wrong a few individuals, the whole community would not take up the quarrel; but if he were to issue orders calculated to injure the interests of the whole community, they would not be obeyed. I draw attention to this in special connection with pepper, and I confess to have made a mistake more than once in stating in the Company's papers that kings and chiefs alone can and should stop the export of pepper, and having examined the subject more carefully, I have come to the conclusion that their power in this matter is small if they do not wish to bring the hatred of the whole nation upon their head. . . .[52]

Royal Interference in Markets Against Local Norms

Where the king ventured beyond his limits, many times people stepped in for some rapid justice. In one such incident in the eighteenth century, Rudraraya, the Maharaja of Khadi and Judi [*sic*] in Bengal, so we are told, proceeded to the market to buy shoes. Negotiation over prices did not proceed according to his satisfaction and he eventually beat up the shopkeeper and threw him out of his own shop. The other shoe merchants went to inform the governor of the Maharaja's misconduct. The Maharaja 'out of fear' sent a minister of his to the governor promising to pay a fine of a 100,000 silver pieces. He felt this might not be enough so he purchased all the shoes for a sum of 10,000 pieces [*sic*] and distributed them among the people.[53]

Decision-making then tended to happen at the level of the *bazaar*, the village, town or community. The landlord or warlord or king, were only brought in when all else failed. The king seems to have seen himself as an arbiter of disputes rather than someone who provided direction or goals. And he nearly always acknowledged the power of the local trader. That is if he wished to keep his crown.

Not only did the rulers leave the traders to their own devices, they did not display much effort to improve their own tax base either.

So why is it then that Indian merchants and rulers displayed little interest in improving efficiencies? Even their pursuit of power and profit was not as vicious as that displayed by the East India Company. Could it be we wonder that this sense of placidity, of a near complete absence of a sense of threat among the Indian merchants of those times, was born of plenty? The idea that plenitude can generate complacency is a theme we shall return to in the next chapter.

WHAT HAS HISTORY GOT TO DO WITH IT: THE PLAN OF THIS BOOK

History is valuable mostly because it brings out these patterns in our behaviour in the very long term. The modern world demands a certain sensitivity to the value of information and the ability to use it systematically.

Market Openness, Enterprise Necessary but not Sufficient for Growth

Free enterprise, open economies, all these merely create opportunities for generating wealth. They represent a window, no more, no less. The mere existence of a window of opportunity cannot create wealth. For that, the country in question, must have the ability to utilize the opportunity. Foreign direct investment, globalisation, imported skills, imported technologies, have little meaning to a country that has no skills to use such resources. Lower order skills will mean a lower level of wealth creation. High order skills will mean a higher level of wealth creation. The ability to systematize information, to improve productivity, the skills to make sense of what is happening and to plan for the future, it is these that are critical to wealth creation.

Intelligent individuals can and do make efforts to improve their skills. But for individuals to be able to learn from each other, to exchange information, institutional mechanisms are essential. Building robust institutions is beyond the capability of any one or even a few individuals. It is here that the role of the state becomes important.

Good Legal Systems, Market Intelligence, Data Management, Technology are Key

The state is also essential as the manager of the legal and regulatory framework. In the modern state, citizens cannot do business easily without a functioning legal system. This has been one of the weakest areas in Indian business history. That this should still be the case is a matter of concern. Clear and transparent rules and laws and a legal system that can apply those rules effectively, is critical to any economy. For trade disputes to linger on for years and even decades till the parties are forced to find informal ways to resolve these, cannot be a healthy situation.

There is a romantic view which says that the English were a rather rigidly protocol oriented kind of people while the Indians were more used to face-to-face negotiation. Perhaps. But following standard rules is a great advantage when it comes to managing money. It is absolutely essential when it comes to managing legal and taxation systems. All such state-wide systems depend on systematic information sets.

The ability to set up systems to collate and manage information, must depend upon the social attitudes to information and to learning with which we have grown up. These skills or absence thereof are so deeply embedded in our history and society that they become visible only when we take a very long view of history.

Now that may be a tall order. But we suggest that unless this basic task is tried out, our efforts might fall seriously short of making India great again.

Therefore, we invite the reader to walk through the portals of history with us. This is the way to understand some of the features that underlay India's past greatness, and to identify or recognise the weaknesses therein. To examine our history is to ensure that as we embark on the journey to make India great once again, we do not commit some of the key errors that our ancestors did.

Individually speaking, Indians do rather well for themselves across the world, in different areas, in rather difficult situations. Indian researchers and businesspeople are counted as some of the most successful ones in the world. Can the systematic use of information facilitate the transformation of individual successes into a collective success for India? Can the use of information make India rich as opposed to just a few Indians? This is a question that leads us to delve into the history of India in this book.

We shall look at Indian history to see what our attitudes to information, to knowledge generation and institution building in the past have been. In this book, we shall examine three different themes in Indian history in order to unravel Indian attitudes to information and productivity and our ability to preserve and transmit information. These stories also help us to look at the learning curve in Indian society. We try to see how Indians in the past looked at long-term institutional innovations.

In the first chapter we shall see that till the eighteenth century, many social groups in India enjoyed a rather low cost of living. Ease of life seems to have generated a certain indifference to information or its systematization.

In the second chapter, we look in greater detail at the relationship between information and productivity as it has played out in modern India. Here we also look at the special role played by institutions in the systematization of information. It is often believed that omission cannot be as important as commission. This is not really true. The failure to systematize information was directly connected with the famines in Bengal towards the end of the eighteenth century, as we shall see in this chapter.

Next we look at the methods of using information in three sectors deemed to be important to any economy: banking, the technology for making iron and steel, and pure sciences in so far as the discipline of mathematics is concerned.

In the third chapter we look at the relationship between banking and value creation. Banking is a sector which requires an immediate return on capital to enable it to pay out interest on its funds. The lives of two remarkable individuals: the ruler of Bengal the Nawab Nazim, Murshid Quli Khan, and the banker, Seth Manik Chand, show how they collaborated to create considerable synergies and improve profits. A brief look at Indian history tells us that India in the past did not lack capital for economic development but it did lack the ability to use capital effectively. There were many banking houses throughout the country that had wealth similar to that of the house of Jagat Seth. The recent unlocking of the treasure vaults in the Sri Padmanabhaswamy Temple located in Thiruvananthapuram, Kerala, revealed a storehouse of wealth estimated at Rs. 90,000 crore. No doubt other Indian temples held similar treasure. It was treasure of this variety which beckoned invaders for thousands of years to invade India. It is not enough for individual businesses to be wealthy—they need to actively involve governments to protect themselves too.

Then we look at other sectors to see how the themes of organization and the effective use of information pan out in Indian history. Innovations that are institutionalized over time are key indicators of this kind of progress.

In the fourth chapter, we look at the iron and steel industry in India. India produced some of the best steel in the olden world but it was simply unable to scale up any of those processes to match the demands of an industrializing world. Eventually all that pre-modern knowledge got lost.

The next theme we study is that most ivory tower of all knowledge disciplines: mathematics. As in all other areas of life, so in mathematics we find that Indians have been a seriously practical-minded people. They demanded high rates of return and returns in the short-term. Profits were of the weekly *bazaar* variety—utility had to be reported in the short run. There were great scientific minds in India's past. Yet much of their great work was not recorded.

What does remain a puzzle is that with Indian mathematics being among the most advanced in the ancient world by the end of the first millennium CE, how is it that we were never able to leverage these individual achievements to scale up production of goods or to increase our turnover to the extent that the Western world was able to.

Till the seventeenth century, India continued to contribute over a quarter of the world GDP but we were already slipping behind. It is not that we stagnated. It was that others grew much faster than we did.

Whether it was the setting up of financial systems, technology or the pure sciences, India had developed a certain skill set that generated wealth. In all three sectors, Indians gained considerable renown in the ancient world. Still, we were unable to generate institutional systems to improve productivity.

Lack of robust institutions might be one reason why the distribution of skills in the Indian population, has been so uneven. A high level of skill depends above all on functional institutions, and on information exchange in society. Technical information in India has historically been confined to small groups that barely interacted with each other. We shall see how the lack of institutions has affected the learning curve.

A common problem in the modern world and in history in general is that brilliant individuals and their life histories make for good reading. What institutional support these brilliant people received or failed to receive, is much less exciting. No one is interested in knowing about the scaffolding that was essential for the construction of a building. It is great to know that Bill Gates was a college dropout. It gives a comforting feeling to know that formal education is not so great as it is touted to be and great individuals can beat all odds. What does not find its way into the popular narrative is the fact that Gates developed some of his skills in computer programming in high school by using computer time made available by local computer companies which were reaching out to kids to find flaws in their security systems. That kind of interface between knowledge systems and innovation has not yet been imbricated into our formal institutions or our private companies to become a self-sustaining on-going activity, a national habit, if you will.

But, be warned, while knowledge was important, knowledge systems remained distant for Indians in the past. We have ignored the role of institutions and long-term perspectives for too long, and the results are there for all to see. Countries which have, for whatever reason, managed to also take care of institutions and long-term perspectives, have been able to leverage individual talents and scale up these to benefit society and country.

This book then, explores how even in the absence of sufficient structures to up-scale individual efforts, geography and society combined to facilitate an economy that was the largest in the pre-industrial world till roughly the seventeenth century. Then we sum up all the strands to tell the story of resurgent India in the twenty-first century; of our signal successes and of the dysfunctionalities that remain to be addressed. It is our fervent hope that the study of some of the strengths and weaknesses of our history will show India the path ahead.

NOTES

1. These are figures at current prices. For India 1950-1 figures, see Ministry of Finance, Government of India, 2016-17, *Economic Survey*, vol. 2, A-12. For conversion rate of Rs. 4.77 to 1 USD in 1950, RBI figures used. For US figures for 1950-1, see U.S. Bureau of Economic Analysis, GNPA, retrieved from FRED, Federal Reserve Bank of St. Louis; https://fred.stlouisfed.org/series/GNPA, 4 January 2019. For 2017 figures for India and USA, see World Bank, 2017; URL accessed on 4 January 2018: https://data.worldbank.org/indicator/NY.GDP.MKTP.CN?locations=IN
2. Ibid.
3. World Bank, 1990, p. 29.
4. World Bank, 2018 http://databank.worldbank.org/data/download/poverty/33EF03BB-9722-4AE2-ABC7-AA2972D68AFE/Archives-2018/Global_POVEQ_IND.pdf, accessed on 14 November 2018.
5. Bhagwati, 2013.

6. Tone, 1800: 137.
7. Broughton, 1892: 134-5.
8. Alavi, 1993.
9. Ibid.
10. Sykes, 1847.
11. Hedges, 1887, vol. I: 139.
12. Basu, 1967: 110.
13. Chaudhuri, 1978: 438.
14. Prakash, 1985: 44-5.
15. Ibid.
16. Chatterjee, 1992.
17. Ibid.
18. Moosvi, 2008, rpt. 2010: 253.
19. Ibid.: 244-5.
20. Ibid.: 247.
21. Malekandathil, 2010, rev. edn. 2013: 120-1.
22. Foster, 1921: 203.
23. Gupta, 1998: 372.
24. Gupta, 1994, rpt.: 77.
25. Ibid.: 96.
26. Ibid.: 98.
27. Ibid.: 99.
28. Ibid.: 100.
29. Chaudhuri, 1978: 113.
30. Gupta, 1994, rpt.: 114.
31. Ibid.
32. Askari, 1961
33. Foster, 1906, vol. I: 4-6.
34. Gupta, 1994, rpt.: 149-50.
35. White, 1995: 46-7.
36. Ibid.: 73-80.
37. Chaudhuri, 1975: 64-5.
38. Chatterjee, 1992.
39. Ibid.
40. Chaudhuri, 1978: 210.
41. The word Gentoos was used by Europeans to refer to Hindus. Muslims were mostly referred to as Moors.
42. Banyans means 'banias', a common name for a mercantile group.
43. Grose, 1772: 105-6.
44. Ibid.: 106.

45. Chaudhury, 1995: 209.
46. Chaudhuri, 1975: 69-76.
47. Malcolm, 1823, 2: 98-9.
48. Little, 1960: xvii.
49. Chaudhury, 1995, 99-100.
50. Tyagi, 2014: 34.
51. Ibid.: 28.
52. Gupta, 1967: 15-16.
53. Mukherjee, 2009.

CHAPTER 1

India: Rich in Resources

Natural resources abounded in India. Indian emperors were some of the richest in the world. William Hawkins, Captain of the first East India Company ship, *Hector* to arrive in India in the early seventeenth century, commented that, 'India is rich in silver, for all nations bring coyne, and carry away commodities for the same; and this coyne is buried in India, and goeth not out'.[1] Hawkins spent about three years at the court of Mughal emperor Jahangir from 1609 to 1611. He reported the annual revenues of the Mughal emperor to be around 50 crores of rupees.[2] At the exchange rate of Rs. 8 to the pound, this would have been more than 62 million pounds sterling. The figures cited by Hawkins may or may not be correct; certainly the riches of the Mughal court dazzled him. Seeing that crown revenues in England were around 535,000 pound in 1603,[3] which was less than 1 per cent of the figure he attributes to the Mughals, it is not surprising that the Mughal court made such an impression on Hawkins.

Yet human effort to increase the bounty of nature is hard to find. India for all it's riches, continued to be troubled by low productivity, whether in agriculture, in iron and steel or in trade. India produced some of the best steel in the world at the time or wootz steel as it was called. But we always produced it in small lots of a few hundred kilograms. Any efforts to up-scale production have not been recorded. We had some of the most fertile soil in the world anywhere and grain was so abundant that little effort was required to get a good crop. Still, yields per hectare did not improve noticeably. The Mughals or any other Indian ruler for that matter, seem to have made little effort to improve credit and banking, to improve productivity or to increase trade.

We always seemed to be reasonably content with what we had. Why should this be so?

Aurangzeb Feels Short-changed in His Education

We get a marvellous insight into Aurangzeb and his ideas from a conversation between him and his old teacher. It so happened that one Mulla Shah of Badakshan, was tutor to both Dara Shukoh, elder son of Shah Jahan, and also Aurangzeb. So when Aurangzeb won the war of succession, Mulla Shah rushed to Delhi to seek an interview with the new Emperor. Obviously, he hoped for promotions and favours. In the beginning, Aurangzeb would not see him. When he finally did agree after three months, this is what he reportedly told his old teacher:

> Pray what is your pleasure with me, Mullah-gy [Mulla-Ji] Monsieur the Doctor? Do you pretend that I ought to exalt you to the first honours of the State? . . . But what was the knowledge I derived under your tuition? You taught me that the whole of Franguistan (Europe) was no more than some inconsiderable island, of which the most powerful Monarch was formerly the King of Portugal, then he of Holland, and afterward the King of England. In regard to the other sovereigns of Franguistan, such as the King of France and him of Andalusia, you told me they resembled our petty Rajas, and that the potentates of Hindoustan eclipsed the glory of all other kings; that they alone were Humayons, Ekbars, Jehan-Guyres, or Chah-Jehans; the Happy, the Great, the Conquerors of the World, and the Kings of the World; and that Persia Usbec, Kachguer, Tartary, and Catay, Pegu, Siam, China and Matchine (MahaChina or the Great China) trembled at the name of the Kings of the Indies. Admirable geographer! Deeply read historian! Was it not incumbent upon my preceptor to make me acquainted with the distinguishing features of every nation of the earth; its resources and strength; its mode of warfare, its manners, religion, form of government, and wherein its interests principally consist; and, by a regular course of historical reading, to render me familiar with the origin of States, their progress and decline; the events, accidents, or errors, owing to which such great changes and mighty revolutions, have been effected? Far from having imparted to me a profound and comprehensive knowledge of the history of mankind, scarcely did I learn from you the names of my ancestors, the renowned founders of this empire. . . .[4] [*sic*]

Yet, despite his obvious feeling of being short-changed in his education, there is little to show that Aurangzeb found better tutors for his own children.

This quality of life; this sense of inertia, is something visible in the life of the times too. Weavers, farmers, artisans, mostly everyone in India were simply contented with their lot. Could it be that the cost of living was so low and land so plentiful that eking out a living was an easy task?

However, paradoxical it might sound, so rich were we, that Indians were content with what they had. The cost of living was low. Six to eight months of work was more than enough to keep body and soul together. We were content. Let us look at how some groups of people in different parts of the country lived in the past to find some clues to the problem.

COST OF LIVING FOR WEAVER OF BENGAL IN EIGHTEENTH CENTURY

The weaver was a key figure in the textile industry of Bengal in the seventeenth and eighteenth centuries. For two hundred years at least before Plassey changed the political economy of the region, the weavers in this region, produced cloth of such high quality that it out-sold European products in the international market and made Bengal one of the richest provinces in the Mughal empire.

A major part of the reason that weavers here enjoyed so much competitive advantage was that the cost of living in Bengal was rather low. In addition, the raw materials were available close by and transport by river provided cheap logistics. Let us try to see what an average weaver might have been able to earn and what he needed to spend on the basic necessities of life in those times.

Combination of Weaving with Farming Good Risk Protection

Contemporary records say that most weavers in Bengal were also part-time peasants. Some weavers may have worked full time but it was the combination with agriculture that gave many of them a peculiar flexibility. In the monsoon season, they busied themselves with family labour in cultivating paddy in their fields. The rest of the year they devoted themselves to weaving, again with the help of family labour. The women in the family spent a lot of their time in spinning cotton and winding silk. It was no doubt his connection with farming that gave the weaver significant risk protection. When times were not so good, he could return to farming.

Robert Orme, the official historian of the English East India Company said of Bengal that, it was difficult to find a village in which every man, woman and child was not employed in making a piece of cloth.

Capital investment required was rather low. In a detailed survey report of Bengal commissioned by the English East India Company from its Calcutta Headquarters, Scottish physician Francis Buchanan-Hamilton writes in the early nineteenth century that at most an investment of Rs. 20 was required in loom and house by a weaver. Within this amount, he could build a house and buy a loom, pots, silk, cotton and dyes sufficient to weave one cloth. A man and his wife could generally weave and dye a cloth in one month that sold for Rs. 20 and still make Rs. 5 in profit.[5] This Hamilton wrote for the period 1807-11 when he conducted the survey.

But let us go back to the seventeenth century before the assumption of rule by the East India Company changed the economy irrevocably.

For those times, the English and Dutch sources tell us that a weaver's earnings would be about 30 to 40 per cent of the price of the items he wove and sold. The information from English sources comes from the report of one Matthias Vincent at a time when the English were still trying to find a firm foothold in Bengal.[6] A profit margin of 38 per cent as recorded by the British is indeed rather high. The Dutch sources give a more modest figure of the weaver's earnings as being from 32 to 34 per cent. So we take an average of one-third of the price of the item, as being the net earning of the weavers.

Now let us see how many such pieces he could weave in a month using only the labour of his wife and children at most. The amount of labour required for textile products can vary immensely depending on a number of factors—the material itself, the number of warp threads, with higher thread counts taking more time and effort, the intricacy of the design and so on. A man, his wife and perhaps a child could between them, weave about 0.75-3.5 yards of silk on one loom in a day, depending on all these factors.[7] For this, they might earn a net profit of Rs 1.75 in good times on one piece, 10 yards in length, in the late seventeenth century. Assuming they were able to weave three and a half ordinary silk pieces in the month, the average earning on the ordinary pieces would be roughly Rs. 6 and two annas in a month. If they chose to work for only seven months in the year they would make Rs. 42 in cash income roughly in the year.

Since he was also a farmer, the weaver might have spent four months of the monsoon season in raising a paddy crop. For the rest of the time, he might get his land cultivated by family labour, since land easily brought in two to three crops a year. No statistics on landholding is available but a farmer with less than 10 *bighas* is called a poor farmer. Assuming a small landholding of 5 *bighas* of ordinary land and given local productivity of 8-10 maunds to the *bigha*, one single crop could get him 40 maunds of paddy.[8]

We must also account for the taxes he paid. Taxes could be anything from 25 to 30 per cent of the crop plus overheads. Indian peasants have never been particularly enthusiastic about paying taxes, probably rightly so. In an entertaining account dating to 1612, Father Sebastian Manrique, a friar of the order of St. Augustine describes his journey in India including the province of Bengal. He has rather nasty things to say about the oppressions of the Mughal rulers. We learn that in case the peasant did not pay his taxes, not only his property but his wife and children could be seized. And then Father Manrique gives some eye-witness accounts of the process of recovery. He says the Indian peasants are a spiritless lot; kindness is wasted on them. For one who gives blows is a master and one who does not, is a dog. 'The Bengali ryot made it a rule never to part with money without the application of a whip, while the necessity of this painful preliminary was strongly insisted upon by the ryot's wife who, if she learnt that her lord has dispensed with it and paid without a struggle, put him on short rations for a time as a punishment.'[9] The fault then was not entirely that of the Governor. Wives it seems were a domestic force to contend with and a threat of keeping her husband on bread and water, would be intimidating.

However, for the sake of our narrative, we assume that the peasant did indeed pay his taxes regularly without raising any such protests. After paying all his taxes and de-husking, he might be left with 16-17 maunds of rice.[10]

Now let us see what his expenses might have been. For the prices the Indian population would have paid, we take the time period of the first quarter of the eighteenth century. We also take it that he would need to support a family of six people and that he and his wife would be the main earning members.[11]

Since this is a Bengali family, we shall assume that the family liked to eat fish and that they ate fish at least half the time.

It is not easy to know what people might have eaten in those days. For help, we take as a base, the diet recommended by the Indian Council of Medical Research in 2010. But we need to remember that those were difficult times. People had to do hard physical labour. This might have included working on ploughing the land, harvesting the crop, winnowing the grain, working on an old fashioned loom. Much more energy would be needed. So it would be reasonable to add another 50 per cent to this. The resulting diet is similar to what a contemporary English observer records.[12] The one major difference is that Indians in those days used to consume much more by way of dal; roughly they ate about 15 per cent as much dal as rice. Indians also preferred a far saltier diet—this was a common complaint of Englishmen. With these adjustments, we can estimate what a family of six might have eaten three hundred years ago in Bengal (see Table 1.1. All Figures are approximations). We do not include vegetables here. A peasant family would have access to home grown vegetables; and vegetables do contribute to micro-nutrients but not to calories.

Eating *dal*, *chawal* and *ghee*, with the occasional dose of fish, evidently worked for the Bengali weaver. When dietician Rujuta

Food Group	Total daily intake in grams for days of fish based diet*	Total daily intake in grams for days of non-fish diet	Annual intake in kg	Converted to Bengal Seers** of 933 grams	Annual Cost in Rs.	Prices of Commodities
Rice	3,735	3,735	1,344.6	1,441	2.56	We deduct 16.8 maunds of home-grown rice and put a value to the rest. Coarse *kanakhali* rice was available at 300 seers a rupee[14]
Pulses	280.125	560.25	151.27	162	4.05	40 seers per rupee.[15]
Milk	2,250	2,250	810	868	0.00	Milch cattle at home
Mustard Oil	306	280.5	105.57	113	4.71	Oil of the second sort available at 24 seers a rupee[16]
Ghee	54	49.5	18.63	20	1.79	11.2 seers per rupee[17]
Sugar and jaggery	125	125.0	45.00	48	2.49	19.3 seers per rupee[18]
Salt	125	125.0	45.00	48	1.33	32-40 seers per rupee[19]
Fish	250	0.0	45.00	48	6.00	Half a rupee a month sufficient to feed family of six for 15 days.[20]
Total					22.93	

Notes: * For those eating fish, as per ICMR recommendations, the daily dose of pulses is reduced by 50 per cent and an extra 5 g of oil is added to those days when fish was eaten.

** Bengal seer measured at 2.057 pounds or 933 grams (*Useful Tables*, 1834: 67). Figures rounded off after conversion to seer to nearest whole number.

Source: See endnotes 13-20. All prices are approximations.

Diwekar hails the virtues of local foods and most especially *dal, chawal* and *ghee*, she is right on target. Even more interesting is the fact that more than half the protein component of the diet was contributed by rice! Today we consume polished varieties of rice which are far poorer in nutrition content as compared to traditional varieties.

This budget (Table 1.1) suggests that a family of six could meet all recommended dietary needs happily at an annual cost of roughly Rs. 23 which would be half of the family's cash income.

Of course, there was considerable variation in prices. We do not have any consistent year-wise data for the different rice varieties. But information in the English factory records shows that rice prices could shoot up by three to four times, while other necessaries of life sometimes did double.

Even in Adverse Times, Budget could meet Food Needs

We take one scenario where rice prices shot up by 4 times and oil prices doubled. To make things difficult, we can assume fish prices rose by 50 per cent. In this case the weaver would spend roughly Rs. 42 per annum on consuming the above diet. In case the earnings of the weaver rose marginally only by a quarter this would mean a cash income of about Rs. 50-2 annually. In this case, he would be spending roughly 80 per cent of his income on meeting his food needs. This would leave him a little to cover other expenses. But his food needs would still be met.

The coming to power of the English East India Company in Bengal changed the happy situation of the weaver. By the later half of the eighteenth century, incomes had crashed and prices had risen. Even by the 1750s, with persistent attacks by the Maratha *Bargies* and disturbed conditions, things were difficult. Still, the English officials could report twenty-five years after Plassey, in the late eighteenth century that a family of two men, women and children could subsist perfectly well on Rs. 9 per year and spare money for other necessaries of life!

Now we go to a different region of the country to see how poor people might have fared.

COST OF LIVING FOR THE PEASANT IN MARWAR REGION

Munhot Nainsi was the Diwan of Marwar state in the time of Raja Jaswant Singh in the seventeenth century. Something of a polymath, he compiled extensive information about the land revenue administration and life in the Marwar region. His writings give us some idea of how the people of those times lived, ate and earned their livelihoods. While spare cash was limited for the middling peasant, it still seems to have been a happy-go-lucky kind of life. The most difficult event to deal with was the occasional famine.

Land was available in plenty, so much so that it was routine to leave cultivable land fallow after two or three seasons. Up to the end of the nineteenth century, nearly one-third to one-half of area under cultivation in the Marwar region, was left fallow. This also meant that the land-man ratio was very comfortable. A farmer who cultivated about 10-20 *bighas* of land, would have been called a poor farmer.

The availability of plenty of land and scarce manpower meant that rulers had to be careful about oppressive taxation in difficult times, otherwise they might be faced with wholesale desertion. A scholar tells us of a pargana official writing to the Diwan Kalyan Das in 1685 AD,

> The raiyatis (probably khud-kasht peasants) have gone to some other places in famine years. Therefore, I have instructed all the chaudhari and qanungos, patel and patwari and ijaradars of pargana Bahatri, Piragpur, Jalapur and Bhankok, to console the paltis who have gone to Malwa, Burhanpur, Kulibhit, and Purab and towards Agra and Sri Mathura. To attract them inducements for patta batai (concessional sharing of patta), bullocks and seed were to be offered. I (Kesho Das) have also granted concessional pattas to the patels of two out of four villages who have gone to bring the paltis back.[21]

Land revenue demand could range from 15 to 33 per cent but the *hasil* or actual collected, was lower. The *hasil* is reported to be anywhere from a low of 30 per cent to a high of 85 per cent of the estimated demand.[22] Tax could be collected in cash in the *zabti* system or also in kind. Information available about tax collected in kind from certain villages in this region indicates collection of roughly 25 per cent of the produce by the state from the ordinary peasants.[23]

In a land rich society, it was access to resources like bullocks, Persian wheels and ploughs which determined the wealth or poverty of the farmers, rather than the land available to them. In pargana Chatsu in the Jaipur region for instance, the average land available per farmer was 90 *bighas* but if he had only one plough then he could not cultivate more than 50 *bighas* of land, without any other capital.[24]

For cultivating land in rainfed conditions, capital required was limited and one plough was enough to sustain a family of six. The area under crops in *rabi* and *kharif* in Jalor pargana in Marwar indicates that two-third land was cultivated in *kharif* and one third in the rabi season.[25] The ratio of *kharif* to *rabi* could vary from 90:10 to 70:30 in the neighbouring parganas.[26] Millets like *bajra* and *jowar*, pulses like *mung* and *moth*, cotton and sugarcane, were major *kharif* crops. Intermixing of cereals with pulses was the norm. Wheat and gram (*chana*) were major *rabi* crops.

Daily Diet of Marwari Farmer

People ate cereals like *jowar*, *bajra* and other millets as staple food. *Dal* or pulses was probably eaten daily. A liberal dose of ghee or oil depending on the pockets of the family and some pickle, added relish to the meal. *Gur* was another common ingredient of diet.

Tax Paid could Depend on Social Status

A very interesting feature of the village community in Rajasthan was that tax rates seem to have depended on position in the village hierarchy much more than on caste. So we find three different land revenue rates were imposed on peasants from the kunbhar caste. The *mehtar-kunbhar* (potter headman) paid one sixth of his produce as revenue. This is the lowest rate in the entire revenue schedule. Then there were the ordinary kunbhars who seem to have been obliged to render services to the village: they paid one-fourth of the produce as tax. Those kunbhar peasants who were not on the village establishment at all, paid one-third of the produce as tax to the government.[27] This was among the highest rates.

We shall try to see how a poor farmer might have survived. It has been calculated from the information available in Nainsi's writings that roughly 50 maunds of grain was available per peasant, before tax, in some of the villages in Marwar region.[28]

Let us say he produced about 50 maunds of foodgrain in *kharif* and *rabi* put together. 40 maunds of this might be millets for home consumption, 5 maunds of *moong* and 5 maunds could be wheat grown for sale. If he paid 25 per cent tax to the state, he might be left with 30 maunds of millet, 3.75 maunds of *moong* and 3.75 maunds of wheat for his use. We further deduct a little for seed requirement. Routinely such farmers grew some oilseed for home use, probably sesame (*til*) in this case. Farmers also grew cane for *gud* (jaggery) at home but let us say he still needed to buy a quarter of his needs from the market. In addition, our farmer may have grown some *guar* (cluster beans) as a cash crop on say 2 *bighas* of land. Tax on such cash crops was fixed in cash; for vegetables, it could range up to Rs. 1.37 per *bigha* in the Merta pargana of Marwar for the last quarter of the seventeenth century.[29]

Farmers normally supplemented this income with dairying and sheep rearing. The cattle and sheep population in this part of Rajasthan was considerable. Tharparkar was and continues to be an excellent milch cattle of the Jodhpur region. Milk yield is in the region of 1,100 to 2,000 litres per lactation cycle. Given a fat content of roughly 4.5 per cent it might take 22 to 25 litres to produce 1 kg of *ghee*. And sheep were reared for wool for sale. Sale of ghee and raw wool is widely reported for the Marwar region.

Now let us see what the economics of this peasant household might look like (Tables 1.2 and 1.3) (all figures are approximations).

To the present-day reader, all the rupee figures in three decimal points might seem like a lot of nit-picking but it is important to remember that the value of money in those times was much larger than in the present. Re. 0.125 (8 paise) was the grazing tax on one

TABLE 1.2: INCOME IN CASH AND KIND FOR THE MARWARI FARMER IN THE LATE SEVENTEENTH CENTURY

Category of cash income	Quantity for sale in maunds[30]	Market rate in Rs. per maund	Annual cash income in Rs.	Annual cash income if prices increase by 30 per cent	Remarks
Sale of wheat	2.75	0.8	2.20	2.86	5 Maunds of wheat produced, 25 per cent tax paid in kind plus 1 maund for seed. Prices of wheat reported for Eastern Rajasthan in seventeenth century.[31]
Sale of *guar* seed	10	0.6	6.0	7.8	Value of 10 maunds of *guar* produced from 2 *bigha*.[32] Prices of *guar* reported for Eastern Rajasthan in the seventeenth century.
Sale of wool	0.75	0.875	0.66	0.66	Roughly 25 kg wool produced from 15 sheep per annum.[33] Wool prices remain stable.
Sale of *ghee*	1.65	6.5	10.725	13.94	72 kg *ghee* produced from 2,500 litres of milk from 2 milch cattle. After deducting 700 litres for home consumption, 25 litres milk used per kg *ghee*. 0.5 maunds *ghee* for home consumption leaving 1.65 maunds for sale.[34]
Total cash in Rs.			19.585	25.26	

TABLE 1.2: contd.

Category of cash income	Quantity for sale in maunds[30]	Market rate in Rs. per maund	Annual cash income in Rs.	Annual cash income if prices increase by 30 per cent	Remarks
Annual Income net of cash taxes			17.19	22.335	
Income in Kind	For home consumption				
Millets (*bajra* and *kodon*)	30 maunds				
Pulses	3.75 maunds				
Guar for home consumption	Green fodder used for cattle. *Guar* also cooked as vegetable.				
Milk	700 litres				
Ghee	0.5 maunds				
Oil	3 maunds				
Jaggery	4.5 maunds				

Source: See endnotes 30-4. All prices are approximations.

TABLE 1.3: CASH TAXES PAID BY FARMER IN MARWAR REGION

Category of tax	Rate of tax	Cash value of tax in last quarter of seventeenth century in Rs.	Cash taxes in Rs. if taxes on *guar* and *ghee* increase by 30 per cent
Grazing tax for cows	5 *dugani*[35] per cow for 2 cows	0.25	0.25
Grazing tax for sheep	1 *dugani* per sheep for 15 sheep	0.375	0.375
Cash tax on *guar*[36]	25 per cent tax on income	1.50	1.95
Tax on *ghee*	1 ser per maund on 1.65 maunds	0.27	0.35
Total tax		2.395	2.925

Source: See endnotes 35-6.

cow per annum. This was enough in the 1660s to buy *bajra* ration for an entire family for two and a half days. We have seen that the normal daily consumption of a family was roughly 4 *ser* or 3.7 kg of cereals. In the 1660s in Rajasthan, you could buy 10.25 kg or 11½ *ser* of *bajra* in 8 paise. Prices had risen till the 1740s but you could still buy 1.9 kg or half the daily ration of a family in 8 paise at that time. One of the smallest units of the rupee was the *dhela* and there were 128 *dhelas* to the rupee. In 1740 in Rajasthan you could still buy 120 g of *bajra* in 1 *dhela*.

Table 1.4 shows how much a family would be spending every year on food.

Tables 1.2, 1.3 and 1.4 show that a family that paid all their taxes, would be spending nearly 60-6 per cent of their cash income to eat comfortably with some left over to buy clothes for the family and occasional entertainment. Given that the *masalachi* in government employment earned Rs. 2 a month and 1 *payali* (4-5 *ser*) *bajra* and 2 *chhatak ghee* daily as rations and that the lowest paid agriculture labourer got 4½ *ser bajra* and 1 *chhatak ghee* daily,[37] government employment then and now was much better than labouring in the fields! Still, the farmer could lead such a life with

TABLE 1.4: FOOD INTAKE OF A FAMILY OF 6 IN THE MARWAR REGION FOR THE LATE SEVENTEENTH CENTURY[38]

(*Figures in Rs.*)

Food group	Total daily intake in g for vegetarian diet	Monthly intake in kg	Annual intake in kg	Annual intake in maunds[39]	Bought from Market in maunds	Prices in Rs. per maund in normal conditions[40]	Cash ex-penditure in Rs.	Cash expenditure prices of pulses, millets increase by 60% and gud by 15%
Millets/Cereals	3,735.00	112.05	1,344.60	40.20	10.00	0.4	4.00	6.40
Pulses	560.25	16.81	201.69	6.03	2.28	1.21-1.29	2.85	4.56
Leafy vegetables	420.00	12.60	151.2	4.52	0.00		0.00	0.0
Other vegetables	495.00	14.85	178.2	5.33	0.00		0.00	0.0
Roots and tubers	345.00	10.35	124.2	3.71	0.00		0.00	0.0
Milk	2,250.00	67.50	810.00	24.22	0.00	0	0.00	0.0
Oil	280.5	8.42	100.98	3.02	0.00	2.16-4	0.00	0.0
Oil–*ghee*	49.5	1.49	17.82	0.53	0.00	4.57-5.93	0.00	0.0
Sugar and jaggery	573.75	17.21	206.55	6.17	1.54	1.48-2	2.7	3.105
Salt	125.00	3.75	45.00	1.35	1.35	0.52-0.67	0.81	0.81
Total							10.36	14.875

Source: See endnotes 38-40. All prices are approximations.

barely 4-6 months of labour in the year, so life could not have been too hard.

A Serendipitous Existence

With little pressure of work and low costs of living, it is not a wonder that setting up systems to collect information was hardly a priority. If the necessities of life are easily obtained, then planning for a distant future makes less sense. After all information is collated with the idea that it can be of some use later, either to ourselves or to others. It is when we have such a long-term perspective that matters are different. Information is of value only if it is collated for many years and then used for decision-making. Individual bits of information are less useful.

Systems that can keep track of information are not set up in a day or even in one lifetime. That takes several lifetimes to do. Systems might increase the reach of the individual but they also take a lot of maintenance. Above all, they require long-term thinking.

Planning for the future requires that states invest in capacity building and information gathering. Even when they are weak and inefficient, the mere fact that they exist, enables businesses to operate. The various traders of Bengal had played one company against another to maximize their profits. The weavers of Bengal might not have been particularly rich but the existence of a state machinery had meant that they could not be coerced by the various East India companies. Their independence and ability to negotiate on prices with the companies, depended on the neutrality, if not the active assistance of the state. After Plassey, that neutrality vanished and so did the independence of the weaver. Incomes crashed for anyone who had hoped to exist independently of the company's coercion.

For Visibility, State Needs to provide Visible Goods and Services

The trouble with state mechanisms is that mostly their value remains intangible. For businesses to see the value of the invisible state, it is important for the state to generate visible goods and services that are of value to society. In India, this was hardly the case. Average per capita incomes might have been sufficient for a comfortable existence, but they still remained low.

No doubt unrestricted free trade had made Bengal a rich province, perhaps the richest province in India. In the process, many businessmen had got rich too. As did many weavers. But incomes still stagnated. To raise those incomes, active effort was needed to supply better services to all the artisans and merchants who had contributed to the riches of the province. These were things that the nawabs of Bengal had not done. They had never invested in improving the capabilities of the state to recover taxes. Or to use those taxes for the public good.

Indian merchants seemed to believe that power has no role to play in making profits. They can hardly be faulted for that. If Indian rulers had by and large left them alone other than for the occasional extortion, the European Company was likely to be the same. They showed little curiosity about the behaviour of the company. They never seemed to feel a sense of threat.

In case they shared information with each other about these new entrants in the market, they have left no record of it behind. Some rulers perhaps did entertain apprehensions. So an official of the French East India Company reported that Alivardi Khan, Nawab of Bengal in the first half of the eighteenth century, was extremely wary of the English Company and of the way it had behaved in the Coromandel. He also asked the English company why they needed fortification when they were only merchants. But he never went out of his way to contest the growing power of the company. In case he shared his fears with anyone else, there is no record available. Networks of information and of trust have been rather scarce in India. Whether between rulers and merchants or within different merchant communities, information is hardly shared.

In the end, it was the accession to power in Bengal that mattered the most to the fortunes of the English East India Company. With Plassey, the independence of the *subah* of Bengal came to an end. It was Bengal that gave the company access to the land revenues of the *subah*. After the battles of Plassey and Buxar, the Company was able to use Indian land revenues to hire Indian soldiers to fight Indian princes. Other Indian princes were unable to learn from what was happening till it was too late.

Within thirty years after the Battle of Plassey, life changed irrevocably for the people of Bengal. Gradually as the English East India Company took over other parts of the country, it changed there too. What we do know is that incomes stagnated all over India and we got left behind while others raced ahead.

Writing in the early twentieth century, an Indian historian imagined with some sadness, how a middle-aged weaver in Bengal of the 1790s might have seen the world. This weaver would have been born around Plassey and the world he saw would have been completely different from the world of his fathers. His father's stories about the competitive bidding among the 'hatmen' (the Indian name for the Europeans) or their agents, for the produce of his loom, would have seemed distant. When Bengal was free,

> an upcountry Indian merchant's agent or an occasional Armenian would turn up, praise the cloth that was being fabricated upon the loom, secure it by paying a higher price to his father than any European would pay. There was then no muckeem or peon, no seizing and beating, no disgrace to the family. . . . He would now have to provide cloth surreptitiously to the European private trader or the Indian merchant to meet the expenses of the funeral obsequies of his father.[41]

Some weavers continued to protest the oppressive working conditions and the rock bottom prices that the officials of the East India Company forced upon them. The weavers of Shantipur even wrote 1773 onwards, several petitions to the Company complaining among other things that the local agent forcibly deducted one rupee per piece from their earnings so that they were not even left enough to cover the cost of their raw material. The Company pretended to listen and turned a deaf ear. The clamor in England against manufactured goods from India was rising and they knew that the case of the Indian weavers was a losing one.

From an Indifferent to a Hostile State

William Bolts, an English merchant from eighteenth century Bengal later wrote eloquently,

> From a society of mere traders, confined by charter to the employment of six ships and six pinnaces yearly, the Company are become sovereigns of

extensive, rich and populous kingdoms. . . . In this new situation in the society, so widely different from its original institution, their true commercial interests appear almost entirely misunderstood or neglected; and it may be safely said, there is scarcely any public spirit apparent among their leaders, either in England or in India. . . . The questions, How many lacks should I put in my pocket? Or How many sons, nephews or dependants shall I provide for at the expense of the miserable inhabitants of the subject dominions? Are those which of late have been the foremost to be propounded by the Chiefs of the Company on both sides the Ocean. Hence the dominions in Asia, like the distant Roman provinces during the decline of that empire, have been abandoned, as lawful prey, to every species of speculators; insomuch as many servants of the Company, after exhibiting such scenes of barbarity as can scarcely be paralleled in the history of any country, have returned to England loaded with wealth. . . .[42]

Bolts continues,

There is in Bengal no freedom in trade, though by that alone it can be made flourishing and importantly beneficial to the British state. All branches of the interior Indian commerce, are without exception, entirely monopolies of the most cruel and ruinous natures; and so totally corrupted, from every species of abuse, as to be in the last stages towards annihilation. Civil justice is eradicated, and millions are thereby left entirely at the mercy of a few men, who divide the spoils of the public among themselves. . . . In this situation while the poor industrious natives are oppressed beyond conception, population is decreasing, the manufactories and revenues are decaying, and Bengal, which used not many years ago to send annually a tribute of several millions in hard specie to Dehly, is now reduced to so extreme a want of circulation that it is not improbable the Company . . . will soon be in want of specie in Bengal to pay their troops. . . .[43]

Connection between State Power and Trade Remained Invisible to Indians

This connection between the power of the state and the trade of the country, seemed invisible to Indians. Till the mid-eighteenth century, the numerous peasants, weavers, artisans, traders of India had been living happily, perhaps at a low level of productivity, but with all the basic necessities of life. Their existence had been predicated on the assumption that the state would remain neutral and that it would not work against them. With the rule of the East

India Company, that particular assumption no longer held true. And when the state started working against the people whom it ruled as foreign subjects, whatever risk protection people had, collapsed.

Perhaps the insouciance with which they lived came from a sense of the beauty and invincibility of their way of life. It can be easy to ignore information that contradicts your world-view. Sir Thomas Roe, English ambassador to the court of Jehangir, reportedly gifted him a copy of Mercator's Book of Cosmography of the world. Initially, Jehangir was most intrigued by the gift and then he wanted to know where his dominion lay on the map. Roe showed him that the world was divided into four quarters and that his dominion lay in one quarter along with Persia and Tartary. At this point, Jehangir who had believed he was Conqueror of the world, was troubled and then he returned the book to Roe, saying that he and his people could not understand the language of the book and that he could not deprive Roe of such a jewel.[44]

The Europeans did not need to be told that armed trading produced more profits than peaceful trading. They did whatever they believed necessary to increase those profits. Still, Indians did not see or understand this fundamental difference in perspective in over two hundred years of living and transacting with the people of the various East India Companies. The indifference of the government of the day to the concerns of businessmen, a dysfunctional legal system, an unregulated market, an ineffective taxation system, the absence of information networks and low levels of trust, created the conditions that led to the rise of colonialism in our country. That systematized information networks are of value, that learning is of value, that thinkers are valuable and that we can import them only to our own disadvantage, have been rather costly lessons for us.

NOTES

1. Foster, 1921: 112.
2. Ibid.: 99.
3. O'Brien & Hunt, *European State Finance Database: English State Taxes and Other Revenues, 1559-1603.*

4. Bernier, 1916: 155-61.
5. Hamilton, 1833: 296.
6. Vincent's report tells us that a weaver could earn about one and three quarter rupees on a piece of silk (taffeta as he called it) 10 yards long and 27-36 inches wide (Temple, 1911, vol. II: 13). The ordinary silk taffeta pieces cost roughly Rs. 4 each to the company at this time.
7. Mukerji, 1903: 52, 100, 126. Mukerji says that for tasar silk a man could weave 2.5 yards in a day. For better quality silk, it depended on the number of threads in the warp and design. Plain silk corahs produced in thousands could be woven at the rate of 3.5 yards a day. Silk *dhutis* of size 9.5 cubits by 2.5 cubits (about 5.9 sq. yards) might be woven in 8 days which means a rate of 0.75 yards of silk in the day. All rates assume a man working with his wife and child on one loom. This is similar to the details given about weavers by Francis Buchanan Hamilton in his study of Dinajpur.
8. The maunds referred to are Bengal maunds which were made up of 40 Calcutta *seers* weighing 82 $^{2}/_{7}$ pounds or 37.32 kg. For productivity of land, see Datta R., 2000: 41 for productivity in Comilla, Rangpur, Midnapur and Burdwan which ranged from 8-10 maunds per *bigha* at the end of the eighteenth century. Ten years later, in Buchanan's survey, he puts it at 6-8 maunds per bigha of rice for ordinary land. So we take 8 maunds per *bigha* as a modest figure.
9. Oaten, 1909: 98.
10. We deduct 40 per cent tax and factor in another 30 per cent loss due to de-husking of paddy.
11. A family of six we take it, may reasonably have one adult male doing heavy work, one working female, a boy and a girl aged between 10-12 years and two infants below 6 years of age. The weaver would be the main breadwinner, using family labour to earn his bread. His wife, as was normal for women in peasant families, would perhaps spend her time spinning thread, helping with weaving cloth and working the family farm, as would the children.
12. Hamilton, 1833: 126.
13. The ICMR report (Indian Council of Medical Research, 2010) recommends that an adult male doing heavy work requires 3,490 calories daily, an adult female also doing heavy work requires 2,850 calories, a boy of age 10-12 years requires 2,550 calories, a girl in the same age group needs 2,350 calories, children from age 3-6 need 1,350 calories and infants below 3 need 1,060 calories. This means a daily calorific need of 13,650 calories for the entire family of 6 people. ICMR works out the diet keeping these needs in mind. To these figures we add another 50 per cent and

then we adjust pulses upwards so they constitute 15 per cent of the rice consumption.

14. Sixth Report from the Select Committee, Appointed to take into consideration the state of the Administration of Justice in the provinces of Bengal, Bahar and Orissa. Appendix No. 15. Extract of Fort William Revenue Consultations. 29 November 1776. Prices reported at Murshidabad for the year 1136 AH (1723-24 CE).
15. Herklots, 1829. An average of prices recorded for 26 years in the period 1700-40 comes to 39.75 *seers* per rupee rounded off to 1 maund per rupee.
16. Sixth Report from the Select Committee, Appointed to take into consideration the state of the Administration of Justice in the provinces of Bengal, Bahar and Orissa (1782). Appendix No. 15. Extract of Fort William Revenue Consultations. 29 November 1776. Prices reported at Murshidabad for the year 1136 AH (1723-24 CE).
17. Sixth Report from the Select Committee, Appointed to take into consideration the state of the Administration of Justice in the provinces of Bengal, Bahar and Orissa. (1782). Appendix No. 15. Extract of Fort William Revenue Consultations. 29 November 1776. Prices reported at Murshidabad for the year 1136 AH (1723-24 CE).
18. Bayly, 1816, v. 12: 560. Prices available are for Calcutta for the period 1753-6.
19. Bolts, 1722: 174. According to merchant Bolts, salt sold in the times of Alivardi Khan for Rs. 40-60 per hundred maunds. An average wholesale price of Rs. 50 for a hundred maunds might mean a retail price of Re 1-Rs. 1.2 to the maund.
20. Temple, 1911, vol. 1: 321.
21. Kumar, 2013: 14.
22. Bhadani, 1999.
23. Sato, 1987: 172.
24. Singh, 1990.
25. Bhadani, 1999. In modern times too, 70 per cent of land in Jalor is cultivated in kharif and the remaining 30 per cent in *rabi*.
26. Bhadani, 1999.
27. Bhadani, 1999.
28. Sato, 1987: 172.
29. Sato, 1987.
30. Maunds used in this table refer to *man-i-shahjahani* of 33.45 kg. Secondary sources have normalized weights and prices from their primary material to rupees per *man-i-shahjahani*.

31. S.P. Gupta, 1982; Hasan & Gupta, 1967. Average taken of prices reported for parganas in Eastern Rajasthan for the period 1660-90.
32. Rainfed Guar yield reported at 10 maunds/acre in late nineteenth century in Meerut. See Watt, 1899, vol. 2: 673. The *bigha* used in Marwar was the *bigha-i-sikandari* which was about 78 per cent of the *bigha-i-ilahi*. This would make the *bigha-i-sikandari* about 0.48 of an acre. For prices, information from Marwar is scarce but we do have some prices for eastern Rajasthan in seventeenth century, see S.P. Gupta, 1982.
33. Prices of raw wool back calculated from tax on sale of raw wool which amounted to Re 1 and 3 annas on 24 maunds in the Marwar region (M. Kumar, 2017, unpublished thesis, 212). While tax rate is not reported generally on goods, in few cases it was reportedly 1 *taka* per rupee which means about 5 per cent. Calculating backwards this means a price of Rs. 21 for 24 maunds or 13-14 annas per maund. For wool yield, the Marwari sheep, common in the Jodhpur and Jalor region produces 1-2 kg of washed wool of medium and coarse quality per year (Sen, 1981: 33). Assuming that a poor farmer might maintain around 15 sheep these would yield about 15-30 kg of raw wool. We take around 25 kg or 0.75 maunds as the production in this case. Also given that the wool market was relatively stable, these prices have been kept the same even when other prices increase.
34. Prices of *ghee* as reported by Prof. Bhadani from the *Vigat* of Nainsi for the pargana Phalodi in the Marwar region. Prices reported in rupees per maunds/ *man-i-shahjahani*: Bhadani, *The Pastoral Secor in the Economy of Seventeenth Century Marwar*, 1996. Milch yield of Tharparkar cattle is reported at 1,100-2,500 litres per cow per annum so 1,250 litres per cow in dryland conditions is a conservative estimate. See Choudhary et al., 2018.
35. Dugani was 1/40th of a rupee.
36. Taxes were assessed in cash on crops like pulses and vegetables. We take 25 per cent tax on the cash value of guar which would make it Rs. 0.75 per *bigha* tax at a price of Re. 0.6 per maund for 2 *bighas* of *guar*.
37. Sato, 1987: 161.
38. Based on ICMR diet plus 50 per cent and with pulses increased to 15 per cent of cereals. Please see footnote 13.
39. Weights are calculated in maunds of 33.45 kg since prices have been normalized and reported by Prof S.P. Gupta in terms of *man-i-shahjahani* of 40 *seers* with each seer equal to 40 copper dams.
40. S.P. Gupta, 1982. Bhadani, 1999: Prices of millets, pulses, oil, jaggery and salt taken as reported by Prof. S.P. Gupta for eastern Rajasthan and varied

by 60 per cent to generate two different scenarios. Gupta says that variation in prices across villages was low for the same time period. Overtime however there is a definite increase in prices hence we take a 60 per cent increase.

41. Sinha, 1956, vol. I: 164.
42. Bolts, 1772: iv-v.
43. Bolts, 1772: vii
44. Terry, 1707: 350f.

CHAPTER 2

Information and Productivity: The Missing Link

Systems to collate and manage information, depend above all, on a certain respect for the written word. The maintenance of records that are reasonably accurate over long periods of time in turn has important consequences for the ability of any social group to go up the learning curve. These are qualities that it is difficult to find in Indian history. Till today, record keeping systems in India remain rather weak. To the question why such systems are mostly dysfunctional in India, most people look slightly uncomfortable. The reply more often than not is that well, we have our own methods and that *jugad* seems to work most of the time. *Jugad*, the Indian workaround, is an end in itself. It is a typically Indian word to indicate a resistance to finding a lasting solution to any problem. *Jugad*, when allowed to exist in large and complex systems over years and decades, can render systems extraordinarily inefficient and ineffective. Omissions can be just as important as commissions. One graphic historical illustration of the impact of omissions and a general indifference to the written word is to be found in the Great Bengal Famine of 1769-70.

The famine of Bengal has been attributed to the general indifference of the English East India Company to the welfare of their new-found subjects and to their desire to maximize revenue at all costs. Much of the charge is no doubt true. The company was certainly indifferent to the plight of the peasant and made little effort to check profiteering in grain on the part of English traders at this time. But there is one qualifier. When the English company increased land revenues to such high levels as to bring the farmer to the brink of famine, it was only doing a rather literal reading of revenue records maintained by Indians themselves for hundreds of years.

THE MUGHAL SYSTEM OF RECORD-KEEPING

The Mughal system of record-keeping was dependent to a large extent on a bureaucratic machinery that was expected to maintain itself directly from the proceeds of the revenues itself. Their salaries did not come from the state exchequer. In this sense, the entire system was built on a conflict of interest. To the extent that revenue officials could game the system, they did do so. Mughal emperors made some desultory attempts to identify and punish fraudulent record-keeping but these were hit and miss efforts.

The term used for Mughal revenues was *jama.* What was actually collected was called the *haasil.* For years where both figures are available, they often show that the *haasil* lagged behind the *jama.* Whether *jama* or *haasil,* these included revenues from different streams—land tax, customs duties on export and import of goods, transit duties on internal trade, proceeds of royal monopolies such as salt, minting charges on coinage, judicial fines and so on. The information system that existed at the level of province or *subah* did not maintain any distinction between all these sub-categories. It was all the *jama.* There might have been a break up of the sub-categories at the level of *tahsil* but it was in the interest of revenue officials to obfuscate information.

This presented the Mughals with a serious problem. They knew well that customs duties for instance were an important source of revenue but getting accurate information from day-to-day and year to year required systems to function. That required time and effort. So they found a workaround—revenues from import and export duties on goods were to be credited directly to the state exchequer. Alternatively, customs duties from important ports like Surat in Gujarat were often reserved for the *jagirs* of royal princes and princesses. These were perquisites to be handed over to royal favourites.

Within the *jama,* there were two broad divisions of revenue between the *khalisa* lands which were directly under the Crown and the *jagir* lands that were administered by the *jagirdars.* The *jagir* lands formed a far larger proportion of the royal dominions than the *khalisa* lands did. In the specific case of Bengal, one of the major reforms brought in by administrator Murshid Quli Khan was to greatly increase the proportion of *khalisa* land. The *jagirdars* were allowed to deduct the costs of collecting revenue from the collection before remitting it to the emperor. They were allowed to levy internal transit duties on trade. Numerous toll posts or chowkies were set up to recover these duties from traders. The *jagirdars* also had the freedom to set-up markets at different locations which could be either temporary or permanent. At these markets, traders were charged both ground rent for their stalls and tax on sale of goods. The proceeds of all such revenues from *jagir* lands—whether transit duties or market rents or land revenue or judicial fines were clubbed together in the *jama*. The transit duties, market rents and such miscellaneous taxes were referred to as the *sair* duties (*sayer* in the English records).

Towards the end of the seventeenth century and the beginning of the eighteenth century, the practice of farming out taxes on lands was often resorted to by royal officials. This only made the maze of revenue records even more difficult to navigate. Sometimes the officials themselves either directly or through their business associates, took the revenue farm. This made it difficult to ascertain what the different revenue streams might be.

A Conflict of Interest: Revenue Collectors directly Concerned with Trade

Writing in a memoir from central India in the mid-nineteenth century, Sir John Malcolm writes,

> There is no branch of their revenue in which the Mahratta governments are more defrauded than that of customs. This arises chiefly from ministers, collectors, and renters, being almost without exception concerned in trade. From the death of Alia Bhye[1] till within the last two years, large commercial speculations in Central India had more the character of military enterprises than the occupation of industrious merchants. Every trader had his party of armed men, formed connexions with ministers and commanders of armies, contracted engagements with plundering chieftains and robbers, and had

his goods, whether exported or imported, guarded like the baggage of an army. The insurance companies at Oojein, Indore, and Mundissor, kept small corps, which were supported by the high premiums charged on articles that were exported or imported between Malwa, Guzerat, the Deckan, and Hindustan. These companies were compelled to bribe the most powerful plunderers of the day, who, in their demands upon them and the merchants, had no other standard than their own temporary interests. It is impossible to form an estimate of the Sayer or customs of a country under such circumstances. . .[2].

Much the same situation prevailed in other parts of the country. For collection of land revenue, the audit systems set-up by the Mughals were weak. Fudging of revenue records, when it was discovered, attracted strong penalties. But discovering such instances or an audit, required setting up systems and building state capacities that the Mughals had never done. The conflict of interest built into the system was heightened by the arrangement that the appointment of a key official at village level, the *patwari*, was mostly hereditary. Appointments in the same family could remain for decades. This in turn meant that the families of *patwaris* controlled revenue records—the distinction between private and public remained hazy.

It has been pointed out that the prosperity of revenue officials in the Mughal empire down to the lowest rungs was very visible and had much to do with the industry of faking village records. So we see the spectacle of a normal *karkun* (clerk) by name Surat Singh, buying a house in a respectable locality of Lahore for Rs. 700, a princely sum in the mid-seventeenth century. At about the same time, Khwaja Udai Singh, a petty official, spent Rs. 3,000 on the construction of a well attached to a *dargah* at Lahore. The instances go on and on. When during Shah Jahan's tenure, a special officer called *amil* was appointed to check such practices, he merely joined the ranks of those who leeched off the land. As and when the authorities conducted any inquiry into any such case, the local officials banded together to mislead the officials. They might quarrel about sharing of the spoils but allowing it to reach the ears of the authorities would never do. It was almost as though it was an act of piety to mislead officialdom.[3]

THE *JAMA* IN BENGAL

In the 1720s, before the English East India Company came to power in Bengal, the official annual *jama* of the Mughal *subah* of Bengal was reported in various contemporary histories as ranging from Rs. 131 lakh to 142 lakh approximately.[4] The actual collection on the ground could be anything—in the absence of accounts documenting what was actually collected by the machinery, the figures remain a matter of speculation. What is not a matter of speculation, is the amount that was remitted annually to the emperor at Delhi. For the period 1712-27, the average amount of revenue annually transmitted to Delhi is reported to have been Rs. 101.93 lakh. For the period 1727-38, the average annual revenue transmitted to Delhi is reported to have been Rs. 107.57 lakh.[5] The revenues remitted to Delhi include the *haasil* or actual collected plus various presents given by notables on festive occasions and also any arbitrary taxes imposed from time to time to meet contingencies. An entry in the newsletter of the imperial court dated 13 February 1716 about the revenues of Bengal has been translated as follows:

> Murshid Quli Khan, the naib subahdar of Bengal has inquired of his peshkar of the revenue of Bengal. He has written that: The jama of Bengal is Rs. 10,200,000 of which Rs. 7,400,000 is the jama of the khalisa; Rs. 1,800,000 is the jagir of Mir Jumla Bahadur (the subahdar of Bengal); and the remainder [i.e. Rs. 1,000,000 is the jagir of the mansabdars and the jama of the nawara. From the beginning of the reign [about three years earlier], Rs. 24,068,000, including the money of the jagir of Mir Jumla Bahadur, and the money from the unmeasured areas [maujudat] paying tribute, has been sent to the Imperial presence.[6] [*sic.*]

Over and above the regular revenue assessed, especially after the year 1738, many lump sump taxes were imposed from time to time to meet contingencies such as the need to counter the Maratha invasions of Bengal and also to pay the Maratha *chauth* tax imposed after the invasions. The statements of the company officials themselves indicate that much of this kind of contingent expenditure was financed by local merchants. The ranks of the merchants included the English company itself and the European traders.

Richard Becher, later Resident at the Murshidabad court, said in one testimony that he recalled for the period 1744-5, Nawab Alivardi Khan had demanded and obtained a sum of Rs. 3½ lakh from the English East India Company. Further he said that the expenses of defending the country against the Marathas were apportioned proportionately among the various European companies trading in Bengal.[7] But so far as Mughal revenue records were concerned, it was only the figures received that remained on the books, not details of the sources of funds.

So Long as Money Came in, No one Cared from Where

Whether the annual *jama* collected in Bengal was Rs. 142 lakh or Rs. 102 lakh, or even more; how much was *khalisa*, how much was *jagir*, what was the actual collected on the ground and from whom, has remained the subject matter of speculation and conjecture among historians for decades. How much more perplexing would the matter have been to East India Company officials who had practically no knowledge either of the productive capacity of the estate of Bengal and even less of the intricate workings of their administrative setup. No doubt the company had Indian officials working under their supervision who could be expected to have greater knowledge of ground reality. However, we need to remember that these officials were paid by the company and they knew which side their bread was buttered. So much so that in the year 1770 when Bengal was going through a terrible famine, they actually recommended a 10 per cent increase in tax!

Whatever the rights and wrongs of the issue might have been, the *jama* as recorded in the books of accounts including various occasional surcharges levied for contingencies, was all taken at face value and it was taken as a lump sum irrespective of categories. In August 1765 the English East India Company received the *diwani* of Bengal, Bihar and Orissa from the Mughal emperor Shah Alam. Maximizing revenue was an important object for the company. They acted accordingly. It was their understanding that most of this revenue was land revenue; other streams were negligible. The records did little to contradict such an understanding.

For the year 1765, members of the Select Committee of the Company demanded that the gross sum of revenues be fixed at Rs. 1,60,29,016-10-2 and net revenues after deducting costs of collection should be Rs. 1,50,04,887-2-5.[8] The local machinery did not actually succeed in collecting this much from their subjects. The committee took this to mean that the revenue machinery was corrupt and inefficient. They merely enjoined then *naib subahdar* Muhammad Reza Khan and the machinery, to redouble their efforts.

Moving forward to the close of the eighteenth century briefly, a look at the revenues of the East India Company for Bengal, Bihar and Orissa indicate that actually land revenue constituted on an average 60 per cent of the total receipts. Sale of salt contributed 25 per cent and sale of opium another 7.5 per cent (Tables 2.1 and 2.2). Centuries of neglect of the revenue records had created so much confusion that no one really knew where the money was coming from!

To put the taxes together and insist that the Indian farmer should pay these, was in effect what happened. Indian farmers in Bengal, while used to regular tax collection efforts, did not have the kind of risk cushion which would have allowed them to sustain such increases in revenue demand.

COST OF LIVING FOR THE BENGALI WEAVER-PEASANT

We have estimated earlier that till the mid-eighteenth century, a small Bengali weaver-cum-peasant who cultivated 5 *bighas* of land, could enjoy a cash income of roughly Rs. 42 in the year if he practised weaving for seven months and devoted the rest of his time to agriculture. This is for a family of six where the farmer and his wife were the adult earning members. We assume four children in the family and that the elder two would help with some of the tasks of weaving and farming. Now let us see what might have happened to him given a jump in tax demand combined with rise in prices of grain. Tax had shot up to roughly 50 per cent of his produce. So out of roughly 40 maunds of paddy, only 20 maunds would be left.

TABLE 2.1: ANNUAL REVENUE OF THE EAST INDIA COMPANY FOR BENGAL, BIHAR AND ORISSA, 1797-1807[9]

(*in Rs.*)

Year	Total revenue	MINT duties	Post Office collections	Land and sayer revenues collection thereof, inclduing former years' balances	Police taxes, judicial fee and fines	Customs	Sale of salt	Sale of opium	Stamp duties
1797-8	4,67,26,450.0	74,867.00	1,62,862.0	3,09,74,430.00	5,59,207.00	9,22,204.00	1,15,45,245.00	23,80,435.00	1,07,201.00
1798-9	4,77,00,033.0	67,131.00	2,01,926.0	3,07,27,431.00	4,35,414.00	9,57,103.00	1,29,67,227.00	21,03,043.00	2,40,758.00
1799-1800	5,09,23,110.0	1,30,283.00	2,49,527.0	3,21,32,296.00	4,45,265.00	13,54,040.00	1,26,47,667.00	37,20,248.00	2,63,784.00
1800-1	4,97,68,141.0	45,822.00	2,43,862.0	3,21,87,666.00	5,00,214.00	14,11,580.00	1,12,97,197.00	37,25,020.00	3,56,780.00
1801-2	5,17,85,150.0	57,174.00	2,63,719.0	3,29,63,027.00	4,96,647.00	28,57,641.00	1,09,62,842.00	36,76,578.00	5,07,522.00
1802-3	5,76,79,339.0	63,733.00	2,95,837.0	3,29,57,614.00	7,46,726.00	32,23,798.00	1,44,67,745.00	53,46,538.00	5,77,348.00
1803-4	5,97,00,777.0	41,123.00	3,05,017.0	3,25,26,214.00	7,57,176.00	28,98,794.00	1,79,63,544.00	46,31,607.00	5,77,302.00
1804-5	6,13,71,358.0	80,021.00	3,09,693.00	3,22,54,362.00	9,50,190.00	27,23,130.00	1,72,22,338.00	72,58,950.00	5,72,674.00
1805-6	6,04,12,838.0	2,16,353.00	3,61,575.00	3,31,16,730.00	8,93,497.00	29,03,084.00	1,53,51,076.00	69,00,109.00	6,70,414.00
1806-7	5,92,27,493.0	1,91,360.00	3,72,078.00	3,29,66,843.00	9,25,490.00	32,48,305.00	1,59,91,303.00	48,00,692.00	7,31,420.00
Annual average	5,32,06,794.75	70,019.25	2,54,055.38	3,20,90,380.00	6,11,354.88	20,43,536.25	1,36,34,225.63	41,05,302.38	4,60,520.03

Source: See endnote 9.

TABLE 2.2: PER CENT BREAKUP OF THE ANNUAL REVENUES OF THE EAST INDIA COMPANY FROM BENGAL, BIHAR AND ORISSA, 1797-1807[10]

Sub-Components of total revenue of Bengal, Bihar and Orissa

Year	Total estimated revenue	Mint duties	Post office collections	Land and sayer revenues collection thereof, including former years' balances	Police taxes, judicial fee and fines	Customs	Sale of salt	Sale of opium	Stamp duties
1797-8	4,67,26,450.00	0.16	0.35	66.29	1.20	1.97	24.71	5.09	0.23
1798-9	4,77,00,033.00	0.14	0.42	64.42	0.91	2.01	27.18	4.41	0.50
1799-1800	5,09,23,110.00	0.26	0.49	63.10	0.87	2.66	24.84	7.31	0.52
1800-1	4,97,68,141.00	0.09	0.49	64.68	1.01	2.84	22.70	7.48	0.72
1801-2	5,17,85,150.00	0.11	0.51	63.65	0.96	5.52	21.17	7.10	0.98
1802-3	5,76,79,339.00	0.11	0.51	57.14	1.29	5.59	25.08	9.27	1.00
1803-4	5,97,00,777.00	0.07	0.51	54.48	1.27	4.86	30.09	7.76	0.97
1804-5	6,13,71,358.00	0.13	0.50	52.56	1.55	4.44	28.06	11.83	0.93
1805-6	6,04,12,838.00	0.36	0.60	54.82	1.48	4.81	25.41	11.42	1.11
1806-7	5,92,27,493.00	0.32	0.63	55.66	1.56	5.48	27.00	8.11	1.23
Annual average	5,32,06,794.75	0.13	0.47	60.79	1.13	3.73	25.48	7.53	0.73

Source: See endnotes 9-10.

So far as his income from weaving was concerned, studies of contemporary textile prices say that the finer quality of muslins showed little price increase from the 1730s to the 1750s; that there was some increase in prices of coarse calicoes and that raw silk prices did go up by roughly 30-40 per cent.[11] We take a 40 per cent increase in the income of the weaver from the last quarter of the seventeenth century, to meet increased raw material costs. This means a rough cash income of Rs. 60 from seven months of weaving cloth in the year.

For rice prices, these had shot up to six to seven times the levels reported for 1728. In rural areas, rice was selling for 1.1-1.25 maunds to the rupee in the 1760s even before the famine of 1769-70.

The establishment of a monopoly of salt by the company in 1765 led to doubling of salt prices. The Mughals might have maintained a salt monopoly but their ability to enforce it was rather poor as evidenced by the lower price of salt before the arrival of the English company. Given its importance in the local diet, salt deprivation further exacerbated the famine that was to follow. All these changes put together created a situation where the small farmer even if he had a separate income from weaving cloth, was living at subsistence level. As Table 2.3 shows, he was spending Rs. 59.34 or nearly all of his cash income on food alone. In such a situation, if his crop were to fail and he were forced to buy most of his grain requirement from the market at much higher prices, he would be driven to cut down his food intake substantially. If crops failed two years in a row, he might well starve. And for farmers with no supplementary cash income, the situation would be even worse.

This is what seems to have happened in the years 1769-70.

THE GREAT FAMINE OF BENGAL OF 1769-70

Imagination of Reality has Real Consequences

The year 1768 saw freak natural occurrences. First there were floods during the monsoon which ruined many crops. This was followed by a drought that lasted till mid January 1769. Partial failure of crops created much hardship for the farmers. Worse was still to come. 1769 was again a drought year and the crops failed in large

TABLE 2.3: FOOD BASKET OF THE BENGALI WEAVER-PEASANT IN THE YEARS 1760-9

Food group	Total daily intake in grams for days of fish based diet	Total daily intake in grams for days of non-fish diet	Annual intake in kg.	Converted to Bengal seers of 933 grams*	Annual cost in Rs.	Prices of commodities
Rice	3,735	3,735	1,344.6	1,441	20.03	We deduct 14 maunds of home-grown rice and put a value to the rest. Coarse rice was selling for approx. 44 seers per rupee**
Pulses	280.125	560.25	151.27	162	6.04	13-40 seers per rupee.[12]
Milk	2,250	2.250	810	868	0	Milch cattle at home
Mustard oil	306	280.5	105.57	113	15.59	Oil of the second sort available at 6-8.5 seers per rupee[13]
Ghee	54	49.5	18.63	20	6.54	2.25-4 seers per rupee.[14]
Gur/jaggery	125	125	45.00	48	2.96	14-18 seers per rupee[15]
Salt	125	125	45.00	48	2.18	16-26 seers per rupee[16]
Fish	250	0	45.00	48	6.00	8 seers per rupee
Total					59.34	

Notes: * Bengal seer measured at 2.057 pounds or 933 grams (*Useful Tables*, 1834: 67). Figures rounded off after conversion to seer to nearest whole number.

** Post 50 per cent tax and 30 per cent de-husking loss. 14 maunds left. Rice prices fluctuated sharply so average prices in Calcutta for 1765-9 taken. See Bayly, 1816, v.12: 560.

Source: See endnotes 12-16. All prices are approximations.

parts of the province. By November that year, the first signs of disaster had already set in but there was a change of governors that happened. Verelst, the outgoing Governor, was reluctant to recognize the signs officially or to put anything on paper. His successor Cartier was forced to do so once widespread reports of popular distress began to come in. But the company was reluctant to allocate any substantial funds for relief. Rather in April 1770, they actually decide to increase taxes by 10 per cent! Through 1769 and 1770, profiteering on grain was common and when a resolution was tabled in the Calcutta Council to check the phenomenon, the Council rejected the resolution. Rather the company conducted market operations to buy up provisions for the troops lest they mutiny—these provisions were sold to the troops at prices ranging from 9 to 30 *seers* to the rupee. Even here, the company ended up making a profit.

It was only in April 1770 that half hearted measures were taken to distribute half a *seer* of rice per head free to people in some cities. By then, much of the damage had already been done. The rains finally arrived in 1770. By then, Warren Hastings estimated that one-third of the population of the province had been wiped out.

Imaginary understandings can have very real consequences. History telling is important because it is when we take a very long view, that we realize that learning processes in India have tended to be rather slow, even before colonialism put the brakes on whatever economic progress was happening.

What stories like these tells us is that India has always had considerable difficulty in systematizing information.

THE SYSTEMATIC USE OF INFORMATION REQUIRES A DIFFERENT WAY OF THINKING

We suggest that the systematic use of information to improve productivity is what could make India rich. It is inability to store, retrieve and use information systematically, that holds us back as a country. This might seem paradoxical in light of the emergence of India as a major hub of information technology in the twenty-first century but it is not. Information technology is merely a tool to store information. Much before the invention of computers, people did use the printed word to store and retrieve information too. In India, it is the ability to write software code, English language skills and a strong preference to work on a computer interface, that have encouraged the development of the software industry. But the ability to write code is not the same as improving efficiencies.

A society becomes rich when it uses information systematically to improve productivity. Improving productivity means that for the same say hundred rupees, you get more by way of products and services. Information in this sense doesn't mean information technology or computers alone. Those are just means of using information efficiently. The shopkeeper who uses invoice data for the past months to figure out which products move fast and which move slow and uses the insight to draw up his inventory policy, is using information efficiently. The farmer who uses the results of the soil test to figure out what fertilizer to use, is using information efficiently. The engineer who tests the water pipeline for leakages to see how to improve the water pressure, is using information efficiently.

Individuals can use information to improve productivity and also to scale-up operations. A retail chain of stores is not simply a goods provision store multiplied a hundred times; a chain is a different kind of organizational entity. Large organizations need to increase efficiencies all round. They might make a lower percentage of profit. But then even a 5 per cent return on a thousand crores is far larger than a 20 per cent return on a few lakh rupees.

If we were to take a brief look at the growth of a small retail store into a chain, we would notice that the store uses a large number of inputs to facilitate the growth process. It uses technology to process information about the newer stores, to take decisions about what to buy and where to buy and to improve logistics. It uses capital, perhaps from a bank or from personal sources to pump in money that a growing enterprise needs. It uses skilled human resources to perform the tasks needed. Above all, it uses that most intangible, most invisible and yet most powerful of all resources-information. Information, whether about markets, buyers, products or anything else is what helps improve efficiency.

It is here that India has faltered in the past and falters even today. In the Western world, information and it's tools were used to improve productivity across organizations. It was no single invention or even cluster of inventions that was responsible. The change affected sectors across society. Innovation simply jumped from one sector to another.

To use information to scale-up the generation of wealth, required not just capital, or technology or intelligence; it needed a different way of thinking. Systematic thinking that relied heavily on information and evidence is what made a difference. All that systematic thinking really means is that we keep records of information and when making a decision, we use those records to see what strategy might bring better results. Information is used for practically all decisions, even for constructing a problem. This is just as true of routine matters as earth-shaking ones.

Systematic use of Information can Solve Problems

For instance in the year 2015, India was able to eliminate the occurrence of neonatal and maternal tetanus. To achieve this goal, 1993 onwards, the government divided districts according to three different indicators: the incidence of neonatal tetanus defined as numbers per 1,000 live births, tetanus immunization coverage among pregnant women, and the percentage of clean deliveries by trained personnel.[17] Then they drew up plans of action targeting each of these three indicators. By 2015, India achieved the goal they had set for themselves. Information was used both for defining the problem and for achieving a solution.

Where information is not used systematically, problems are more difficult to solve. A routine problem that urban local bodies are confronted with today is the management of solid waste. A commonly proposed solution is waste-to-energy plants. Yet any preliminary look at the data on Indian solid waste would tell us that it is most unsuitable for that kind of plant; it simply has too much wet waste. This means that the energy value of the waste is quite low. To make it a profitable venture would be a herculean task. Yet money is routinely invested in such ventures. It is not the government alone that makes such mistakes. One can see a large number of private sector ventures of a similar nature in India today. The amounts run into hundreds of crores of rupees. Whether the private sector sets up such projects because the money is easily available from public sector banks is difficult to say. The fact is that such costly and ill-conceived projects are a dime a dozen.

They do say that asking the right question is more important even than finding the right answers.

When societies are productive, the use of information for daily decisions becomes a habit. This is not a characteristic of any one group or profession; it is a society-wide phenomenon. Similarly, an ecosystem that sponsors innovation, motivates creativity across the board, whatever the sector might be. If innovation is confined to just one or two sectors, we have taken just a few small steps, not a giant step. The Industrial Revolution was a giant step.

The fact of the Industrial Revolution focussed a great deal of attention on inventions. The flying shuttle, the spinning jenny, the powerloom, the steam engine; all these were no doubt the products of innovation and creativity. What is of interest to us is that in the societies that produced those inventions, innovation in one sector had an impact on another which in turn had an impact on yet another. The effect on productivity simply cascaded. To identify any one of these inventions or sectors as being critical, would be missing the point. All the steam power in the world is of little use when there is little to transport. All the textiles produced, however valuable they might be, are of little use, unless there is a mass market that is easily supplied. And technology that cannot produce on a large scale, cannot meet the needs of a large market.

Capital, technology, great thinkers: all these will have substantial impact when they work with each other. When they work in isolation, the impact can be rather low. When they work together, capacities improve all round. The development of clocks in Europe for instance, provided much impetus to different kinds of processes. The use of gears in clocks, helped in the development of machines. Richard Arkwright, the eighteenth-century English textile magnate, worked with clockmaker John Kay, to develop a spinning frame that could spin 128 cotton threads at the same time. Mughal India knew about many of these developments; they were never used to improve production. Jehangir deposited a clock that had once been gifted to him in his *toshkhana*;[18] to him it was merely an object of curiosity.

It is not the information itself but its uses that are valuable. What we really need to focus on is building an ecosystem that fosters creativity and improves productivity. Information needs to be actively used to build feedback loops to improve our working.

Nor is this issue confined to any specific profession in India. Public servants for insance are taken to task over this all the time. Certainly there is much to be corrected in the public sector. Much more data could be used for making public policy than is currently the case. But then feedback loops tend to be missing across the board in India. If banks, both private and public, have built up such large non-performing assets, surely there was something wrong with the information systems they had built up. If large private sector companies could go sick, again, information had not been well used.

When well-used, information can and does create a cascading effect in productivity. In businesses, the impact becomes much more visible. A 2014 survey by CII on use of information and communication technology (ICT) in the small and medium enterprise (SME) sector said that IT enabled SMEs, grew on an average 15 per cent faster than the rest.[19] Normal wisdom would say that people do learn from each other.

It is little known that the mushrooming of public libraries across Europe in the sixteenth and seventeenth centuries and across USA in the eighteenth century, was critical to the Industrial Revolution. Even today, providing information to small and medium businesses, rather to all businesses, can help them to improve productivity in many ways.

Unfortunately, working with information systematically has never been one of the strengths of our society. Still, we do have many individual success stories.

THE MANY INDIVIDUAL SUCCESSES OF MODERN INDIA

The story of India from the twentieth century onwards is full of rags-to-riches stories that are so common that these are practically taken for granted. Two of the more notable examples are those of a small-time shopkeeper from Sialkot and an even smaller ordinance factory worker from Kamalia in Toba Tek Singh district, both of whom were forced to re-build lives destroyed by the Partition of 1947. The shopkeeper of Sialkot opened a small shop in Karol Bagh, Delhi in an attempt to revive his spice business. The ordnance factory worker opened a cycle shop in Ludhiana and won a small government contract for supplying bicycles.

The shopkeeper from Sialkot, Dharampal Gulati, is known today as the proprietor of MDH spices which incidentally stands for the name of his old shop: Mahashian Di Hatti. MDH *garam masalas* are sold all over the world; a robustly well preserved Gulati features in numerous advertisements of his own products, advising the young on how to lead a fruitful life. The former ordnance factory worker died in 2015, leaving behind a billion-dollar business: he was Brij Mohan Munjal, the founder of the Hero brand of two wheelers.

We have plenty of stories about such people who pulled themselves up by their bootstraps to become part of the economic miracles that happen on and off in India. Yet the minute we proceed from the specific to the average, the picture is very different. Till today, most Indian businesses, whether in the service sector or in industry, show low productivity by world standards.

So how is it that given all the examples of dirt-poor individuals who made it big, the average Indian business is unable to produce more for every rupee invested? In the world of business, there would always be inequalities, but the richness or poverty of a country is defined not by the most brilliant businessmen but the average one.

India continues to lag not just the developed world but also many emerging economies like China where productivity is concerned. We cannot yet lay claim to being 'developed'. Productivity in the manufacturing sector remains low. Official claims are that Manufacturing contributed only 18.1 per cent of Gross Value Added to the Indian economy in 2017-18.[20] India contributes about 7 per cent to the total GDP of the world today. This would be a serious comedown for a country that accounted for over a quarter of world output as late as the seventeenth century.

To the question of why the average Indian business shows low productivity, one likely answer is that information about ways to improve efficiency, filters down rather slowly. The transmission belts of information from the best to the ordinary entrepreneur seem to be so slow, that the conveyor belt almost seems to be stuck. Here we do not talk about individual innovation so much. Innovative ideas of any shape and kind whether it be a new method of selling goods, a brilliant software application or a product that creates a new niche altogether like the pizza in the food business: these will always command competitive advantage.

Rather we talk about the overall use of technologies and strategies that are proven to be advantageous in general. The use of information and communication technology presents the most obvious example. India has been an IT hub for decades now; yet the majority of our software business services the international market. The domestic market accounts for only a small portion of the Indian software industry. In the USA in comparison, the reverse is the case: there it is the domestic market that dominates over the international market.

This should not be taken to mean that Indian businessmen are reluctant to learn. Rather figures show that Indian entrepreneurs are eager to use the benefits that information technology brings. A UNESCO report of 2016 on use of information technology among artisan organizations, says that one-third of the organizations possessed one computer and three fourths of the organizations had an internet connection. Evidently they were sufficiently savvy to use the internet on their phones or other means in the absence of a computer. Similarly, a survey by the Confederation of Indian Industry on the use of IT in small and medium enterprises, found that 83 per cent of SMEs use ICT for finance and accounting, 75 per cent use it for HR and administration functions, 68 per cent for marketing and sales, and 64 per cent for production purposes. The same survey also said that IT-enabled SMEs grew on an average 15 per cent faster than others.[21] Normal wisdom would say that people do learn from each other.

Even in the farm sector, NSSO data shows that 40 per cent farmers do access information about modern technologies to assist in farming practices. It is interesting that for these farmers, the main source of information about such technologies was other farmers.[22] Private dealers in farm commodities and radio programmes formed a close second. Public sector extension services were used only by 5.7 per cent of the farmers who accessed information. If many farmers do not use information routinely, it is far more likely that this is because information is not easily available. It is not that they are reluctant to learn.

THE VALUE OF INFORMATION NETWORKS

So then we need to ask why is the learning process so slow and why information takes so long to reach those who need it. Surely learning processes in society could be faster. It is possible that information networks in India are far too personalized to have wide reach. When making decisions, we tend to depend on word of mouth, on friends, teachers, parents, office colleagues far too much. Ready-to-hand information that has been systematized for the common man, is hard to find.

Market for Information in India Dominated by Fixers

It is routine to find middlemen or fixers who specialize in information. With legal rights to information being enacted by the government through the Right to Information Act, there is far greater transparency today than ever before. But we still have a long way to go. In a widely reported episode not so long ago, a software application for de-mystifying procedures in a municipal corporation, raised a political storm.[23] An application called SARATHI (System of Assisting Residents And Tourists through Helpline

Information) was introduced in the Pimpri Chinchwad municipal corporation in Maharashtra state in August 2013. Standardized information about all civic services was made available on a single platform, in lucid language and with answers to frequently asked questions. The application provided multiple channels for easy and free access to this information through a website, a helpline and Mobile App among others. The councillors were most agitated. So agitated were they that they passed a resolution demanding that the text of complaints received under SARATHI should be made public. Since they were the custodians of their areas, they had a right to know the details of the complaints. Perhaps they felt that their value as suppliers of information, had been affected. Attitudes often can and do lag behind technology.

Opacity characterizes so many sectors in India that people have become inured to poor quality of information in the public domain. Nor is this a special attribute of public sector organizations; the private sector is hardly less opaque. Markets actually thrive on an asymmetry of information between consumer and supplier. Various professional organizations, whether of doctors, architects, builders or chartered accountants have hardly been able to establish information about benchmarks in those sectors. The coming in of the Real Estate Regulator for instance, addressed much of the information asymmetry that had troubled the home-buyer.

Few businesses in India provide detailed information to the consumer about their products whether it be doors and windows, white goods or about their services. We remember a most frustrating time trying to cull information from suppliers of various PVC pipes about how they would install a joint that would not leak, in a home plumbing system. Almost uniformly, they told us to have faith in the skill of the plumber or alternately in God. German and American suppliers in contrast are less religious. They routinely have detailed brochures running into many pages that describe their products and how best to install and use these. Perhaps they are simply more used to consumers who demand a minimum level of information about whatever it is they are looking to purchase.

Could it be that providing reliable information could even out the asymmetries of information and enable people to take better decisions.

We remember on trips to the European continent, that everyone used maps to figure out where they wanted to go. A familiar sight at the railway station or airport in those countries is a tourist counter that hands out maps to all and sundry at a nominal cost. Take the map and you are independent of anyone else, this is the message. In India, our first instinct is to ask anyone on the road for directions. It is a different kind of mind-scape.

Perhaps we believe that friends provide rather reliable information. That at least is how we approach say the decision of how to find the right doctor for a heart problem that a relative needs. Our instinctive response is to ask: which doctor has the best reputation among the people whom we know. All information about how the medical profession is organized tells us that in a hospital, the doctor is responsible in a small degree for patient care. Quality of care depends far more on the nurses and paramedical staff who look after you before and after a surgery. The individual reputation of the physician concerned should not make so much difference logically. Corporate hospitals figured that out long ago. They simply concentrate on building an efficient machine; the doctor is replaceable. But most people still seem to look for that brilliant physician who would save a life.

When we buy an oven for our homes or an electric cooler, a few people would make detailed comparison charts listing the pros and cons of different products in the market in order to decide. But the norm is still to ask your friend. It is that norm which should be modified somewhat; information should have a much wider scope than a circle of friends.

Reliable Information in Public Domain is Serious Asset

All people depend on friends and colleagues for information but if personal opinions are an exclusive basis for making key decisions, the quality of the decision would depend entirely on the reliability of the friend concerned. Whether we wish to use these or not, modern societies need to make institutional sources of information available to the general public. Without those institutional sources, the individual is helpless. Institutionalized information networks simply improve the ability of individuals to decide how best to lead their lives and to make a success of whatever it is that they wish to do.

When we depend exclusively on personalized information networks, then indeed learning is slow. To go up the learning curve faster, individuals need the leverages that groups can provide. The institution is a specialized kind of group that is defined by a greater degree of structure and some rules for working. For better learning and systematized information networks, formal institutions have played a critical role in other societies. These institutions could be of any kind—government agencies, educational institutions, co-operative societies, private sector training agencies or voluntary bodies, to name only the most important categories. The state in times past, has been the largest and most powerful formal institution in societies.

While institutions in general have been weak in India, state systems have by and large shown indifference to information networks. The impact of poor information networks shows itself in numerous ways practically on a daily basis. Yet we have become so inured to the situation that we barely notice it. When the information lag becomes serious enough, it results in societal disasters like the epidemic of farmers' suicides that keeps happening off and on. Over the years, while farm technologies have changed pace pretty rapidly, the quality of farm information networks has decayed.

Nor has this anything to do with who the purveyor of information might be: private sector institutions or public sector institutions. So focused are we on categories and hierarchies as opposed to outcomes, that red herrings take up much of our time. Whether it is the private sector company who informs the farmer what to buy or the agriculture assistant from the panchayat, we have little to indicate that outcomes are any different. Both sources of information are important to complement each other. It is merely that the numbers of institutions that can provide information, is limited and their reach is even more limited.

Wherever information networks have been systematized, the results have been rather remarkable. The setting up of internet based pricing displays in agriculture *mandis* was one such move.

The availability of information on the grading of various universities and colleges by the National Assessment and Accreditation Council in the higher education sector was another such. Gradually we are in the process of setting up means to systematize information but the speed is rather slow. Last mile internet connectivity in villages, still seems far away.

About one hundred and fifty years ago, when traders in Churu, Rajasthan needed to know prices of opium in the markets of Calcutta, they had set-up an elaborate system dependent on human agents. The Calcutta rates were wired to Jaipur. From there, agents would run to a hill outside the city and using pre-arranged signals they would convey the rates using mirrors as reflectors. The signals were sent to other agents on a different hill and so on to Jhunjhunu and then to Churu.[24] Information was gold but getting it was just as difficult. Now that we are into the twenty-first century, perhaps we should find more effective ways to transmit information.

That might speed up productivity and the assimilation process.

LEARNING FROM OTHERS: THE VALUE OF THE WRITTEN WORD

Learning from other people has always been an important source of information. Here the written word is even more powerful than the oral one. Whether the written word is used for teaching students, or for conveying instructions to employees in offices and the shop floor or for simply taking feedback on any programme of action, modern society depends on the written word. Scales of operation have simply increased too much for the oral message to be used as the most important channel of communication. At best oral messages can supplement the written word; they cannot be used as substitutes.

Whether we look at multinational companies or public sector bureaucracies or even smaller operations like kirana stores; organizations with explicit goals depend on written reports. Whether it is detailed account statements, periodical reports, memo or emails, everything is grist to the mill. In times past, letters were a critical source of information about what was happening on the ground, to senior officials. Today much of our information about India from the sixteenth century onwards, depends on various letters written by employees of the Dutch, Portuguese, English and French East India companies, to their overseas employers. Otherwise those companies would never have been able to run profitably.

After their accession to power, English officials wrote reams of reports on whatever they observed, for the office record. Complaints about high prices, about goods being poorly packed and shipped, and the need to buy better and pay lower take up much of the communication. So voluminous was the information they recorded, that those who manned the factory offices, were barely able to organize the material sufficiently to send it back home to London.

Modern Life Depends on Written Records for Decision-making

The large-scale systems that characterize modern society depend on the written word above all. An oral tradition, systems that are heavily focussed on face-to-face personalized interactions, cannot be depended on to manage these. In India today, it is somewhat paradoxical, that with all the lament about bureaucracy and red tape, our governance systems are hardly bureaucratic. Records are barely maintained and difficult to retrieve. It is almost as though record-keeping is seen as a symptom of weakness and not of strength. Governments in India do keep records of expenditure but little more than that.

For instance, English officers over a hundred and fifty years ago were making lists of the farmers in the districts where they were posted. Today we have computerized most of our land records but it is still the rare state government that uses land record systems for constructive purposes like crop insurance. We have finally managed to assign unique numbers to most of our population but we have not been able to identify and number pieces of land uniquely. This in turn has resulted in endless litigation and a substantial criminal element in real estate matters. But the desire to not change, is too great. An opaque land record system creates all sorts of preventable problems. Lack of documentation makes any kind of systems for systematic learning difficult to set-up; course corrections are very rare, and happen infrequently.

There are some exceptions too that are rather instructive. One such exception is the Election Commission of India. At a time when elections in India were fast deteriorating into mafia run murderous assaults on the voting public, the Election Commission stepped in to stop the rot and set-up systems that would ensure some of the fairest elections in the world. It is entirely possible that one of the major reasons for their success was the extensive documentation that the Commission uses. The conduct of elections has become strongly protocol driven; every officer-in-charge of conducting elections and the election observers are given a handbook, which they are supposed to consult for any given situation. Every officer is supposed to document what is happening and send in regular reports. The result has been a high degree of fairness and public confidence in the electoral process in one of the most adversarial of democracies.

Yet, replicating the success of the Election Commission of India in other areas has been tardy. Why would that be? Could there be some kind of cultural imperative at play? That in the absence of a record-keeping culture throughout the historical life of our country, we still find it difficult to keep records and use them as learning tools, as tools to improve ourselves? Rather, we quickly latched on to the flip rhetoric emerging from the West wherein record-keeping and systematic learning was dissed for being 'bureaucratic'? Those societies kept records for thousands of years before some among them started carping about endless paperwork. In India, we have barely begun.

Moving away from the public sector, we find similar issues in organizations of all varieties. Scaling-up from small to large is one of the most serious challenges facing small and medium enterprises today. Report after report says the same thing. Many feel that training might provide some kind of answer to this challenge. No doubt that would help.

Scaling up Depends on Ability to Process Differing Information Sets

In essence, any operation to scale up an enterprise depends on ability to read information of different kinds: about markets, products, competitors, money required, and to prepare a plan to deal with it. Those who can process information faster, do better than others. And information of a specialized nature should be available too. Many of the clusters that have come up in recent times whether it is the automotive and IT cluster in Pune or the biotechnology cluster in Bangalore, have to do with the proliferation of agencies that specialize in specific tasks of which supply of information is perhaps the most important. Information is all.

The ability to read and systematize information has much to do with institutions that can build capacities over time. Here we take a brief look at two such cases that have achieved significant social success in India in the recent past.

THE CASE OF THE TATAS

One such story belongs to the house of Tata. The Tatas are one business group that has been able to use information to increase wealth, not just once or twice but consistently and over decades.

Jamsetji Nusserwanji Tata started a trading firm at the age of twenty-nine in the year 1868. After setting up and making a success out of two textile mills in Bombay and Nagpur, one would have imagined that he would want to do more of the same. But this was no ordinary man. He dreamed of building big and of creating value in sectors that had not been explored by Indians in the nineteenth century. Tata had long been interested in minerals. Once the British government in 1899 opened up the trade in minerals, Tata conceived of the idea of setting up an iron and steel company.[25] This was at a time when India's fortunes were at their lowest ebb. Still he pursued the English authorities for support in his quest. He even visited the USA to hunt for metallurgical consultants and geologists to help him locate a suitable site for such a plant.[26] The experts he met, sent geologist C.M. Weld to India to hunt for the site. Weld did eventually locate the site in the Santhal hills of Mayurbhanj though not in the lifetime of J.N. Tata. It was left to his successor Dorab Tata to fulfil his dream. Many were the obstacles they faced. It is reported that when the Chief Commissioner for Indian Railways, Sir Frederick Upcott learnt of the plan to set-up an Indian iron and steel company, he exclaimed. 'Do you mean to say that Tatas propose to make steel rails to British specifications? Why I will undertake to eat every pound of steel rail they succeed in making.'[27]

Memory is indeed a fickle thing. That the Tatas succeeded in their quest is another matter. Just about a century earlier, English scientists had been examining samples of Indian wootz steel in an effort to unravel its mysteries. So much so that English cutler and metallurgist James Stodart who made and sold knives, used the information that these knives were made of wootz steel from India, to advertise his product! Stodart started his company in 1787. At that time, the market for wootz steel was coming to an end though the fame of the product was still legendary. In a short space of one hundred and ten years, not only did the British forget that Indians had made world-class steel at one time, even the Indians forgot their own history.

Reviving the old tradition was no longer possible. So the Tatas built a new one. The Tata Iron and Steel Company was launched and the Jamshedpur steel plant was commissioned.

While Tata's decision seems to have been rather risky at the time, it was taken after considerable research. The one serious hitch was the lack of trained manpower to advise him about the feasibility of the idea and the location of the plant. Had such manpower been available in India, Tata would not have had to go all the way to the USA in search of a geologist.

Jamsetji Tata seemed to have felt the lack of manpower seriously enough to think about starting a university of science. He set aside fourteen buildings and some of his properties valued at about Rs. 30 lakh in those times, as endowment for the project.[28] His ideas found little support from the British authorities and even from his own community who did not like the idea that the wealth would be used in a project from which the entire community would benefit, not just Parsis. He never gave up the idea though it could not bear fruit in his lifetime. Again it was left to Dorab Tata to lead the project to success. Thus was born the Indian Institute of Science in Bangalore, which today continues to be a top ranked Indian institution of learning.

Tata saw what most of his contemporaries could not: that there is indeed a link between production of industrial goods and the availability of scientific knowledge and learning. Each needs the other to succeed in the long term. It is no accident that two of the companies of the Tata group today, Tata Steel and Tata Consultancy Services, rank among the top ten of their category in the world. Building skills and institutionalizing learning seems to be part and parcel of the tradition of this industrial group.

That the largest and richest steel company in the world which is also owned by an Indian, Laxmi Niwas Mittal, has had great difficulty in setting up a plant in the homeland of its founder, is only a sad commentary on the present state of affairs. At last count, Mittal was negotiating a joint venture with Indian public sector company SAIL, in order to set-up a large scale plant in India. Making clear and easy rules to implement, does not seem to come easily to us. Still there were significant exceptions.

THE CASE OF ISRO

The other story from modern India that can make us proud, is the story of the Indian Space Research Organisation (ISRO). They say necessity is a good teacher. The story of how ISRO developed its own satellite launch vehicle and eventually sent a mission to Mars confirms that. With a world reluctant to share space technology that could have helped develop missile launch capability, ISRO was left pretty much to its own devices. Countries like France and Russia did offer limited help but India was pretty much on its own when developing design capability or even sourcing ingredients. Even ingredients that were locally available were often in short supply. Not only did they have to develop most of the launch vehicle parts and propellants on their own, often the chemicals and instrumentation that made up many of these had to be independently developed. For instance, once the ISRO people realized that the ammonium perchlorate that was the single largest ingredient of a composite propellant was in short supply, ISRO set up a manufacturing plant of its own at Alwaye in Kerala in 1978.[29] Sure enough, the single supplier of the item in the country, stopped supplying it in the mid-1980s but by then the ISRO plant was sufficient to meet its needs.[30]

The second major constraint that shaped the ISRO story was the huge cost of the resources they needed for the launches. Cost alone was only part of the story. If engines of a specific type had been procured from a foreign country in small numbers, it became imperative to use these very carefully. If a launch failed and the engine ended up in the sea, procuring another was not just a cost issue but a foreign policy issue.

Such constraints meant that each individual part of a launch vehicle needed to be tested multiple times before an actual launch.

Over the years ISRO seems to have perfected a method of systematic working. Intense effort by teams, multiple tests, exhaustive recording of all information and feedback loops like failure analysis, seem to have been the sheet anchors of the method. And information was absolute gold. No detail was too insignificant to be ignored. If one single valve leaked, it could mean the failure of a launch that had taken years and hundreds of crores of rupees to set up.

Through all the years of effort, the vision that seems to have driven ISRO was to see that the benefits of science and technology could reach out to meet the needs of the people. Very early on, three specific areas that Vikram Sarabhai, one of the architects of ISRO, identified were: remote sensing, communications and meteorology.[31] The goals were to prove critical to ISRO throughout. That eventually India became only the fourth nation in the world to successfully launch a mission to Mars, after the USA, Russia and China is the result of years of painstaking effort and attention to detail.

INSTITUTIONS HELP PRESERVE INSTITUTIONAL MEMORIES

One feature common to both these success stories was the creation of an institution with a specific goal. Here was a group of people who shared that goal and who regularly exchanged information of mutual interest. It was this community of interest and the long-term collation of information that enabled both bodies of people to produce more wealth. The house of the Tatas generated wealth for the group and also for the nation. ISRO generated wealth for society in general. ISRO does not really keep track of the spin-offs of the technology they produce; keeping track of information is rather alien to our society. But over the years, the spin-offs were indeed considerable. Remote sensing data has been critical to agriculture; communications technology has revolutionized distance education, to name only the most obvious examples.

The very fact that institutions exist, leads to creation of records in the long-term. It is those records and institutional memories that help preserve innovative ideas.

Let us take the case of ISRO itself. In 1994, when the fake spy scandal hit ISRO, Dr. Nambi Narayanan was in-charge of building indigenous cryogenic engines. The scandal and his imprisonment set back India's space effort by decades. It was not till 2014 that India would be able to finally launch an indigenously developed cryogenic engine. Speculations abound that the fake spy scandal was engineered by foreign powers to sabotage the Indian programme. It is a matter of record that till date none of those complicit in the investigation of the case have been punished. Or that the then state government never asked how a technology that had not yet been developed, could possibly be sold. Dr. Narayanan's life was of course destroyed.

Institutions Help Collation of Memories in the Long-term

Its reputation in tatters, ISRO still plodded on. The great thing about institutions is that whatever the setback suffered, records remain and memories remain. So work can go on. And in January 2014, India finally launched a satellite manned by an indigenous cryogenic engine.

One wonders, could it be that many such innovative ideas and much work, could simply have been lost in India over the millennia, for lack of documentation? Oral traditions have their disadvantages.

In modern-day science, every scientist begins from where his predecessors left off. To keep on reinventing the wheel, is hardly a productive exercise.

A second feature of institutions is, that long-term collation of data helps people to identify patterns that help decision-making. Information read in the long haul, can yield very valuable insights. The business world might now be waking up to say that data is the new oil; this is the most routine insight for those involved in the running of institutions. It is individual bits of data that allow us to see the big picture. Both individual bits and the big picture are equally important.

In order to plan the next step, we need a perspective that builds on and includes individual insights. Isolated insights draw upon and contribute to sweeps of information spread across space and time. Just a brief look at the history of ideas shows that ideas have rather long lives, especially ideas that change the world.

If today the effects of economic depressions can be fought and considerably reduced, it is due to the stellar work of economists for nearly a century, dating back to John Maynard Keynes. Similarly, economists like Kenneth Arrow and Robert Merton Solow, for all their individual brilliance, drew strength from the lively dialogue that they engaged in and from a considerable pool of ideas.

It was these last two who talked particularly about the importance of knowledge capital in an economy. They pointed out that all the natural resources of an economy cannot account for increases in productivity. They even provided mathematical proof for this. For increases in productivity, we need to look at knowledge content in the economy. The whole is inevitably greater than the sum of the parts where knowledge is concerned.

Increase in Shared Knowledge is Key to Research

What is true of the social sciences, is even truer of the sciences. However much the history of science might be made up of brilliant discoveries, the process of discovery remains incremental. Eureka moments in science are important but are few and far between. It is the gradual process of adding to the body of knowledge that accounts for the bulk of progress. The research of Norman Borlaug on dwarf varieties of wheat that heralded the Green Revolution, was based on selective breeding techniques dating back to the nineteenth century. It was the Christian priest Gregor Mendel who conducted detailed experiments on selective breeding of pea plants. Once his efforts came into the public domain, it was open to anyone to pick up the technique, if they wanted to.

This process of building upon numerous insights continuously and consistently, becomes far easier with institutions to help. Single individuals, howsoever enterprising and intelligent, cannot collate information in this way.

We in India have a tradition of great sages and wise men stretching back to Aryabhata, Brahmagupta, Madhavacharya and Sankaracharya, to name only a few. Often many of us seem to feel that one man's words of wisdom are in themselves enough. But the modern world is too complex for that. One bit of wisdom, one piece of insight may be important but it is the systematic collation of information and insights that we need. Such collation produces a view far closer to ground reality. No matter how significant the individual be, whether it is a Nobel laureate or a key politician or businessman, individual wisdom can only build on what has gone on before.

Only formal institutions have this kind of reach. Institutions in India have not been so robust. Perhaps this could be one reason for the lack of a vision that we feel around us. A long-term vision in general requires groups of individuals, ideating and interacting with each other; this kind of setting is best found in institutions.

KNOWLEDGE AND INSTITUTIONS: THE WHOLE IS MORE THAN THE SUM OF ITS PARTS

The institution represents the principle that the whole is more than the sum of its parts. Institutions, like all organizations, have certain goals, explicit and implicit. Those goals drive the behaviour of those associated with the institution just as much as their personal motivations. Once an institution comes into being, the goals too exist independently of the individuals who work in the organization.

Let us look briefly at the formal institutions that surround us. Many neighbourhoods in urban areas have residents welfare associations. The Swachch Bharat Mission[32] has been the most successful in precisely those neighbourhoods that have active residents welfare associations. Not only are these associations points of contact between urban local bodies and the residents, they are also repositories of information. The information could be about waste management, about keeping the area clean, about noise pollution, etc. The more successful associations teach the residents how to segregate wet and dry waste and to compost waste. Once residents are able to see the benefits, use the compost, the learning tends to stay. It is not that all residents of such a neighbourhood are passionately committed to the idea of waste management. That is the explicit goal of the association. So the goal serves as a driving force possibly in the face of indifference, or even resistance of some residents.

A slightly more complicated institution is the public library. A public library is a small information system in itself. It is not just a storehouse of books but a forum for exchange of ideas through the medium of books. Libraries were key to the development of the ideas of the Enlightenment in Europe from the seventeenth century onwards. Similarly, subscription libraries based on member subscriptions, were a very important element in building of consensus on social issues in nineteenth-century USA.

The story of the banking house of Jagat seth in pre-modern Bengal provides a signal lesson in the value of institutions. As we shall see in the next chapter, they failed to institutionalize their functioning or their decision-taking process. For that failure, they and the entire country paid a heavy price.

As a society, India still shows a certain inability to set-up long-term systems or institutions. The result is that our ability to manage knowledge systems, also suffers. All this does not imply that an institutional view is always better than individual insight; merely that being better informed, it has more chance of succeeding.

Robust Institutions are the Key to Economic Growth

Without robust institutions to anchor it, growth and progress in India would continue to happen by design and not by default. The design, the ability to use information to devise workable plans, is what is missing in India today.

The very fact that institutions sustain themselves over long periods of time, gives them a great deal of value. Whether public or private, the ownership of the institution is hardly important. It is just that governments having more resources, they are associated with many more institutions. Could it be that given a general suspicion of the government in the public mind, we are reluctant to see the value of public institutions? Perhaps.

If that is so, we need to do a re-think. Modern society and economy depend heavily on institutions for feedback on what is happening, on planning what is to be done and how it is to be done.

India's past has been impressive but, merely noticing India's past greatness is not sufficient to understand the question: how do we translate the great desire today of individuals to do well and make their country great, into reality? To translate that desire, we need to create more and more institutional mechanisms for systematization and sharing of information so that we can go up the learning curve more rapidly. A piece of wisdom can create greater value when it is shared, not when it is kept secret.

We only have to look at the case of mathematics in ancient India to see how the absence of record-keeping acted as a major barrier to learning. India has been home to some of the greatest mathematicians in the world in the past and this is true even today. It is not just the idea of zero and the concept of place value and the number system for which India was known. Seminal ideas like solutions to indeterminate equations and to the infinite series, were also discovered by Indian mathematicians. Yet these were isolated individuals. We do not see much connection between them and institutionalized learning. Is it possible that this is one reason why India lagged behind after showing much initial brilliance?

As institutions grow in scale and complexity, they increase social capacities to manage ever-changing situations. Banks and formal credit systems for instance, were key to the development of the modern economy. Here we do not talk so much about the every-day functions of these institutions. Banks might raise or lower interest rates to reduce or increase credit supply as the context demands. What is important is that a variety of knowledge inputs help the officials in decision-making. What is important for us is that bank officials can draw upon what happened in the last crisis for help in those decisions. In effect, the ability to preserve and transmit memories, knowledge and learned behaviour, is what is important.

Here the story of the banking house of Jagat Seth in pre-modern Bengal is especially insightful. The founder of that house set up a great tradition; he also made a lot of money in the process. But his successors could not institutionalize what he had put in place. It is to this story that we now move.

NOTES

1. Queen Ahilyabai.
2. Malcolm, 1823, vol. 2: 92-3.
3. Khan, 1976.
4. Calkins, 1972, pp. 85-6 & 146-8.
5. Ibid.: 329.
6. Ibid.: 337.
7. *Indian Records Series* 1905: vol. III, 289.
8. Khan, 1969: 113.
9. Accounts, East India Company.
10. Ibid.
11. Chaudhury, 1995: 283-95.
12. Herklots, 1829. Average of prices available for 5 years between 1760 and 1769 in lower Bengal taken.
13. Bayly, 1816, v.12: 560. Average of prices for years 1760-69 in Calcutta taken.
14. Ibid.: 1816, v. 12: 560.
15. Ibid.: 1816, v. 12: 560.

16. Datta, 1990: 46.
17. Annadurai, Danasekharan and Mani, 2017.
18. Literally it means Treasury.
19. Confederation of Indian Industry, 2014.
20. Ministry of Finance, Government of India, 2018, vol. 2: 121.
21. Confederation of Indian Industry, 2014.
22. NSSO, Report No. 499, 2005: 7. Sources of information: other farmers (16.7 per cent), input dealers (13.1 per cent), radio (13 per cent); public sector extension (5.7 per cent).
23. Biswas, 2014.
24. Taknet, 2015: 81.
25. Lala, 2004: 20.
26. Ibid.: 21.
27. Ibid.: 26-7.
28. Ibid.: 38.
29. Raj, 2000: 96-7.
30. Ibid.: 99.
31. Raj, 2000: 22.
32. Clean India Mission launched in 2014 by the Government of India.

CHAPTER 3

Bankers Extraordinaire: The House of Jagat Seth

Sustained growth of wealth requires a systematic collaboration between government and business. A connection between the power of the state and the trade of the country did bring benefits to some individuals on both sides in Indian history; that the connection was not formalized also meant that it was rather weak and could not be sustained. Nor was it very visible to those involved. The impact on the economy was accordingly intermittent. In India, things tended to happen by default rather than by design. Informal relationships are far more vulnerable to hostility and competition as compared to formal ones: this is one of the learnings we get from the encounter between Indian and European merchants in the seventeenth and eighteenth centuries. Still, there was one case of collaboration between merchant and ruler that produced rather remarkable results in the short-term. In the long-term, the relationship simply could not survive a hostile environment. What the results were for the personalities involved and for the region where all this played out, is what we shall see in this chapter.

Today, we take it for granted that the relationship between government and business is critical to the economy of any state. The ability of the state to set-up efficient taxation systems; the ability to keep up money supply according to the needs of trade and the ability to obtain better terms of trade for their business community; all these factors make a lot of difference to the ability of trade and industry to earn more. In turn, if these things work better, the state earns more revenue.

Yet the relationship between government and business is far more likely to evoke snide comments than a clear recognition of the role that the state can play in wealth creation. One reason for this could be that individual businessmen often do make great profits through their nearness to the powers-that-be. In theory, a free market is a great concept. In practice, people try all the time to make it less free through a variety of strategies, all of which have mostly one motive: to make more money. A collaboration between money and power can have a number of general consequences that work to the benefit of all businessmen, not just for the few, provided that there is sustained dialogue between those concerned.

This collaboration is perhaps most visible in state support to the profession of banking. Bankers operate at such a large scale that many operations such as minting, instruments of credit and taxation require positive state policy. In turn, banking is key to providing capital at reasonable rates of interest; and capital can play a critical role in organizing industrial production to meet the demands of the market.

When we look back at our history, we find that India did have a reasonably well-developed money market and credit instruments around the time that the English East India Company entered the country. By the end of Aurangzeb's reign in the seventeenth century, bankers had begun to play an important role even in the collection and transmission of taxes. Some of them had the license to mint money, which is entirely in line with Indian tradition.

What was missing was a relationship of trust and collaboration between bankers and rulers. Once in a while, a few individuals would obtain greater benefits for themselves and make more money. But there was little by way of sustained institutionalized dialogue between the two groups.

When we look back at Indian history, we find that merchants and princes have had cordial relations on many occasions. Merchants have even held important positions in state machinery whether it was Pushyagupta, the governor of Gujarat in the time of the Mauryas or the various positions held by merchants in Mughal administration. What remained missing was anything more systematic that would ensure that the authority of the state synergized with the needs of business and industry.

Moving forward in time, various Mughal nobles, emperors and

local kings, depended upon bankers to meet their credit needs to conduct war and run the administration. Such needs were met through two kinds of strategies—farming out revenue collection in large territories and in obtaining loans from moneylenders. We see this phenomenon in the Bengal subah in eastern India, in Surat and Rajasthan in western India where records are available. But this relationship was never institutionalized. In other countries, monarchs used their constant need for loans, to set-up a centralized bank; not so in India.

The role of the state in wealth creation, has been rather marginal in India. They say that exceptions prove the rule. One such exception is a story from eighteenth-century Bengal: the story of Seth Manikchand and Diwan Murshid Quli Khan.

It is indeed heartening to know that there was someone like Manikchand, a big banker of Bengal, whose banking house got the title *Jagat Seth* who intuitively knew, 300 years ago, what many modern businessmen do not seem to even today: that dialogue and policy support are important for business.

You might ask why we should care about individual exceptions of this variety. We should care because the story of these remarkable characters is tied up in an important way with the history of the province of Bengal and also with the history of India. So long as the alliance between the businessman and the state succeeded, Bengal remained one of the richest provinces of the country. Was it entirely a matter of coincidence that once that alliance broke down, Bengal was ruined and the way was laid open for the domination of India by the English East India Company?

In this story we shall see that Manikchand seems to have instinctively recognized the value of government support for expanding his business. Not so his successor Mehtab Rai who seemed to be indifferent to the ones who ruled. So when a chance did emerge in Bengal, instead of grabbing the chance to rule he much preferred to ask the East India Company to do so. Little did he notice that the East India Company whom he seemed to regard as just another client, was in fact a rival in trade. And the idea that by providing the company access to resources of the state, he was surrendering invaluable competitive advantage, he didn't take cognizance of at all. Perhaps he did not realize the enormity of the advantage, because he failed to realize how much the state had contributed to the rise of his own family?

THE RISE OF MANIKCHAND AND MURSHID QULI KHAN

It was in the early eighteenth century that the Mughal emperor conferred the title *Jagat Seth* (lit. Banker of the World) to the house that had helped make Bengal one of the highest revenue paying regions of the Mughal empire. The Emperor also appointed the head of this banking house the Treasurer-General of Bengal. It was a fitting tribute to this house of bankers; a recognition of their rise to the position of a pillar of society. It is estimated that the total wealth of the house of Jagat Seth at this time was around Rs. 14 crore which in contemporary terms could mean anything between Rs. 4,000 and 10,000 crore.[1] But it is not so much the wealth of this house that concerns us as the extraordinary abilities shown by Manikchand, the founder of the firm. For nearly fifty years, Manikchand and his successors, practically ruled the financial markets of Bengal through a combination of business acumen and political support, a rare occurrence in India at the time.

Manikchand was born in the seventeenth century, to Hiranand Sahu, a Marwari Jain from Nagaur in Rajasthan belonging to the Gailarha *gotra*. Hiranand migrated to Bihar in the mid-seventeenth century in search of better prospects. Hiranand had six sons (some say seven) and one daughter who was married to a businessman from Varanasi.

In Patna, Hiranand made some money in the business of saltpetre, an essential ingredient for making gun powder. Saltpetre from India was much in demand in those times because of its superior quality. The needs of war in Europe and the ease of carrying it as ballast on the ships making the journey to Europe, made saltpetre a valuable commodity.

Hiranand lent out considerable sums to the English East India Company, which had just set up a factory there. By the end of the seventeenth century, he was a man of some influence in Patna but it was his fourth son Manikchand who was destined to go down in history as banker extraordinaire.

Manikchand took up the business from where his father had left off and expanded it in many directions. One of these directions was the profession of moneylending.

Becoming a supplier of capital on a large scale, necessarily meant some closeness with those who needed it. Mughal nobility and rulers were important customers of bankers at the time. They needed money for a variety of tasks: quite apart from personal needs, money was critical to grease the wheels of government. Sale of offices in the Mughal empire was a routine affair. Money was also needed by the *jagirdars*, the officials of the Mughal empire, till such time as they could raise revenue from the lands of their *jagir*. However much personal wealth the *jagirdars* might have had, they needed money to maintain their offices and soldiers.

In the course of expanding his business from Patna to Dhaka, Manikchand struck up a friendship with the newly appointed Diwan of Bengal who would be known later in history as Murshid Quli Khan. The friendship was to last throughout the lives of both men and would have considerable impact on both lives. Murshid Quli Khan had been born into a Brahmin family, adopted by a rich Farsi, who named him Mohammed Hadi. It was with this name that he entered the service of emperor Aurangzeb. Later in service, on having somewhat succeeded in increasing the revenue collection of Bengal, the emperor gave him the title Kartalab Khan ('the seeker of challenges'). Still later, appreciating his efficiency as an imperial officer, the emperor called him 'Murshid Quli Khan', the sagacious one. Once the authority of the imperial Mughals had been suitably weakened, he would be known as the 'Nawab of Bengal'. Under the name of Kartalab Khan a very famous mosque still exists in Old Dhaka. We find some account of his career in a history of Bengal written by Ghulam Husain Salim in the early nineteenth century titled the *Riyaz-us-Salatin*.

Being an efficient sort of person, Murshid Quli Khan seems to have been noticed by Aurangzeb who was looking for a capable administrator for Bengal. Aurangzeb appointed him as *diwan* of Bengal, the Chief Revenue Officer of the province, tasked with collecting tax revenue and sending it safely and securely to the imperial capital. Aurangzeb's own grandson Prince Azim-us-Shan was *nazim* and *faujdar* of Bengal, the chief imperial administrator and military commander. By keeping the offices of the revenue collector and the military commander separate, the Mughals had ensured that power at the provincial level was not centralized in the hands of any one person.

In the past there had been far too many slippages in the revenue estimation and collection within the Mughal empire. The province of Bengal too needed considerable re-organization and reform of revenue administration. The basic record of revenues due, territory-wise, needed to be revised. The original revenue roll which had been prepared by the legendary Todar Mal, revenue minister of Akbar over 100 years ago, had virtually remained unchanged. As a result, as an English officer was to remark with some indignation: the Indian revenue collectors had systematically defrauded their emperor for decades, if not centuries.[2]

In his task of improving the revenues of Bengal, Murshid Quli Khan much appreciated the help and advice that Seth Manikchand provided. Together they tried to stop the leakage of state revenue. *Zamindars* were told that they must pay the revenues on time, on pain of punishment.

One of the first things the new *diwan* did was to resume fertile lands allotted to the Mughal officials in Bengal and re-allot them lands in Orissa. The resumed lands were put to intensive cultivation.

State Guarantee to Farm Loans helped the Banking House

Attention was also paid to improvement in land. On advice from Seth Manikchand, the *diwan* also helped advance 'strength giving' loans to the peasants so they would not suffer from lack of working capital. It was in administering these loans called *taqavi* (lit. 'strength giving'), that Manikchand's genius came into play.

Jain merchant family memories recorded in the late nineteenth and early twentieth centuries, are reported to have said that it was Manikchand who persuaded the Mughal administration to provide once a state guarantee for loans to needy peasants.[3]

State support would have provided an immense fillip to the moneylending operations of Manikchand. Effectively, the revenues of Bengal, then, began to flow through this one banker and his house.

The involvement of bankers and moneylenders in revenue administration seems to have increased the vigour of tax recovery. At all events, the new *diwan* was soon able to increase the revenue sent by Bengal. He is reported in the *Riyaz-us-Salatin* to have remitted over Rs. 1 crore to the imperial treasury.[4] Aurangzeb was extremely pleased. The *diwan* rose in his estimation. *Kartalab Khan* (the seeker of challenges) was the title that the emperor now gave him. In turn, Seth Manikchand, rose in the estimation of the *diwan*.

Such efficiency did not please everyone. One person who was not pleased was the Governor of Bengal, Prince Azim-us-Shan, grandson of Aurangzeb. Possibly because there might have been a contraction in the monies that he could siphon off from the system.

Prince Azim-us-Shan was not known to be too scrupulous in his dealings and prone to misuse his power and authority for personal benefit.

Aurangzeb Disciplines the Prince

Some time ago he had promoted the idea of a *sauda-i-khas* (the trade transactions of the emperor) as distinguished from a *sauda-i-am* (the trade transactions of the common people). Simply put, this meant that he posted his agents to all entrepôts who would then buy up most goods when they came to the market. This would be called *sauda-i-khas*—for, now the goods were with the Prince. Later other traders could buy the goods from the Prince and this was called *sauda-i-am*. Aurangzeb was furious when he got to know of this and had the practice stopped immediately. He also downsized the rank of the prince by reducing the cavalrymen under his command by 500. As far as Aurangzeb was concerned, the world needed to know that the princely knuckles had been administered a rap.

The prince, suspecting the role of the *diwan* in his being disciplined, now began to plot the murder of the imperial *diwan*. Rumour goes that he hired some soldiers to do the needful. The *diwan* escaped the murder attempt by chance. Angry, he went to confront the prince. He knelt before the Prince, accused him of having hired assassins and warned him that he should desist from such practices henceforth. Or else, the *diwan* is supposed to have said, he would kill the Prince with his own hands and then commit suicide. The prince was taken aback and took a conciliatory tone.

SHIFT TO MURSHIDABAD

Murshid Quli Khan returned home a thoughtful man. These were dangerous times. He knew the Prince's nature well and believed in taking precautions. It was at this point in time that Manikchand intervened. He advised the *diwan* to find new headquarters and remove himself from the vicinity of the prince.

The *diwan* agreed with this advice. The town of Maksudabad, some 350 km from the capital Dhaka, was chosen as the new headquarters. Manikchand too shifted along with the *diwan*. The town was now renamed as Murshidabad, after its now most important resident.

From our point of view what is important is that the *diwan* left without informing the Prince and took with him all the public offices attached to his *diwani*. He did take care to inform the emperor though. Manikchand, now with his base at Murshidabad, remained the *diwan's* personal banker till the end of his life. His mansion on the banks of the river at Mahimapur was a few kilometres from the palace of Murshid Quli Khan. The ruins of the old house of Jagat Seth can still be seen. His descendants live nearby.

Manikchand is Put in Charge of the Treasury, Monies Flow in

Now Manikchand was formally appointed in-charge of the treasury. He was invested with the task of managing the revenues of the state. The officials of the English East India Company noticed the almost unending supply of capital to which the local potentates had access and explained this as the consequence of the closeness between the rulers and the bankers.

With trouble brewing in one of the richest provinces of the empire, Aurangzeb promptly administered a stinging rebuke to the Governor of Bengal, his grandson, the Prince Azim-us-Shan, for plotting the murder of a trusted imperial officer. The *Riyaz-us-Salatin* reports that the emperor warned the prince, 'in case a hair-breadth injury, in person or property happens to him (the *diwan*), I will avenge myself on you, my boy'. He also ordered the prince to move out of Bengal to Bihar. The prince was forced to relocate to Patna. The *diwan's* stars shone ever brighter.

The duo of the *diwan* and the Seth now increased their efforts to re-organise the revenues of Bengal. One of the major steps they took was to update the revenue roll of the lands of Bengal. This resulted in Bengal yielding much more revenue for the state as a result.

Now, the rules of the empire demanded that the revenue accounts should be approved by the *qanungo*, i.e. the accounts officer, of the province, by placing his signature on them. Only then could these be passed by the *diwan*. Darab Narain, the *qanungo* of Bengal was duly requested to sign the accounts. The *qanungo* demanded a fee of Rs. 3 lakhs for his signatures. The *diwan* was furious but had little choice. So, he made a counter offer of Rs. 1 lakh, to be paid once he returned from the meeting with the emperor. The *qanungo* refused. The joint *qanungo*, Jinarain by name, however, was more accommodating than his chief. He was willing to negotiate and also willing to take decisions behind the back of his chief. He helped the *diwan* by signing the accounts after accepting a bribe of Rs. 1 lakh. This entire episode is told to us in the *Riyaz-us-Salatin*. As it turned out, the joint *qanungo* had taken a wise decision for, the *diwan* soon found an opportunity to have the *qanungo* killed.[5]

In the meantime, the accounts of Bengal were duly presented to the emperor, Aurangzeb. A very pleased emperor bestowed a new title on this trusted *diwan* for all the sagacity that he had shown in administering the province of Bengal. From now on he would be called 'Murshid Quli Khan', the sagacious one. This is the name with which history too would remember him. In addition to his own office of *diwan*, Murshid Quli Khan was now appointed deputy to the prince in his capacity as the Imperial Administrator of the provinces Bengal and Orissa.

Manikchand, on his side, continued to prosper in his banking operations.

HOW MANIKCHAND RAN HIS BANKING OPERATIONS

Being in charge of the treasury, Manikchand's house received revenues from all the *zamindars* and *jagirdars*. This position provided Manikchand a crucial advantage in his moneylending business. A position in the *diwan's* office meant that it would be a brave man who would try to defraud the Seth.

The firm prospered even more. For the next fifty years, till the middle of the eighteenth century, it was this house, which dictated the terms of trade and the rates of interest on capital. There were already branches in the major cities of north India run by brothers and other kinsmen. Discounted bills of exchange that were issued at one branch, could be presented for encashment at another branch. This increased the scope of business enormously.

In turn the Seth provided important benefits to the state.

State Revenues Begin to Travel via Bank Draft

Till the 1720s, state revenues were sent to Delhi in hundreds of wagons accompanied by a military escort. Sending the revenues physically was a hazardous enterprise. Often the royal cargo was attacked and looted. According to family tradition, Manikchand (but more probably his nephew, Fatehchand) began to use the branches of his banking house run by his kin in other cities, to issue a draft for the revenues, which could then be en-cashed at any other branch. It was a convenient way to transmit revenues.

Perhaps it was on account of such services that the Mughal emperor even gave the title *Jagat Seth* to Fatehchand who was then heading the banking operations of the family firm.

Did this mean that the house of Jagat Seth was running a formal banking operation? Robert Orme, the official historian of the East India Company, did think so. He called the house of Jagat

Seth as the greatest bankers and *shroffs* (money-changers) of the known world at the time.

No doubt if one were to compare the volume of transactions of the house of Jagat Seth and those of contemporary European bankers, Jagat Seth would have rivalled and perhaps outshone the Europeans. But what the house of Jagat Seth never had was an organizational structure for decision taking and record maintenance rivalling the Europeans. Everything was based on a closed, secret kinship group. To this day, we are only able to construct the finances of the house, on the basis of European records of the time; not on the basis of the banking records of the house. All decisions were personalized decisions made on the basis of whatever information was available.

Personalized Working left Behind no Memories

A personalized way of working also meant that the very real benefits to this alliance were never put on paper, or calculated in real time. After all, the fact that the state was now able to transmit its revenues to Delhi by way of a draft instead of a large armed troop of soldiers escorting a physical treasure, saved the state a lot of money. It was a much more efficient way of working. For the banker's house, this kind of function, gave it tremendous legitimacy.

A centralized bank is much more effective in controlling rates of interest and in money supply, than individual moneylenders could ever be. It was the institution of the public debt that in other countries led to the development of the bond market. But none of this was ever formalized in Bengal. Since none of this information was ever recorded, there was nothing to guide future generations.

Without any written information emerging, it was in turn difficult to build a community of interest around some shared goals.

Institutionalization of Decision-Making Helps the Company

The English East India Company, in contrast, had over the years, formalized a system of taking decisions, which while privileging certain individuals, always allowed constant evaluation and re-evaluation of those decisions. Also there was considerable decentralization of decision-making in the Company. Perhaps this was a product of necessity given the very long distance between company headquarters in England and the sphere of operations in India. Even while the officials of the Company took local decisions that sometimes went contrary to Company policy, there were still a large body of decisions that were actuated by what the Company desired.

The difference was to prove a crucial one. It meant that so long as there were intelligent, far-seeing people at the head of affairs in Indian family enterprises, the house prospered. But a single foolish leader could ruin in one stroke what the forefathers had built.

The second major difference in the operations of the Company and Indian bankers was the emphasis of Europeans on standardization and an attempt to organize production according to the needs of the market. This was something Indians never seem to have shown an interest in doing. The Company used Indian middlemen to supervise the working of weavers who supplied piece goods to the Company. The Company liked to prescribe standards of quality in a written contract with which the middlemen were expected to comply. The Indians were content to sell the goods which they traded at what they believed were reasonable rates of profit, which were seldom less than 15-20 per cent. They never seemed to see the need either to increase the rates or to organize production to improve efficiencies. Investments in fixed capital were uniformly low. But this did not seem to lead to any reduction in the fortunes of Indian trading houses.

So let us see how stable were the revenues of the house of Jagat Seth.

In those days bankers like Manikchand had a few main sources of income:

1. Lending money on large scale to those who needed it; and here the Mughal nobility and often the emperor himself were frequent clients;
2. Buying bullion and old coins for re-coining in the mint for a charge;

3. Discounting bills of exchange for immediate cash;
4. Wholesale trade in the major commodities of the time like raw silk, cotton cloth, saltpetre, etc.

Manikchand participated in all four activities. What distinguished him from the others was the large scale of his operations; this in turn was made possible by state support and a state guarantee.

In 1757, Luke Scrafton, then working with the East India Company, made the following estimate of the annual income of this house in a communication to Robert Clive:

TABLE 3.1: SOURCES OF INCOME OF THE HOUSE OF JAGAT SETH[6]

Category of Income	Revenue in Rupees
On 2/3 of revenue at 10 per cent	10,60,000
Interest from *zamindars* at 12 per cent	13,50,000
On re-coining 50 lakh at 7 per cent	3,50,000
Interest on 40 lakh at 37½ per cent	15,00,000
Interest from Batta or Exchange Rates 7 to 8 lakh	7,00,000
Total	49,60,000

Source: Chaudhary, 1995: 114-15.

An annual income of Rs. 49.60 lakh or so was no mean sum.

THE CRUCIAL RIGHT TO RUN THE MINT

At first glance, the income of the house from re-coining was a small part of their total income but the leverage this operation provided was a considerable one. In practice, the Mughals maintained an open minting system. Coining of bullion brought to the official mint, seems to have been a custom in India from time immemorial. From the days of the Imperial Mauryas when five symbols were stamped on silver punch-marked coins (one of the first currency systems of India), we find many instances of kings licensing out the minting of coins to private agencies like guilds and merchants, provided the government's conditions were observed. Of the five symbols stamped on the punch-marked coins, while four are commonly accepted as royal symbols, there were as many as 200 varieties of the fifth, leading numismatists to estimate that this fifth symbol might be associated with the mint where the coin was issued.[7] The practise persisted and in Mughal India, people could take their bullion to the nearest mint for coining after paying minting charges. Mostly the officials staffing the mints were Mughal officials but the Mughal state could and did make exceptions. It was on account of this that the English East India Company was granted the license to coin rupees in their mints at Bombay and Madras; provided they conformed to the standards prescribed and provided they used the dies supplied by the Mughals. No one in the Mughal state system saw that in licensing the right to coin money, they had shared an attribute of the sovereign state. For them, it was the output that mattered.

Once in fact the English went so far as to coin rupees bearing the image of William III and Mary, the English sovereigns. Khafi Khan, a Mughal official, says that the news writers of Surat reported that the English had coined some rupees at Bombay with 'a superscription containing the name of their impure king'.[8] As soon as this came to light, the Mughal officials put a stop to the practice. But this was as far as their assertion of sovereignty went.

In the market, there were different series of coins issued in different years, although conforming to the given standard in the year of issue. In practice, the freshly minted coins enjoyed a premium in the market and old coins were discounted at rates which could go up to 3 per cent. This also generated a flourishing trade in money changing where old coins were accepted at a discount in exchange for new ones. This was the function of the *shroffs*. One foreign traveller of those times remarked that it would be a small village indeed which did not have a *shroff* of its own.

So in Mughal times, anyone could carry their bullion or old coins for minting or re-coining as the case may be, for a 5 per cent charge. The silver for minting was normally brought in by trading vessels and Indian goods were mostly paid for in currency. Often the timing of shipping operations meant that the bullion arrived for minting at specific times of the year. This in turn meant that there was a long queue for minting bullion. From the English records of Surat, we learn that it could take up to 33 days to get your bullion minted. Given that time was at a premium, the traders had only so much time to get their money, make their payments, collect goods and to ship those out. In such conditions, anyone who had special access to the mint, had a huge advantage. His proximity to Murshid Quli Khan provided Manikchand that crucial advantage. He did not have to wait to get his bullion coined.

The ever-fluctuating political relations of the Company with Murshid Quli Khan meant that the Company directors were reluctant to depend too much on the Mughal mints. They displayed a great sensitivity to power relations in this as in other matters. They had already secured the right to coin money in Madras and Bombay. Now they wished to secure similar rights in Bengal. The directors showed a clear desire to avoid dealing with the Mughal mints. One of their letters even goes so far as to say clearly that if dealing with the local *shroffs* for coinage meant a loss, so be it; but this was preferable to dealing with the Mughal mints. Inevitably, the work of the English company went to a large number of shroffs; the house of Jagat Seth also enjoyed their custom.

Income from interest earned on moneylending amounted to nearly half the profits of the house of Jagat Seth and the European companies were significant customers. For, the Europeans were almost permanently in dire need of capital. Bullion was the major item of import into India; between the time when the ships departed for Europe and when these arrived again, the European companies needed money for making cash advances to artisans to buy goods. Manikchand's banking house could always be relied upon to advance money. Manikchand's seemingly unending supply of funds for the Company made the directors of the English East India Company wonder, once in a while, whether they were dealing with a person or an institution.

Manikchand was advancing working capital loans not only to the East India Company but also to its servants for their private trading ventures—an activity that ate into the profits of the Company. In 1710, Josiah Chitty who was the Company's paymaster and storekeeper, was dismissed for misappropriating cash. But

Chitty had run up huge loans and he could not leave the country till all his debts were settled. Eventually he was only allowed to leave after he had paid up the Rs. 7,000 that he owed to Manikchand.[9] The brokers of the East India Company undertook to take care of the rest. Evidently Seth Manikchand was important enough for the East India Company and they could not afford to annoy him. Indications are that he was lending them on an average Rs. 4 lakh per year at this time.

We learn from other sources that by 1750, a very large part of the credit needs of the East India Company were met by the House of Jagat Seth.

RIDING TWO HORSES: THE FIGHT FOR TOLL-FREE TRADE

Manikchand, however, was riding two horses. While his primary allegiance was to Murshid Quli Khan, the English too were important clients. If the local government of Bengal was in conflict with the English East India Company, Manikchand did not want to let his loyalty to the government drive away an important client. But such personalized relationships need constant nurturing.

Meanwhile, Murshid Quli Khan continued to depend on the banker a great deal. Family memories have it that it was Manikchand who helped purchase the *diwan's* confirmation of his office from the emperor Bahadur Shah who succeeded Aurangzeb. Mughal officials hoping to purchase an office, often remained heavily indebted to local bankers who alone could provide large loans to facilitate the purchase of such offices.

At the same time the banker while extending all these services to Murshid Quli Khan, continued to offer loans and other services to the English. His chosen strategy was to persuade both parties of his commitment while making money on both.

The conflict of interest could not be postponed indefinitely; it came to the fore over the East India Company obtaining a *firman* (in this context, a royal permit, edict) from the Mughal emperor in 1717, exempting the Company from all custom duties in Bengal.

The royal *firman* touched two crucial privileges that the English were angling for: the right to run the mint and to be free of any taxes on their trade. Running the mint would end their dependency on Indian bankers like the house of Jagat Seth. Not paying taxes would reduce overheads. We have seen that the extant system of custom duty payment in Bengal, as in most of the country at the time, was riddled with corruption. The prevalent rate of custom duty was 2.5 per cent for Muslim traders and 5 per cent for Hindu traders. In practice, tax recovery varied a great deal and the Mughal officials were quite open to the taking of bribes. So far the English had resorted to bribing individual officials on a need-to-do basis for reducing their tax liabilities. Still, the English, while not averse to cheating, hoped to have some sort of a permanent arrangement with the authorities of the state. To this end, they had been approaching the emperor for years in the hope of obtaining a license for duty free trade.

At first they tried hard to obtain an official order for duty-free trade from Murshid Quli Khan. He agreed to recommend their case to the emperor for a flat payment of Rs. 30,000. In today's world such payments would be called 'bribes'. Somehow, the deal fell through.

The Company then decided to approach the emperor directly. They sent an embassy to Delhi in 1714. For some time, the embassy simply hung around the Mughal court, soliciting interviews with the emperor and anyone whom they thought might procure for them the longed for order.

THE ROYAL *FIRMAN* OF 1717: THE FIRST STRIKE AGAINST THE COLLABORATION OF MERCHANT AND RULER

As luck would have it, the Mughal emperor fell ill. An English doctor, William Hamilton, managed to cure him in 1715. This allowed the English direct access to the Emperor. In due course, after suitable personal gifts had been given to the Emperor, Farrukhsiyar (for he was the one who sat on the Mughal throne at this time), gave the English the much longed for permit for duty-free trade throughout the empire. The permit was issued through an imperial edict, the *firman* of 1717. The English obtained a cash advance in Delhi from Gulabchand, elder brother of Manikchand, to pay to the emperor for this *firman*. The house of Jagat Seth could be credited with helping the East India Company obtain the firman. In Bengal, though, as we shall see below, the same house of Jagat Seth managed to stymie the implementation of the *firman* in full.

There were three main parts to the royal order:

1. grant of customs-free trade for the British throughout the empire and;
2. the right to coin bullion at the Bengal mint free of charge and;
3. right to purchase some 38 towns and villages near Calcutta.

These were what the English East India Company had been looking for, for the past fifty years.

Murshid Quli Khan, refused to obey the imperial edict and called it 'foolish'. By now the power of the Mughal emperor had waned to such an extent that his deputies in far off provinces like Bengal could easily flout imperial orders without fear of consequences. On the excuse that it would be against the interest of the empire, Murshid Quli Khan refused to give the English the right to purchase towns and villages. Seth Manikchand seems to have convinced him that even minting rights for the English would be contrary to imperial interests. So the English were not given the right to mint bullion either. They had to continue to depend on Seth Manikchand's mint.

Thus the English could get only one part of the *firman* implemented in Bengal, namely, the permission to trade free of duty. The *nawab* of Bengal simply would not agree to the second and third parts of the order, the parts that allowed the English to mint money and to become owners of large territories. The words of the *firman* were, 'The Bengal government should afford facilities for the coining of the Company's gold and silver in the mint at Murshidabad in the season of coining other merchants' money *if it was not against the King's interest*'.[10] The latter phrase was sufficient for the Nawab of Bengal to wriggle out of any commitment to the English that might emanate from the imperial *firman*.

The English sought the intercession of Seth Manikchand. Manikchand seems to have made a few sympathetic noises which the English duly reported to the emperor.

Family memories have it that an annoyed emperor ordered that the *diwani* be taken away from Murshid Quli Khan and be given to Manikchand. Such elevation worried Manikchand even more for Murshid Quli Khan seemed to believe that all this was due to a conspiracy by Manikchand.[11]

Murshid Quli Khan believed that his friend and collaborator had stabbed him in the back. He told Manikchand with some sarcasm that now all officials would bow before him, Seth Manikchand, instead. Manikchand was quick to explain that he had never wanted the *diwan's* position. Rather, that it was he who always bowed before Murshid Quli Khan and believed in their lasting friendship. As for the emperor, Manikchand explained that he would tell the emperor that Murshid Quli Khan was far more capable than himself and hence he had relinquished his post in favour of Murshid Quli Khan. At the same time, Seth Manikchand also counselled Murshid Quli Khan that the English were traders, cunning and also fighters and that it was not wise to get into a hostile position with them.[12]

For us the point to note is the voluntary abdication of power by the banker. This was a quality which the merchants of India were to display again and again. It seems as if they did not find that the exercise of political power had much value. Murshid Quli Khan, on his side, had shown his power by defying the Emperor a little and interpreting the firman of 1717, in a manner to his liking. The resultant imperial ire seems to have been quelled with the intermediation of Seth Manikchand.

The different privileges granted in the royal order affected the provincial *nawab* and the *seth* differently. Duty free trade and the right to purchase nearby villages meant a loss of income to the *nawab* but it did not affect Manikchand. Losing the privilege to run the mint, would take away a substantial portion of Manikchand's profit and it meant some loss of revenue to the *nawab* as well. For the alliance to work, both parties needed to recognize their mutual interests.

And yet, it was the house of Jagat Seth which is reputed to have helped the English to have obtained the *firman*. It is entirely possible that Manikchand had no idea that the English were using his good offices to ask for the right to run the mint along with the benefit of duty-free trade. He might even have rationalized it as a case of profit maximization. At all events, now that the damage was done, he did whatever damage control was possible. So long as merchant and ruler recognized that their mutual interests lay together, the alliance worked. But personal alliances that depend on friendships and implicit understanding, find it difficult to last beyond the lives of the persons involved. Subsequent events show that clearly.

Mint Provides House of Jagat Seth with Critical Leverage

Murshid Quli Khan did not allow the English to purchase the towns and villages as specified in the *firman*. Nor would he allow the British to coin money at the Murshidabad mint. Not only that, from now, it was the house of Jagat Seth that was given the privilege to run the Murshidabad mint. Manikchand's family now had almost total control over the coining of all the bullion imported into Bengal. It was only after Plassey when the English East India Company acquired sufficient power that this privilege was taken away.

The house of Jagat Seth put their privileges to good use for their own good and also in some sense, in the interests of empire. By helping systematize revenue administration in the province of Bengal and by sending the provincial revenues to Delhi by draft, they improved their power and fortunes immensely. But none of this was ever recorded on paper. Their successors simply forgot such recent events.

After the death of Seth Manikchand, his nephew and successor Seth Fatehchand continued the same policy of active collaboration with the *nawab* of Bengal. Nawab Murshid Quli Khan and his numerous successors continued to resist, with the help of the house of Jagat Seth, all English attempts to coin bullion at the royal mint at Murshidabad. At the same time, the house of Jagat Seth also continued to provide capital and services to the English East India Company.

In 1756, both Seth Fatehchand and the then *nawab*, Alivardi Khan, died within a few months of each other. Siraj-ud-daulah succeeded Alivardi Khan and Seth Mehtab Rai succeeded Seth Fatehchand. Seth Mehtab Rai seems to have decided to stop riding two horses and actively colluded with the English against Siraj.

THE SECOND STRIKE AGAINST COLLABORATION OF MERCHANT AND RULER

The opportunity for taking sides came up when Siraj, soon after ascending to the office of *nawab*, objected to the abuse of the privilege of duty free trade that the *firman* of 1717 had allowed to the English. Servants of the Company routinely used the privilege that had been accorded for the Company for their own private trade. They were willing to even carry goods of Indian traders under their own name—at the payment of a small fee by the Indians, of course. This hurt the revenues of Bengal so the *nawab* tried to stop it. To show the seriousness of his intent, Siraj once entered the English stronghold of Calcutta with his troops in 1756. That triggered a series of events which resulted in the creation of a conspiracy to dethrone Nawab Siraj-ud-daulah.

The English now looked to appoint Mir Jafar, an uncle to Siraj-ud-daulah and commander of his army, as the *nawab*. Narratives about the Battle of Plassey which took place in 1757, usually focus on the perfidy of Mir Jafar who took a bribe from the English, allowed them to defeat Nawab Siraj-ud-daulah, himself became the Nawab of Bengal and enabled the English to set up an empire in India. This is a well-known story in Indian history.

NAWAB'S OPEN INSULT ALIENATES HOUSE OF JAGAT SETH

What is not so well-known is that the conspiracy was only possible due to the active treachery of Mehtab Rai. One story goes that Siraj-ud-daulah had slapped Mehtab Rai in open court for failing to obtain his confirmation in the office of *nawab* from the Mughal court. Not content with such humiliation, he had even imprisoned Mehtab Rai for a few days.

Seth Mehtab Rai then seems to have abandoned the fifty-year long collaboration with the house of the *nawab*. One is forced to conclude that in the eyes of Mehtab Rai, one ruler was as good as another.

When Seth Manikchand was faced with a similar choice in 1717, he had chosen his loyalty to Murshid Quli Khan over the Company. Perhaps there was an element of personal choice involved here. Was Mehtab Rai being scared of the volatile nature of Siraj? We shall never know for sure. What is certain, though, is that it was the support of the House of Jagat Seth, which ensured success for the machinations of the Company to set up a puppet *nawab*.

The increasing power of the English East India Company worried Jean Law de Lauriston, the head of the French settlement at Kassimbazaar, who was at this time freebooting across India with a small troop of men and ten canons. He wondered about the reasons why the house of Jagat Seth had not laid a claim to the governorship of Bengal in 1756. 'Among Indians such undertakings proceed slowly and take their own time, and that did not suit the English. Moreover the bankers were Gentiles (Hindus) and averse to taking risks', he noted in his diary.[13]

THE NEXUS BETWEEN MONEY AND POWER: A PUZZLE

This then is a puzzle that confronts us. How was it that Mehtab Rai could not recognize that all the power of his forefathers had come from the upgradation of scale of operations that royal backing had made possible?

In hindsight, the house of Jagat Seth had benefited in many ways from their long partnership with the *nawab* of Bengal but two privileges stand out:

1. their position in the office of the *diwan* made it possible for them to recover all their debts in an era where enforcement of long term contracts was no easy matter and;

2. their privileged access to the royal mint meant that they could get their bullion earnings from trade coined immediately and at the same time delay those of all others.

Put together, the two rights gave them much control over interest rates in Bengal and over other merchants.

Did Indians Feel One Ruler was as Good as Another?

Apparently the benefits of such an association were not so visible to Mehtab Rai at all. He made a bad decision. It was not just a case of him backing the wrong horse, for, that was something that could be remedied; rather, it was about bringing in a new player into the game who would change the very rules of the game. The English of course as soon as they came to power, put the privileges of the Jagat Seth to an end speedily. The fortunes of the house of Jagat Seth went into an irreversible decline.

How could they not realize that by backing the British in the Battle of Plassey, they were in fact helping their own competitors? This, when the English Company was more or less a wild card? Was Mehtab Rai too clever by half? They might have lent them money for the past fifty years but in the words of their own ancestor Seth Manikchand, the English were not just traders but fighters and a cunning race. The *nawab* and his cohorts, howsoever whimsical, were known quantities.

So why did Mehtab Rai seem to feel that one ruler was about as good as another? One explanation for such indifference to the vast resources of the state machinery might be that in India, states had made little effort to support business in general. We see similar indifference to using state resources for making greater profit in the case of other merchants too. At most, state power was used for personalized profit.

Similar behaviour patterns could be observed in other parts of the country as well. At this point we shall take a quick look at the northern Malabar region to see what was happening there.

THE ALI RAJAS OF CANNANORE

From the writings of Ruchira Banerjee, we come to know how the power of the Ali Rajas of Cannanore, one of the most powerful trading families in northern Malabar in the early eighteenth century, was destroyed by the East India Company.[14] The Ali Rajas were descended from a prince of the Arakkal clan, Arayan Kulangara. The Arakkal chieftains were Nairs and part of the ruling Kolattiri house. Arayan Kulangara converted to Islam sometime around the eleventh-twelfth centuries CE; he took the name Muhammad Ali or Mammali. Due to conversion, his family lost the right to stake a claim to the throne or to be custodian of temples, but they acquired considerable freedom to conduct maritime trade.[15] By this time, maritime trade seems to have been looked down upon as a socially degrading activity in this region. At the same time, the Ali rajas continue to enjoy the rights of *deshadhipatyam* in the lands they controlled. This right gave them the authority to monitor sale of produce and to regulate the movement of goods. This was a powerful combination and the family went from strength to strength. Over the centuries, the Ali Rajas also obtained the allegiance of many Mappila merchants who were mostly descended from Malayali fisherwomen. While the Ali Rajas were socially inferior to other Nair chieftains, they were a force to be reckoned with.

The European companies' entry onto the scene, changed equations all around. First the Portuguese and then the Dutch East India Company tried to introduce some degree of monopoly in trade by trying to get the local rajas to force their subjects to sell pepper to them at prices below the market. The rajas signed the treaties but expressed helplessness in enforcing these.[16] The local merchants for their part, did their best to evade the monopoly by smuggling and by finding ever newer routes for their produce. Many nobles simply ignored the treaties. When the monopoly could only be partially enforced, the Dutch East India Company looked for ways to increase local control and hopefully their profit margins.

The English East India Company had set-up a factory at Tellicherry in northern Malabar. It made no effort to enforce a monopoly but it did use the system of passes for trade and regularly fished in troubled waters. The English were rather hostile to the Ali Rajas as trade rivals, perhaps because they ran a trans-oceanic trade network. In the circumstances, the ability of the English company to coerce traders to take their passes, gave them considerable advantage; one which they used to the fullest. In 1736, they even refused to issue passes to the Arakkal family on the ground that the family 'smuggled' pepper to Calicut.[17]

The Ali Rajas for their part had tied up with one faction among the Nairs, in an attempt to obtain supremacy over another Nair faction. The Nairs looked to the English company for financial support in the fight. The attempt of the Ali Rajas failed and the impact on them was substantial. They lost the right of *deshadhipatyam* in part of the territory (Dharmapatnam island and Rhandaterra district) in 1728-9. This was a huge loss. It allowed a handle to the English both to manipulate inland trade and to gradually settle Mappila merchants friendly to them, in these areas.[18]

In the 1760s, things turned temporarily in the favour of the Ali Rajas with the attack of Haider Ali in this region. The Ali Rajas allied themselves with Haider Ali; in return he declared them rulers of the Mappilas living in the region from Karwar to Kanyakumari. Perhaps the Ali Rajas had some idea of regaining the legacy of Arayan Kulangara. Now they were restored to full chieftain status. The European companies uniformly reacted to the new developments with considerable hostility. The Dutch East India Company lost its privileges and often had to pay large sums in re-negotiation; the profit margins of the others suffered too.

The Ali Raja chieftain Kunhi Amsi, used his new found power as tax collector to try to establish a relationship of superiority even over Mappila merchants. The merchants did not like it at all. Kunhi Amsi's efforts to collect taxes on the farm produce on behalf of Haider Ali, were especially disliked. It is reported that even the Kolattiri Rajas had never imposed agricultural taxes on the populace; they derived their income from toll dues and from trade. In these tax collection efforts, Ali raja used some of the Mappila merchants as agents. The traditional authority of the Nair chieftains was bypassed in this tax collection effort. They were extremely upset—both at being so bypassed and by the fact that the tax collectors were Mappilas. The result was that many groups were dissatisfied with their share of the new-found power and prosperity of the Ali Raja family.[19]

In the circumstances, it became possible for the English East India Company to set up a rival faction among the merchant community.

At the same time, Haider Ali's resources were increasingly stretched and he could not offer much support to the Ali Rajas. When the Ali Rajas failed to collect sufficient tribute, Haider Ali demoted Kunhi Amsi and restored the Nair rulers.[20]

Irrespective of the fate of the Haider Ali family or its fights with the East India Company, the ascendancy of the Ali Rajas gradually came to an end. It was the rival merchant faction set up and supported by the English Company which grew richer until in 1792, the company established its dominion in Malabar.

MONEY AND HIERARCHY WERE ALL

Whether it was the case of the fluctuating relationship between the house of Jagat Seth and the *nawabs* of Bengal or the case of the Ali Rajas of Cannanore or earlier, the case of the merchants of Surat, what we cannot see is the ability to make long-lasting alliances. There was no community of interest.

To the Indian merchants, the two elements that seemed to matter were individual wealth and their position in the hierarchy. Everyone else including the government and the East India Company were of use so long as they could contribute to the game. Few people in India had made any attempt to know the English beyond what was required for trade dealings.

Idea that Power could change Terms of Trade Seemed Inconceivable

To the merchants, the English East India Company was just another rival trader and an inferior one at that. They routinely dealt with the merchants of the company both in the latter's capacity as representatives of the company and as private traders. Perhaps they believed that the merchants of the company were motivated only by money and social prestige. We suggest that to the Indian merchants, the idea that power could change the terms of trade, may have been historically an inconceivable idea. Surely the Mughal nobles had used their official positions to get some individual leverage in their trade transactions. We have seen this in the behaviour of the nobility from the queen downwards. But such individual activities never had much impact on the community of merchants as a whole.

One can only speculate that Mehtab Rai and others like him had generational memories of the past thousands of years of a situation where the king hardly mattered. The typical Indian king, even when of some consequence, did little either to interfere or influence trade or even to promote it beyond ensuring law and order. Sometimes he did not even do a good job of keeping the peace. Consequently, Mehtab Rai simply seems to have decided that whoever was willing to demand less for the privilege of ruling, was the better option. Mir Jafar would be a good puppet ruler since he had taken such a large bribe.

Mehtab Rai may well have believed that Mir Jafar or someone else of his ilk would continue to provide services to his banking house and to the company in exchange for a percentage of profit. That is what most of the Mughal nobility did. To understand that the merchants of the East India Company were merely acting on behalf of an abstract entity that had a life and goals of its own, may have been beyond the ken of the Indian merchants.

KNOWING THE ENGLISH: THE VALUE AND PRICE OF ROYAL BACKING

The crucial point in India had always been that Indian rulers simply had never used the authority of the state to help businessmen in any significant way. The corollary of this behaviour was that the rulers seldom demanded undue favours of the merchants; and dutifully paid interest on the loans that they took.

It is mentioned in the records of Aurangzeb's court, that when he in 1702, had requested an interest free loan of half a million rupees from the moneylenders of the Imperial Camp so that he could pay the salary of his troops, they politely refused. It was the moneylenders' contention that if this practice were to spread to the provinces, if other officials were to start demanding such loans, that would be the end of their profession. The emperor meekly accepted the rebuff.[21]

The English were of a far different breed: they seemed to realize very well the value of royal backing and were willing to pay a price for it. Economic historians like to use the word 'mercantilist' for it. The East India Company from its very inception was based on the idea of a monopoly of trade enforced by royal charter. That is how it was incorporated in its original charter dated 31 December 1600, which had an initial validity of fifteen years. In order to renew the charter and to maintain this monopoly, the Company had to offer repeated loans to the English Crown for whom it served as a significant source of funds. In England, there were many traders who resented the special opportunity offered to the Company to make a profit and who wanted a piece of the action, so to speak. So over the years there were many attempts by rival groups of traders to encroach on the monopoly of the East India Company. Many people also attacked them for causing a huge drain on the bullion in England since for nearly 200 years, this was most of what Britain exported to India in exchange for textile goods, saltpetre and much else.

The public stance of the Company, articulated by one of their directors Thomas Mun in his essays,[22] was that they might be exporting bullion to India but the commodities they imported from that country, were re-exported to the rest of Europe; all the bullion was recovered and much more. Privately, in order to protect its monopoly, the Company had to shell out money to the Crown. The sums grew larger over time. The Crown also used the Company to conduct its various proxy wars with the French and the Dutch in Asia.

The efforts of rival interlopers began almost immediately, the first being that of Sir Edward Michelborne in 1604, who was granted a charter for trade by King James I, to trade in the territory of the East India Company but this was not a successful attempt. Soon after this, there were other attempts. In 1617, a Scottish East India Company was set up; this time they were authorized to trade under the Scottish royal seal. The English East India Company later bought out this company. In 1624, King James I offered to set out ships under the royal standard but the East India Company refused the offer saying that there could be no partnership with the king.[23] The failed attempt only encouraged other rivals.

When in 1635, a charter for trade with the East Indies was granted to Company's rival, Sir William Courten, the reasons given for this action were, 'the East India company had neglected to establish fortified factories, or seats of trade, to which the king's subjects could resort with safety; that they had consulted their own interests only, without any regard to the king's revenue; and in general that they had broken the condition on which their charter and exclusive privileges had been granted to them'.[24]

The king was allotted stock worth £10,000 in this Courten Association and the secretary of state was allotted stock worth £1,000.

In 1636, the king raised the custom duties on pepper by 70 per cent, which in turn led to a significant increase in the revenue from customs duties. In 1641, the King forced the Company to hand over its pepper stock to the Crown as 'loan'; the said stock was valued at roughly £63,000. This loan was to be repaid in four instalments. But the King, Charles I, was executed in 1649, by rebels, and the 'loan' was only partly recovered. After this incident, many other demands were made on the revenues of the Company. The Company complained all the time, but they paid-up the money—they were well aware of the value of royal backing.

Another well-known case of the attempts to encroach on this monopoly, was the formation of the New East India Company in 1697. The financial difficulties of the Crown had led it to ask the Company for a loan of £2 million at 8 per cent to finance a war with the French. But the East India Company only offered a loan of £500,000 at 4 per cent. The Crown would not be so easily fobbed off. It promptly encouraged a rival group of merchants to set up the New East India Company.

Soon the two companies seem to have realized that the competition would only hurt them. So in 1709, the two companies were merged and they agreed to give a loan of £1.2 million to the Crown—free of interest. The monopoly of the Company was renewed.

ENGLAND AND INDIA: TWO DIFFERENT PERSPECTIVES

To return to our story of India, the contrast between the behaviour of traders in England and Bengal is clear enough. The alliance between government and business in India always remained an uneasy one. No doubt the Mughal officials indulged in private trade and had their own investments. But to use the services of a group of traders to carry out significant tasks for the state government, is something that was not common. Even Manikchand and Murshid Quli Khan, and Fatehchand and Alivardi Khan, never formalized the association other than to give the house of Jagat Seth the authority to run the mint and to remit the royal revenues to Delhi. Nor did the house of Jagat Seth set-up a formal institution, which could then negotiate with successive *nawabs*. All efforts were individual efforts. Every deal was an individual deal.

Using Coercion to Promote Trade has been Alien to India

Most importantly, while Manikchand and Murshid Quli Khan both profited from their association, they never used the coercive power of the state in the shape of military force to promote the ends of trade. In contrast, the use of coercion, military troops, naval force and fortification was integral to English strategy. The English always demonstrated a belief that it was legitimate to conduct trade over the barrel of a gun. Whether this was on account of their backing by the Crown or because of how that society was organized, is immaterial; the fact is that they did use force repeatedly. They used many excuses to justify what they did: that the Indian rulers made incessant demands for payment; that the conditions in the country were so unstable that the use of force was needed for defence, etc. The fact remains however that India had traded with the world for more than a thousand years before the English arrived. And did not much bother about using the authority of the state as a device to increase trade or to beat down rivals.

No doubt Indian rulers and merchants worked in collaboration; this is amply borne out by the methods of their working. But the army was not used to promote, protect and defend traders without a specific payoff. The Indian merchants and rulers alike, seemed to know the price of everything and the value of nothing. The value of state protection to merchants was a sunk cost with benefits in an unknowable future. Long-term thinking has that drawback.

It was here that the English won out. They believed that their Indian agents were under their protection and that all those who lived in their settlements at Madras, Bombay and Calcutta, were entitled to their protection. Indian rulers did not offer protection of this variety.

The most definitive factor in this whole story was the failure of the Mughal state to offer protection to the banking community. Siraj-ud-daulah simply did not inspire enough trust, nor did he make much effort to build bridges. We see similar behaviour in other parts of the country too. In 1732, when the Marathas raided Surat, the Mughal governor simply refused to do anything to intercede. It was the bankers of Surat who drove off the Marathas with the help of the English East India Company. In the end, bankers whether in Bengal or Gujarat or the Malabar, simply seem to have decided to throw in their lot with the Company as it made good business sense to do so.

FAMOUS LAST WORDS

A closer look at the Mughal state itself, reveals an insouciance about the English company similar to that displayed by the merchants. Had they pooled information, they might have seen the threat looming on the horizon. Neither the rulers nor the bankers, ever did do so.

It is entirely possible that the monetary operations of the East India Company and its servants were so small in comparison to the country's internal trade and to the individual wealth of the bankers and officials, that most Indians simply dismissed the Company as a creature of little account. In his history of Aurangzeb, Khafi Khan the coeval historian of Mughal India, notes contemptuously that:

> the total revenue of Bombay, which is chiefly derived from betel-nuts and cocoa-nuts, does not reach to two or three lacs of rupees. The profits of the commerce of these misbelievers, according to report, does not exceed twenty lacs of rupees. The balance of the money required for the maintenance of the English settlement is obtained by plundering the ships voyaging to the House of God, of which they take one or two every year. . . .[25]

Here it is useful to recall that the total wealth of the House of Jagat Seth is estimated at Rs. 14 crore in then currency. Their annual income was estimated to be Rs. 49.60 lakh.

In comparison, the English East India Company on a high in 1743, had an annual trade of £2.04 million. The average annual trade of the East India Company in the early eighteenth century was around £1.3 to £1.8 million. At the estimated exchange rate of Rs. 8 to the pound in the early eighteenth century, this would have meant that the company turnover at its peak was Rs. 1.63 crore in one year and that normally it hovered from Rs. 1.04 to 1.44 crore per year. The profits of the company amounted to an average annual return of 9.7 per cent on share capital for the period 1710-45, which would mean an average annual profit of roughly Rs. 24.75 lakh.[26]

If we take the entire share capital of the East India Company at its height before the battle of Plassey, it comes to roughly £3.19 million which at the then estimated exchange rate would be Rs. 2.55 crore.[27] If the entire share capital of the English Company was less than one fifth the worth of one banking house, it is no wonder that the Indians counted them as being so unimportant.

These sums could not hold a candle to the wealth of the Mughal officials. Khafi Khan estimates that at the death of Abul Hasan, a prominent Mughal official, his wealth amounted to Rs. 6,80,10,000 besides jewels, inlaid items and gold and silver vessels.[28] No wonder then that the Mughals counted the English as being of small account. Yet the company did display qualities that were to prove critical to their success: namely the ability of the English to generate a high quality of protection, to manage their money well as also their ability to systematize information and to improve efficiencies. It is these that were crucial to the making of money; not the volume of their trade.

In 150 Years of Doing Business with the Company, Indian Traders Never Saw that the English did Business Differently

One question that is frequently raised is whether we can blame the English East India Company for the looting of India. That they looted the country is a matter of record. Before 1757, and the disaster at Plassey, the Company was exporting ever increasing amounts of gold and silver bullion to Asia on account of an unfavourable balance of trade. In the period 1700-50, there were at least three years from 1703 to 1705 when the company's exports to India consisted of treasure at 100 per cent and commodity exports were zero. In other years, the export of treasure ranged from a high of 91.7 per cent of the value of all exports to Asia, to a low of 65.3 per cent of all exports. Needless to say the amounts plummeted as soon as the Company got access to the treasury of Bengal. In the year 1757, 70.1 per cent of company exports consisted of treasure. As a percentage of exports, treasure fell to 61.1 per cent in 1758, further to 32.4 per cent in 1759 and still further to 27.8 per cent in 1760 while commodity exports shot up.[29]

At one stroke, the English East India Company addressed the complaints made by its employees over the last 150 years. Company employees had variously complained that they were unable to execute their orders fully because of competition from Asian merchants, that they were unable to drive down prices as much as they wanted, that they were forced to pay bribes to the local rulers, that they were unable to mint money at Bengal, etc. Interestingly, the English East India Company which had bribed English rulers for over a hundred years at least for maintaining their monopoly, with the bribes often running into figures of the order of £10,000, when asked to pay up less than a tenth of that amount to an Indian ruler, complained of political extortion! Now they could remedy all this and use their coercive power to do what they wanted.

However, we need to note that the English East India Company did not coerce the Indian soldiers who fought in their armies against Indian rulers: they merely paid them regular salaries. Nor did the Company coerce Indian bankers like the house of Jagat Seth to cooperate with them in overthrowing their rulers; this the bankers did out of their independent judgement. The real question to be asked is why the Indians soldiers and bankers had so little faith in their own rulers and if they did have little faith, which is manifest, then why they did not wish to be rulers in the first place. Why did they invite a foreign agency to rule over them?

The English after all had been in the country for the last 150 years and they had given everyone plenty of notice about the direction in which they were slowly moving. They had been asserting the privileges of sovereignty at the first opportunity. Not only did they fortify themselves and coin money, they constantly used armed force to not only defend their trade but to block that of others. The Mughals knew this very well. In 1686, the East India Company directors initiated a policy of war against the Mughals. Childs' War, it was called, after Sir Josiah Child, the director of the Company who suggested it. They initiated hostilities in Bengal and entered the river Hooghly with warships and cannon. The Mughal response was tardy and initially designed to ignore the infractions by the Company. Later, the Mughals forced the Company out of Bengal; they also took control over Surat and blockaded Bombay. Finally, the Company apologized to Aurangzeb for their mis-behaviour. The entire adventure for the Company had lasted some four years. Child had estimated that with the English ships blocking off the sea trade going through the Arabian Sea, the Mughals could be forced to concede trading and minting privileges. French observers of those times noted with pleasure the disciplining of the English, the reparations that they had to pay to Aurangzeb in order to be able to trade in India once again. Later also in Bengal, Murshid Quli Khan had to take retaliatory measures against the Company when they seized the ship of an Armenian.

This is not to say that there was any long-term design to the Indian conquest or to the Battle of Plassey. Merely that the English were very sensitive to power relations and also well aware of the relation between power and profit. That was not the Indian business tradition.

That the Indians saw no unique pattern in the English behaviour is what should interest us. They did not even care to study the Englishmen out of mere curiosity if nothing else. The Europeans were such bit players in the trade of India that they did not attract any attention. By the time the battle of Plassey happened, the English company had already marginalized many large merchants in different parts of the country. They had even put some large merchants in Bengal to trouble by stopping the system of *dadni* advances and choosing to deal directly with weavers. Yet Mehtab Rai had seen nothing risky in striking a deal with a business rival he could not hope to control. No doubt he thought he was making a good business decision. Where business decisions are so personalized and have little relation to evidence on the ground, events can take unforeseen shape.

The English company had developed strong organizational capabilities. When the opportunity arose, they could scale-up operations. It was their ability to manage money, to protect themselves and to maintain institutional memories that provided them resilience that the Indian business community never had. We may not have shown similar behaviour; what is more important is that we did not notice that others thought and behaved differently. The learning curve remained rather flat.

In the absence of any institutional memories or any effort at documentation, most of the history re-told here has been forgotten. The once proud house of Jagat Seth is only a memory. All that remains are the ruins of their house at Mahimapur. The knowledge that the house was wealthier than the East India Company at one time, has faded to the extent that the occasional visitors to the site conclude that it must be a myth that when the king needed money, he borrowed it from the Jagat Seth. History surely is a great leveller.

NOTES

1. Little, 1960: xvii. [A comparative idea of what this wealth meant can be had by looking at the price of wheat: which between 1700-50 in Bengal ranged from Re. 0.60 to Rs. 1.25 per maund (one Bengal maund being 37.32 kg) as compared with the modern-day support price of Rs. 1,735 per 100 kg which means Rs. 647 per maund. So there is an increase of the order of 517 to 1,078 times in wheat. For ghee there is an increase of the order of 2,917 times; for moong dal of the order of 2,500 to 3,348 times and for mustard oil of the order of 762 to 2,450 times. Conservatively then the increase is of the order of 760 times].
2. Firminger, 1812, rpt. 1984, vol. II: 191.
3. Doogar, 2013.
4. Salim, 1902: 248.
5. Salim, 1902.
6. Chaudhary, 1995: 114-15.
7. Discussion with Prashant Kulkarni, numismatist.
8. Elliot, 1877, vol. 7: 351.
9. Little, 1960: 19-20.
10. Little, 1960: viii, emphasis added.
11. Bhandari, 1934: 1F-1G.
12. Ibid.
13. Lauriston, 2014.
14. Banerjee, 1998.
15. Ibid.
16. Ibid.
17. Ibid.
18. Ibid.
19. Ibid.
20. Ibid.
21. Habib, 1964: 408-9.
22. Mun, 1664 (1895), pp. 12-14.
23. Scott, 1910, vol. 2: 108.
24. Bruce, 1810, vol. 1: 331.
25. Elliot, 1877, vol. 7: 354.
26. Chaudhuri, 1978: 440.
27. Chaudhuri, 1978: 451.
28. Elliot, 1877, vol. 7: 335.
29. Chaudhuri, 1978: 512.

CHAPTER 4

The Unsung Artisan

In this chapter we shall look at a rather different sector from finance, namely manufacturing, to see what kind of skills Indians possessed. Till the eighteenth century, India was famed as a nation that specialized in high quality steel. It is no accident that today India is the second largest producer of crude steel in the world after China. High steel production is in keeping with Indian history. What is new is that India is also the third largest consumer of finished steel in the world and it is a net importer of finished steel. Specialized steel forms only 8.3 per cent of the finished steel output.[1] A brief look at history so far as iron and steel are concerned, tells us that at one time, India was known through the world for specialized steels. Till the early nineteenth century, a kind of steel that was called wootz was so widely made through the country that variations of the word from which it is probably derived, *ukku*, are found in many Indian languages. It was known as *uruku/uruki* in Tamil, *urku/ukku* in Kannada, *ukk/urukku/ukku* in Malayalam and *ukku* in Telugu to name a few. It was the existence of this kind of skill that made India famous for small arms and swords. Yet within a hundred years, memories of their prowess had vanished from Indian minds and from the minds of customers who had bought it. In this chapter we shall tell the story of Indian steel.

THE STORY OF WOOTZ

Wootz steel, a special kind of steel, was a unique product perfected in India over thousands of years. The earliest physical evidence for its production dates to around the first century CE. The fascination of the ancient world for wootz steel is about as old as the product itself. Some of it even passed into myths about the Damascus swords. While the steel came from India, many of the sword blades were worked and sold in the city of Damascus; hence the name 'Damascus sword'. Wootz steel was characterized by a wavy pattern resembling watered silk; this pattern was what was noticed about the Damascus blade. In the ancient world, these sword blades were widely known and highly prized for their sharpness, flexibility, and strength. The Scottish author, Sir Walter Scott wrote a famous story that perpetuated the legend. He described the Damascus blade as one that could slice through a silk handkerchief floating in the air. He tells of a fictional meeting between the English Richard the Lionheart and the Muslim Sultan Saladin. Trying to impress Saladin with his prowess, Richard chopped a tree trunk with his sword. Saladin, more civilized and restrained, simply threw a silk handkerchief in the air and allowed it to fall on his blade that sliced through the handkerchief with nary an effort on his part.

The legend gives us clues about the unique qualities of wootz steel. In knives and swords, one looks for a sharp cutting edge. This sharpness was characteristic of wootz blades. At the same time, swords also need a hardness and strength that knives do not. When your blade clashed with the sword of the enemy, you would not want it to shatter on impact. This was the second quality that the blade possessed. But it was perhaps the third quality that seemed almost miraculous to all those who wrote about it. This was its flexibility or the ability to bend without breaking. It was this combination of sharpness, hardness and flexibility that gave the Damascus sword its legendary quality.

This combination was quite difficult to achieve.

Today steel is a generic name given to a large family of carbon-iron alloys. Any engineering handbook tells us that steel derives most of its qualities from three kinds of factors: the presence of microscopic elements that provide it special attributes, the percentage of carbon present and the method of heat treatment and cooling. The various classification systems devised by scientists and engineers for steels, tell us about the elements present in the steel and might also inform us about the proportions of carbon in hundredths of a per cent.

Unique Combination of Malleability and Hardness

Modern science tells us that carbon is mainly responsible for giving hardness and strength to steel. Too low a carbon content means that the steel will be malleable and can be worked easily but it will not be hard enough; too high a carbon content means that it will be hard but it can also be brittle and can shatter on impact. So, there is always a trade-off between hardness and malleability. Another factor that has an important role to play in the properties of steel is quenching (rapid cooling). The rate of cooling, the medium in which cooling is done and so on, determine the end product.

Artisans of wootz steel may not have had this kind of knowledge. They perfected their art by figuring out what they could observe about the variables in the process. How much charcoal was to be added to the furnace, the rate at which bellows were to be pumped to determine the temperature, what the iron looked like, whether it was to be cooled in the furnace itself or with water, whether the cooling was more effective in oil, water, or whey, and so on. Today we can only make intelligent guesses about how the artisan might have produced wootz for, present-day scientists are still trying, unsuccessfully, to produce this specialty material from pre-colonial India.

Archaeological remains of iron weapons tell us that Indian artisans seemed to have found a way to achieve a carbon content ranging from 1 to 1.8 per cent in wootz steel. This made it a high carbon steel which had both the requisite hardness and malleability. One of the first physical samples of high carbon steel from India dates to the first century CE; it was discovered at Taxila by Sir John Marshall. A double-edged sword, a fragmentary blade and an axe like tool that may have been used by a carpenter, found at this site were specimens of high carbon steel in which carbon content was found to be from 1.3 to 1.7 per cent.[2]

It was not just swords that were made from wootz steel but also body armour and helmets. By the medieval age, it was being used for making small firearms such as for the barrels of matchlock and flintlock guns. It has been suggested that it was also used for making steel wires for musical instruments. It remains a mystery how the artisans achieved the special properties that this material had.

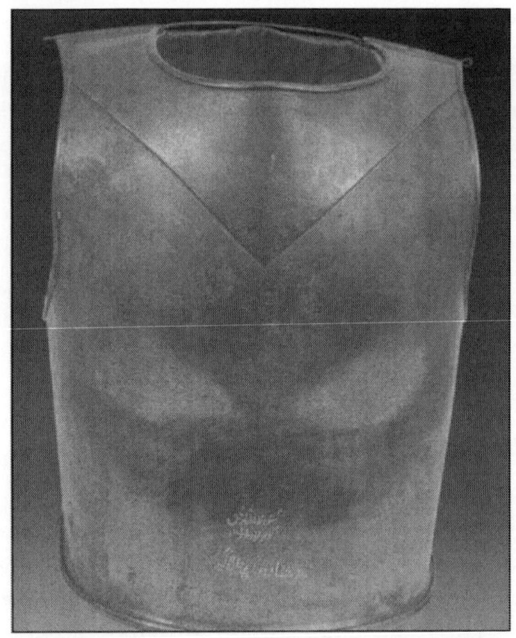

Figure 4.1: Aurangzeb's Waistcoat Armour, *c.*1680
(Image from National Museum, New Delhi, India)

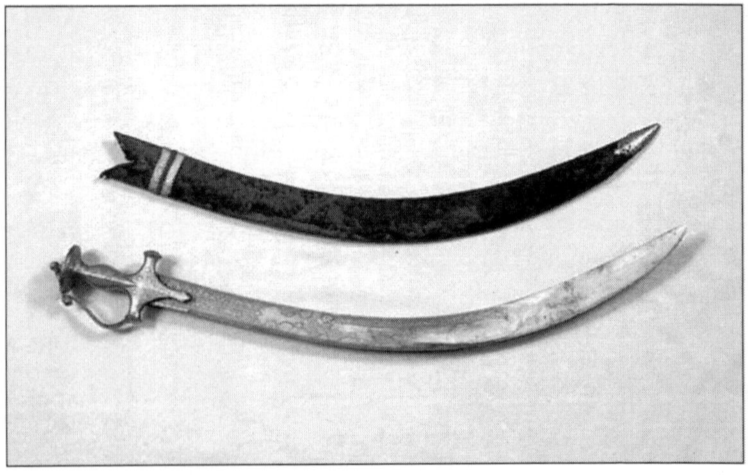

Figure 4.2: Tipu Sultan's Sword, *c.*1790
(Image from National Museum, New Delhi, India)

Scientists have spent many years in figuring this one out. No one is entirely sure how it was done. But we do have descriptions and some archaeological remains that have been used to reconstruct the process. What science has succeeded in doing is figuring out the principles underlying the whole process.

GERMAN RESEARCHERS UNLOCK THE SECRET OF WOOTZ STEEL

Marianne Reibold, a German researcher, found that unknown to themselves, Indian artisans had been using what later came to be called nanotechnology to produce the wootz steel.[3] Reibold and her team of researchers at the University of Dresden, obtained a sample of a seventeenth-century Damascus blade from the Berne Historical Museum and immersed a portion of it in hydrochloric acid for one week. It dissolved and after a week, the carbon that remained in the acid was picked up with a copper grid and analysed.[4] They concluded that the particles found were carbon nanotubes occasionally filled with nanowires of cementite.[5] This then was the secret of the amazing material. Cementite is a brittle material and it would tend to make the steel brittle enough to shatter at too much pressure; it was the carbon nanotubes protecting the nanowires of cementite, which would have provided the material its elasticity and strength.

Now it seems that Indian artisans did not know all this science or at least they did not put it down on paper. So, what was going on? Moreover, if wootz steel was so superior, why was it that it died out in such a way that today it merely remains the stuff of legend. We shall try to find some answers based on what archaeological and literary evidence has been reported from different parts of India about iron production and subsequent processing into wootz.

HOW WAS IRON MADE

The first step in the making of iron, is producing sponge iron which is an intermediate product. Sponge iron was made in iron smelters throughout the country, using iron ore, at temperatures below the melting point of iron. India has always been rich enough in iron ore. Many forest dwellers from central India, in Jharkhand, in Orissa and in southern India, specialized in producing iron. Iron smelting in India dates to even before the beginning of the first millennium BCE. Remains of furnaces have been found across the country ranging from Naikund in the Vidarbha region to Ujjain in central India, Dhatva in Gujarat, Karnataka, Andhra Pradesh and Tamil Nadu.

Scholars have reconstructed the processes of making sponge iron extant in earlier times by studying the remains of ancient furnaces and through observing blacksmiths at work in tribal areas in contemporary times. In the 1980s an Indian and a Japanese researcher went into Bastar in central India, to Bailadila that has been a major source of iron ore, to meet the blacksmiths who worked with the ore. These smiths came from the Mundia and Halbi tribes. In the village of Lohārpārā they found people making iron. The iron-workers were most reluctant to show their iron furnaces but were finally won over by scholarly curiosity. The workers were essentially digging a square pit in the ground; devoting one side of the pit to constructing a furnace. The fire in the furnace was stoked by workers using foot operated bellows. This is the description of the scholars:

> The bowl shaped furnace was built below the ground level by digging a square pit of about 2000*2000 mm and 500 mm depth, and with steps on one side to go down. . . . The furnace was made by digging a hole in one of the vertical faces of the pit. . . . The front part of the furnace was made by layering stiff mud, and two bamboo tuyeres, having 5 to 10 mm inner diameter were fitted in the bowl of the furnace. . . . The furnace had a total height of about 800 mm and the diameter of furnace at the throat 200 mm. The shaft of the furnace was 600 mm in depth and had a tapered wall. It ended into a bowl-shaped hearth having about 240 mm maximum diameter and 100 mm depth. A hole was provided in the bowl to tap out slag. The furnace was made below the ground level to cut down the access of air . . . the air blast to the furnace was supplied by a pair of foot operated bellows. . . .[6]

At the mouth of the furnace a platform was built to pre-heat the ore and charcoal before pushing it down into the furnace. A drawing of the furnace and how it was operated is given below.

Source: Prakash and Igaki, 1984.

Figure 4.3: Schematic Diagram of the iron-making Furnace as found at Lohār Pārā in district Bastar, Chhattisgarh

Men and women in the family could easily operate these bellows by stepping on them alternately.

Alternate layers of red-hot charcoal and ore were pushed into the furnace till it was full. It could take about 15-20 kg of charge at a time and the entire process took about 6 hours. At the end of this, a mass of sponge iron of about 1 kg in weight was formed which was separated from the slag. The furnace normally operated at temperatures of up to 1150 °C.[7]

The sponge iron was then taken to a forge. Repeated heating and hammering squeezed out the remaining slag in the iron and the spongy mass got converted into solid bars of wrought iron.

In Tamil Nadu, there appear to have been furnaces ten to 15 ft high which could produce up to 250 kg of iron per day.

Knives made from this kind of wrought iron, could be sharpened by applying carburization paste to the edges. Physicians like

Sushruta mention applying carbonaceous paste to a surgical knife, then heating it red-hot, hardening and tempering the knife to obtain a sharp edge.

Many tribal communities in India still produce sponge iron in this way. One obvious constraint on scaling up this process was the use of human power to operate the bellows. In India, the scaling up that may have been possible by using a source of power other than human, such as water to power the bellows, never happened. Could it be that there was little curiosity about scaling up production because there was never any shortage of human labour? Also such basic production of iron may have been sufficient to guarantee a comfortable livelihood. The people who made iron in this fashion, nearly always had a supplementary source of income whether from farming or animal husbandry and farm-related activities. So a low level of productivity was still sufficient to bring in enough money. And being of some market value, there were enough traders who plied the product across India and overseas as well.

At all events, about all that we know today of olden iron making techniques is the making of sponge iron and wrought iron. Knowledge about making weapon-grade crucible steel, wootz, out of these materials, died out in the nineteenth century.

Perhaps the oldest description of the making of wootz dates to the second century CE; it is in Greek and is supposed to have been written by Alexandrian chemist Zosimos of Panopolis. His description of the method was: take four measures[8] of soft, malleable iron with low carbon content and cut into small pieces; add 15 parts by weight of a part of the date peel known to the Arabians of the time as *elileg* (without the core of the fruit); add 4 parts by weight each of other components of date palms known at the time as *belileg* and *amblag*; and two parts of glass worker's magnesia. Crush together all the parts of the date palm and the magnesia but not too finely, and add to the iron. The mixture was to be heated in a crucible. Four measures of iron required 100 measures of charcoal for heating until it all melted.[9]

Zosimos cautioned that the magnesia was not to be used if the iron was relatively soft since the magnesia made it dry and brittle. He ended by saying that the material could create marvellous swords.

It was discovered by the Indians so he says, transmitted by the Persians and from there, it reached the Egyptians.[10]

So how then was this material made?

MAKING STEEL OUT OF IRON: INDIAN TEXTS

We get a little information about Indian processes of steel making from the sixth century CE text *Brihat Samhita.*[11]

Varahamihira informs us, that to obtain a sword that will not break even against rocks, the sword must be rubbed with sesamum oil. Then it must be smeared with a kind of ointment prepared with the milky juice of the *arka* plant,[12] mixed with the ashes of sheep's horn and the droppings of doves and mice. After being so anointed, it must be heated red hot and then given a 'drink' or quenched. Varahamihira now refers to Shukracharya, a sage of ancient times, as having prescribed different kinds of quenching for the heated iron, or 'drinks' for the sword, to achieve different qualities in the end product. The results of the drink, Shukracharya is supposed to have said, was not just confined to obtaining a superior cutting blade.

Different kinds of qualities demanded different fluids. For cutting the trunk of elephants in battles, a drink of fish-bile and the milk of deer, horse, and goat, mixed with the toddy of palm trees was needed.

Yet another recipe was that the iron weapon should be treated with a day-old drink made of burnt powder of bananas (or its ribs), mixed with buttermilk and then sharpened properly. A sword of this kind, Varahamihira says, would not break on stones, or become blunt on iron instruments.

The trouble is that Varahamihira spends just three verses of his chapter on *Khadagalakshnam* (signs of swords) to give any details, almost as if everything else about making a sword was already known. He spends the rest of his chapter on describing various auspicious shapes of swords: the cow's tongue, blue lily petal, bamboo leaf, etc. and on the shapes of dents on the swords. So, we get to know that dents shaped like chameleons, crows, herons, and scorpions were inauspicious. We also get to know that dents resembling the *bilva* tree, Vardhamana figure, umbrella, Shiva's emblem, lotus, *svastika*, etc. were auspicious. This gives us plenty of information on the likes and dislikes of Indians of Varahamihira's times but little on how they made their weapons. Perhaps they just took knowledge of the processes for granted, and did not feel the need to systematically record these.

What ancient Indians seemed to be doing, was making lists of various organic sources for the chemicals which would improve the qualities of the steel. For instance, the juice of the *arka* plant is rich in anti-oxidants and it provides anti-corrosive properties to steel. Pigeon/dove droppings are rich in nitrates and nitrates are very important for the hardening of steel.

Indian Professors Piece Together Myriad Varieties of Indian Iron and Steel

By the thirteenth century CE, we have a little more information about the different kinds of iron that were produced in India. An Indian text from the thirteenth century CE, the *Rasa-ratna-samuccaya* (रस-रत्न-समुच्चय) classifies iron into three basic categories: *kanta*, *tiksna* and *munda*. The first two were the commercially most valuable types. A professor of industrial technology at Banaras Hindu University Varanasi Prof. Prakash says, that *kanta loha* was probably soft iron with relatively low carbon content which was quite malleable; it also had significant magnetic properties.[13] Some varieties of this *loha* like *chumbaka* were used to make magnets. It could also be converted into *bhasma* for use in ayurvedic medicine.

Tiksna loha as the name suggests, could produce a very sharp cutting edge. So, it was valuable for making arms and also in agricultural implements. It could also be used to make *tiksna loha bhasma* for medicinal purposes. One variety of *tiksna loha, kala ayasa*[14] seems to conform in description to cakes of wootz steel: bluish black in colour, dense, smooth, heavy, and bright in appearance, with sharp edges which did not get spoiled even with hammering.[15] Interestingly, Kautilya mentions metals like *kala ayasa* and *tamra* (copper) in the section devoted to a discussion of forest products. It was the forest dwellers who seemed to specialize in the making of iron.[16]

The third and last variety, *munda loha,* was probably named after the Mundia people, expert artisans who lived in the Bastar region. This was most likely cast iron. In price terms, it was the least valuable. While one of the subtypes in this variety was deemed useable (*mridu* or soft), other varieties were brittle. A.K. Biswas, a professor of materials and metallurgical engineering from IIT Kanpur says that these brittle varieties were produced unintentionally when the temperature of the furnace rose too high and the amount of charcoal used was too large, resulting in high carbon iron.[17]

Today there is little detailed record of all the different varieties of iron that must have been produced in India over the centuries. Ironically, it was this kind of cast iron which would be useful for casting cannon in the medieval ages. And yet casting iron for cannon, was something that was never developed to any useable extent in India. Medieval metal workers continued to forge weld rings of wrought iron into cannons rather than cast as one piece.

WHO WERE THE TRADERS IN WOOTZ?

Given its immense applications in warfare, there was much profit to be made in the wootz trade. References to the trade in iron and steel go back to the beginning of the first millennium CE. The unknown author of the famous *Periplus of the Erythraean Sea* in his descriptions of navigation and trading opportunities from Roman Egyptian ports like Berenice along the coast of the Red Sea, and others along north-east Africa and the Sindh and south-western India, refers to the export of iron and steel from the West coast of India to North Africa. It seems to have been known to the Romans also since Ferrum Indicum is one of the taxable commodities mentioned in the times of the Roman emperors Marcus Aurelius and Commodus. The Romans considered Indian steel to be superior to and costlier than steel of Persia, the other country where steel was produced. The Persians for centuries were the among the largest trade partners of India as far as iron and wootz steel were concerned, right down to the sixteenth century. Persian rulers, it seems preferred to fight with swords made from Indian steel, the *shamser-i-hindig.*[18]

The Cairo Geniza records come in handy here. These are fragments of some 300,000 Jewish manuscripts found in the store room, i.e. the geniza, of the Ben Ezra Synagogue in Old Cairo. Covering the period from 870 CE to nineteenth century, they allow us to get a glimpse of the world of trade and commerce of those times. Of interest to us here is the life of the Tunisian Jewish trader originally from al-Mahadiyya, Abraham Ben Yiju. He came to India to make his fortune. He left North Africa in the year 1132, and with some gaps, he stayed in India, on the Malabar coast, continuously till 1149 CE when he left for good. During this period, he set up a factory for the manufacture of bronze ware; he also traded in Indian iron. He bought and freed an Indian slave girl whom he married and who bore him three children.[19]

In this period, he invested in many shipping ventures for himself and for his friends and business partners. Right at the beginning of his career, he lost two ships and it took him many years to recover from this loss. From the correspondence between him and these partners as preserved in the Geniza records, we learn about the chief commodities of the India trade, the prices at which these were sold and the profits to be made. Chief among these items were spices, aromatics, drugs of various kinds and second in value came metals, principally iron and steel and bronze ware. Textiles came a poor third. The balance of trade was in favour of India so the difference had to be paid in bullion. In order to reduce the bullion outlay, importers in Yemen and Egypt shipped out old utensils and copper scrap, which could be used in the metal industry. These documents show clearly that India at the time was importing raw materials extensively and that these materials were used for artisanal production on a very significant scale.

One of the letters for instance which records one such India trip lists the value of the assets sent from India to Aden as being 535 Maliki *dinars* net of custom duty: this consignment consisted of pepper worth 315 *dinars*, and iron worth 220 *dinars*. In return the Aden end of the trade shipped 423 *dinars* worth of copper and other assorted household goods and a little cash.[20]

Iron sold was of many types; six different kinds were mentioned in the letters. The most frequent reference is to it having been sold in the shape of solid cakes or ingots; this is inferred in the use of the word *bayd*, which refers to its egg like shape, *bayd* being the Arabic term for egg. The other five kinds of iron mentioned are: *muhdath* (refurbished); *rasmi* (regular/standard); *raqs* (shiny); *kufi* (round) and *amlas* (smooth). This iron then seems to have been worked into swords and other items in the Middle East. These products are described in some Arabic accounts of this period.

The twelfth century geographer Al Idrisi wrote,

> the Indians are very good at making various compounds of mixtures of substances with the help of which they melt the malleable iron; it then turns into Indian iron, and is called after al-Hind. There, in al-Hind, are workshops where swords are manufactured, and their craftsmen make excellent ones surpassing those made by other peoples. In the same way, the Singhi, Sarandibi, and Baynimani iron vie with one another for superiority as regards the climate of the place, skill in industry, the method of melting and stamping and beauty in polishing and scouring. But no iron is comparable to the Indian one in sharpness.[21]

EIGHTEENTH-CENTURY ACCOUNTS OF WOOTZ

It is when the Europeans arrive on the scene, that we begin to get descriptions of the process by which the actual steel furnaces were made and operated. By the eighteenth and nineteenth centuries, the Industrial Revolution had already begun in Europe. Curiosity about the superior kind of wootz steel that India produced, was at an all-time high.

The English cutler and metallurgist James Stodart used wootz steel extensively for making his knives. His company, set-up in 1787, advertized the superiority of its surgical instruments by announcing that they were made from Indian steel—specifically wootz!

Here is the trade-card used by James Stodart from the late eighteenth century. This card, a copy of which is with the British Museum in London, announces proudly that he made 'Surgeons Instruments, Razors and other Cutlery from उत्स (Wootz) a Steel from India'. It also announces that a certain Mr. S. prefers a steel from India 'over Steel from Europe' and that this was 'after years of comparative trial'.

Figure 4.4: Trade Card of James Stodart, late eighteenth century, British Museum

His fascination with the material led him into a collaboration with the scientist Michael Faraday and together the two re-invented a variation on the making of crucible steel in early nineteenth-century Britain.

At about this time, another Englishman by name David Mushet took a patent for the process of converting wrought iron into steel and sold it to a Sheffield firm for £3000. The Industrial Revolution in Britain had revived interest in a material known to the premodern world.

Many English officials of the East India Company recorded their high opinion of the material. Captain Campbell writing in 1842, says that, 'From what I have seen of Indian iron, I consider the worst I have ever seen to be as good as the best English iron, and that its supposed defects arise from its almost always containing a considerable portion of steel'.

MAKING WOOTZ STEEL THROUGH CARBURIZATION

From European accounts we find that there were at least two different kinds of processes for making wootz steel in India. The first method involved heating sponge iron with organic matter like leaves in a sealed crucible for the iron to absorb carbon. The other method that was popular in the Hyderabad region, involved fusing together two different kinds of iron in a sealed crucible. This latter was Deccani or Golconda steel and was the more valuable of the two.

A description of the process of making wootz steel through in-situ carburization can be found in the reports of the Scottish doctor, Francis Buchanan of the Bengal Medical Service. Serving under the English East India Company, Buchanan was assigned the task of surveying first, the Mysore territories of the now defeated Tipu Sultan and then the territories of Bengal. During his journeys through Mysore starting in 1800, Buchanan found many of the smelters and watched the working of the iron furnaces closely. The following is based on what he reported.[22]

First he described the process of making sponge iron. In two districts of Mysore that he visited, Buchanan tells us that the iron smelters used the local black sand as ore, along with charcoal as fuel. The sand was brought down from the hills by the torrents in the river, during the rainy season. It was found only during these few months so the smelters ran for only that period. For the rest of the year, the men worked as cultivators and supplied wood to the townspeople.

Magnetic Sand into Sponge Iron

Three distinct processes were involved in smelting the iron ore. Accordingly, there were three kinds of workers: those who washed the sand, those who made the charcoal, and those who worked at the bellows. Eleven men including the foreman worked at the smelting furnace.

The first group of people washed the black sand extensively in open troughs in running water and then used it as ore. The business of the black sand brought some income to the village headman also. This was quite apart from the money paid to the collector of customs and the keeper of the forest.

The second group of workmen made the charcoal in the woods.

Probably they simply heaped the wood into a pile and set it on fire. Once the wood charred, they would have doused it with water.

It was the third task of working the furnace that was the hardest. The workmen put baskets of charcoal in the furnace along with handfuls of the black sand. Once the charcoal got burnt, the cycle was repeated. It seems that around 47 per cent of the ore could be recovered as sponge iron.[23]

Three furnaces were smelted every day and the sponge iron so produced was sent for forging. Ten men worked at the forge. The men were divided between four tasks: one man to work the forceps, two men to manage the bellows, three men to work the hammer and four men to supply the charcoal. The charcoal for the forge was made from bamboo.

This kind of iron produced from sand was sold for roughly 1.7 annas per kg.[24]

Iron made from a different kind of ore, that is stone ore in other districts, was cheaper but it was of no use for making steel.

Next, Buchanan tells us of the furnace that processed some of the iron into steel. Here is a sketch that he drew:

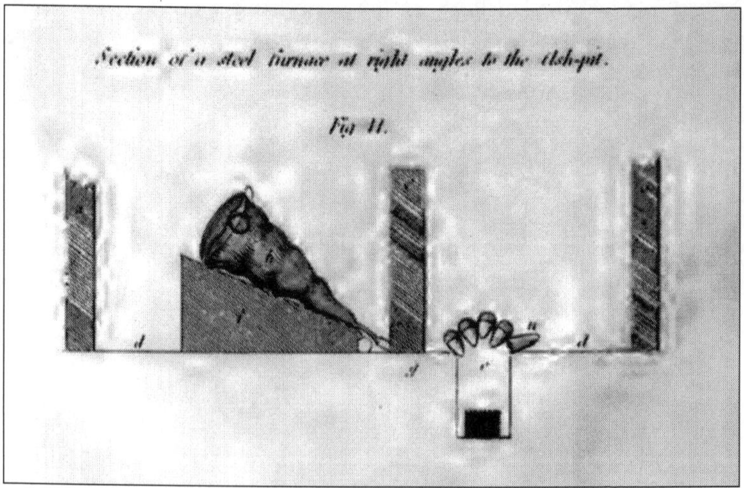

Source: Buchanan, 1807, 2: 19.

Figure 4.5: Section of a steel furnace at right angles to the ash pit

The steel furnace was a circular pit sunk into the ground and was built inside a hut. The pit was 18 inches in diameter and 36 inches deep. Below the pit they dug another separate pit for receiving the ash from the coal in the furnace. The furnace was filled with coal. The bellows made of bullock's hide, rested on banked earth. The fire was stoked by blowing air from the bellows shown in the picture above, through an earthen tube that connected the bellows with the furnace. The workers at the bellows were protected from the blazing heat by building a five foot high mud wall between the bellows and the furnace.

Steel through Carburization of Iron

Once the furnace had been set-up in this way, the crucibles containing iron were arranged. The crucibles were conical in shape and made of unbaked clay. In each crucible, they put a third of a wedge of iron (about 275 g of iron) along with approx. 35 g worth of the stem of a plant, the Cassia Auriculata along with two green leaves of a plant of the Convolvulus family (or Ipomea). The plant material provided the organic material needed for carburization. Then the mouth of the crucible was closed with clay and the junction sealed. The crucibles were arranged in the shape of a double arch inside the furnace. In all, there were fifteen crucibles. Opposite the muzzle of the bellows, an empty crucible was placed.

In this way, there were five sets of fourteen crucibles each, which produced steel daily. At the end of the process, each crucible contained a single button of steel which the smiths said was around 1.25 *seers* (344 g in local weight). Buchanan says the button mostly weighed only about 1 *seer* (278 g in local weight) but it was never sold by weight.[25]

Thirteen people worked at each steel furnace. All were cultivators and only managed the furnace in their spare time. The thirteen included a head workman who built the crucibles and loaded these, and four teams of three workmen each. At any point of time, there were three people at the steel furnace: one to work the fire and the other two to work the bellows. There was also an owner who was paid when the steel was sold.

Of the steel that was produced, the good steel in the Mysore region was sold at 6½ annas to 8 annas for a kilo (depending on whether you took the local worker's estimate of the daily produce or Buchanan's). The bad steel sold at 2.7 annas a kilo to 3 1/3 annas per kilo. Compared to the value of 1.7 annas to the kilo of sand iron, this represents a value addition of three and a half to four and a half times for the good steel.

Much of the steel was made based on advances from merchants since most of it seems to have been exported, so Buchanan reports. It was being used for arms and ammunition, making wires for musical instruments, etc.

MAKING WOOTZ THROUGH CO-FUSION OF DIFFERENT METALS

The second process of producing crucible steel by co-fusion of different kinds of iron, has been described by an English traveller, Henry Wesley Voysey, from the nineteenth century. Voysey was a physician by training and in addition a geologist and mineralogist. Some refer to him as the father of Indian geology. Voysey in the course of his travels in Andhra Pradesh, tells us that Konasamundram (literally corner of the sea) which was located 12 miles south of the river Godavari and 25 miles from Nirmul, was famous for manufacture of steel. Most of this was exported to Persia.[26] The main differences that we note in his description of the process from the steel furnace described by Buchanan are: the contents of the crucibles, the method of cooling and the larger volumes of the Deccani process.

In this region, the smiths used a special kind of clay for the furnace and also for the cone shaped vessels (crucibles as these are known) in which the steel was made. Voysey reports that the granitic clay of the furnace was found in the neighbourhood and that it was formed by decomposition of granite rock with small pieces of quartz and feldspar. It was even exported to other areas for manufacture of crucibles. For the making of crucibles, this clay, so he said, was ground into a fine powder, and mixed with equal parts of chaff of rice and oil. Others report that the mixture was ground finely by the feet of oxen for producing the material for making the furnace and crucibles.

Golconda Process of Co-fusion of Iron to Steel

Regarding the contents put into the crucible, Voysey says that no charcoal was put into it but small pieces of glass were put at the bottom to serve as a flux. Two different kinds of iron were fused together: three parts of Mirtpalli iron to two parts of Kondapur iron were mixed together. The Mirtpalli iron was of reddish brown colour and porous in texture while the Kondapur iron was dirty brown in colour and very frangible; it was moderately compact and 'of a brilliant white fracture'. The furnace was heated for 24 hours at the end of which the crucible was taken out and cooled. The resulting cake of steel was about one and a half pounds in weight. It was then covered with clay and annealed in the furnace for 12 to 16 hours. Three to four annealings were done till the steel was soft enough to be worked.[27]

Many crucibles could be put together at one time into the furnace and there were furnaces with provision for as many as 48 crucibles. Golconda wootz steel was much more valuable than the steel made from the black sand in the Mysore region. It sold for roughly 6½ to 13 annas to the kg.

Essentially the artisans of wootz steel seem to have been fusing different kinds of iron in the crucible. One type was probably high carbon cast iron and the other was some low carbon iron. The patterned appearance of wootz steel may have been due to these different kinds of metals, some hard and some soft, being fused together at high temperatures.

Artisans Maintain Strict Temperature Controls

A.K. Biswas, a professor of materials and metallurgical engineering at IIT Kanpur, has suggested that perhaps the combination of hardness and flexibility that characterized wootz was achieved by maintaining a very narrow range of temperatures in the steel furnace from about 650 °C which was blood-red to 850 °C which was cherry-red.[28] Any higher and the product became too brittle. He also suggested that the reason that Europeans could never achieve the same was, that they were simply heating the material to white heat which was over 1200 °C.

The French traveller Tavernier too had noted this tendency of Indian made steel. He reported that when Indian workmen put the wootz into the fire for working it, they needed to give it the redness of a cherry. If the workman were to heat it to the same high temperatures as did the Europeans, it would grow hard and break like glass.

The other reason identified for the special qualities of wootz steel has been the slow cooling period and the repeated cycles of annealing (heating to and holding at a suitable temperature followed by cooling at a suitable rate). In the annealing process, the artisans were cooling the steel at a slow rate. That way the steel could acquire malleability and ductility while retaining its hardness. But it required repeated cycles to achieve this result. The higher the number of cycles, the better the steel. Is it possible that the carbon nanotubes that the German metallurgists discovered during their analyses of wootz, were formed as a result of the repeated annealing cycles? Investigations are still on.

PRODUCTIVITY PER FURNACE AND EARNINGS OF LABOUR

The one thing that was common to both processes was a heavy use of labour and a rather low level of output. In the carburization process described by Buchanan around the year 1800, eleven men worked on three furnaces for smelting iron from sand and another ten worked on the forge. Together they produced roughly 27.21 kg of iron per day. Since all eleven men were able to run three small furnaces at the same time, we shall take this equivalent to one furnace. Since they worked six months in the year, annual output of sponge iron per furnace was around five tons.

For the steel forge described by Buchanan in Mysore, around thirteen people worked on one steel furnace to produce about 1.5 to 1.85 tons of steel in six months every year. In the cofusion process that was common in the Hyderabad region, the furnace was more productive and may have produced upwards of 10-13 tons in the year.

In the absence of any detailed survey, it is difficult to estimate the number of iron and steel furnaces and forges operating in the country at the time but Dharampal has estimated that there might have been about 10,000 furnaces in the country.[29] Taking an average of 5 tons per furnace, India might have been producing 50,000 tons of iron and steel in the eighteenth century.

Small-scale Production in India became Costlier

When we compare with England, we find that right up to 1750, England was producing upto 25,000 tons of iron per annum. The quality of the iron might have been poorer but each furnace produced around 340 tons per furnace per annum. The scales of operation were entirely different. The main constraint England faced was a shortage of charcoal. Then in 1709, one Abraham Darby came up with a process for smelting ore using coke. Initially the iron that was produced was of poor quality and could not be converted into bar iron. But by the 1750s, the younger Darby had improved the process so that iron smelted with coke could be converted into bar iron. After that, and with the application of steam power to the furnace, English production rapidly rose to roughly 80,000 tons by 1790 with one furnace producing up to 1,000 tons per annum. There was no looking back for them. India never saw any rise in productivity and over time, Indian iron and steel grew to be costlier in the market.

In 1830, Swedish steel was selling between 7⅓ and 9¾ annas per kg which was similar to Mysore steel but cheaper than Golconda steel. At 4.16 to 4.8 annas per kg, English steel was even cheaper. Golconda steel was much costlier than the English variety.

No doubt the average annual earnings of the workmen in these furnaces were sufficient to yield a comfortable livelihood. Here is a basic comparison of earnings for the period 1800-10 in the region of Mysore based on the information provided by Buchanan:

TABLE 4.1: MONTHLY EARNINGS OF IRON AND STEEL WORKERS IN MYSORE *c*.1800[30]

	Mysore Region Sand Iron Smelter	Mysore Region Steel Furnace
Category of worker	Total Earnings in 6 months in rupees	Total Earnings in 6 months in rupees
Washing sand	19.70	–
Making charcoal	19.70	–
Bellowsman	19.70	19.70
Foreman	31.50	39.30
Owner	41.21	137.81

Both Buchanan and Voysey were clear that these workmen tended to their fields in their spare time. These earnings supplemented by farm income, would have made for a comfortable life indeed. But it did not stand up against the competitive edge that better technology and productivity provided to English producers.

WHY DID WOOTZ DIE OUT

Wootz was fast becoming too costly. There were other reasons too. By the sixteenth century, trade in wootz had declined in importance in the subcontinent. One reason could be that warfare had changed and now cannons were far more important in warfare than swords ever were. While wootz steel was of great value for forging swords, small arms like pistols and surgical knives, etc., it was not of much use for cannon making.

For cannon, Indian blacksmiths continued to prefer forge welding techniques. A massive iron cannon found at Thanjavur is estimated to consist of as many as 291 different wrought iron rings that were forge welded together. The Delhi iron pillar is an example of forge welding. Indian blacksmiths are not known to have cast iron. Casting iron would have meant achieving much higher temperatures at which the molten iron could be cast into moulds of the desired shape. This was a crucial limitation in warfare since the Europeans used cast iron for their cannon. Wootz, however, was used for producing a superior quality of small arms.

When the Europeans came into the country, they noted that the Mughals did not have efficient cannon. The Mughal cannon were mostly made of bronze or brass. Moreover, such cannons were not of much use, the simple reason being that the Indians produced metal in such small furnaces that products of many different furnaces had to be used to produce a single cannon. The French traveller Thevenot comments on the arms of the Mughals, 'They have Cannon also in their Towns, but since they melt the metal in diverse Furnaces, so that some of it must needs be better melted than others when they mingle all together, their Cannon commonly is good for nothing'.[31]

Basically, the iron and steel industry in India produced high quality products but it remained a small-scale industry. It was already dying when in 1860, in the aftermath of the Mutiny of 1857, the British banned production of wootz steel in India, ostensibly to save India's forests from destruction for charcoal.[32]

No doubt, the Indian economy was doing well in comparison with the past but it stagnated. Others raced ahead and we stayed wherever we were. In 1800, iron production in India was at least as much as and perhaps more than what was being produced in England or Europe. But things had already started changing. The United Kingdom was producing 80,000 metric tons of iron per annum in 1790. After 1800, they raced ahead and by 1870 they were producing 50 per cent of the world production of iron.[33] They had found the methods to scale up all their processes. We never did.

But the fascination with wootz remained. In the late nineteenth-century Indologist Horace Hyman Wilson could write, 'The Hindus have the art of smelting iron, of welding it, and of making steel, and have had these arts from times immemorial'. He was reiterating the words of Al Idrisi uttered 600 years earlier. And yet no one wanted the wootz any more, not enough for the production to remain viable at any rate.

Today we only have memories left of thousands of years of wootz production. A scholar in modern times who studied over 1,100 villages in the Telangana region, reports that he found evidence relating to iron and steel manufacture in as many as 425 villages.[34] In most of these villages there is a temple dedicated to the goddess Mammayi who is the goddess of metal work. One of the families in these villages recalled that one of their ancestors was employed as a wootz steel worker in the local Jagtial fort and that he used to knit wootz metal wires into coats of mail armour.[35] But once the market for this kind of steel was gone, those artisans gradually moved out into other kinds of employment.

WHY COULDN'T INDIAN ARTISANS SCALE-UP

So why is it we wonder that the Indian artisans with the best product in the known world, simply could not scale-up their production to meet the needs of an expanding economy? We can only estimate the reasons. One factor seems to be that while the Indian artisans had a great storehouse of information, they never documented any of it; nor did anyone see fit to do it for them. In the absence of any systematic documentation, they were unable to come up with ideas to deal with the problem of providing more mechanical power to increase the strength of their bellows or the scale of their furnaces. Europe by the fifteenth century was already using water power to drive bellows but not Indian artisans. They never moved to the blast furnace or the Bessemer converter. Small-scale artisanal production, however superior, simply could not cope with the ever-increasing demands of the modern market.

To the question as to why the artisans could not innovate, perhaps they did not have any sufficient reason for doing so? Their method of making steel, however wasteful of resources such as charcoal, could continue happily till such time as the forest cover started decreasing. That there was no shortage of forests in India till the twentieth century is another matter. In England on the other hand, when the demand of the iron industry came into conflict with the increasing demand for timber in the ship-building industry, their sovereign simply banned the use of charcoal for making iron, thereby forcing the smiths to shift to coke which required much more power than charcoal.

INDIAN ARTISANS LED A SERENDIPITOUS LIFE, WHY INNOVATE

Let us look at another reason. The artisans in India were independent producers who owned their own equipment and who bought their own raw material. The artisans perhaps did not have much incentive to innovate or re-organize themselves in line with the changing demand, given their more than adequate earnings.

Using the information provided in the record of the Englishman Buchanan's journey from the early nineteenth century, a scholar has estimated the average earnings of different classes of workers and entrepreneurs in then Mysore. He uses the broad measure of two separate baskets of food: one of coarse millets and the other of coarse rice each amounting to 2,040 calories per day for three family members. This is a base subsistence ration and only a surplus would ensure a decent living. His estimation is that the annual wages of the foreman of a smelter who worked for ten months in the year amounted to 2 times the coarse millet basket and 1.22 times the coarse rice basket. For the owners of the iron smelter, their earnings ranged from 3.37 to 14.32 times the coarse millet basket and 2.05 to 8.72 times the coarse rice basket. These earnings were not only comparable to but higher than their counterparts in contemporary England. And the earnings of those engaged in such a high value product as wootz would be even higher. Such earnings not only met their daily needs, it would give them surplus to meet other needs also.[36]

No wonder then that Buchanan found such a relaxed pace of life among the local workers. He noted this serendipitous quality of existence in India in the record of his journeys. He has the following to say about how agriculture servants in India led their life in the Shimoga region of Karnataka:

> The greater part of the cultivation is carried on by the tenants, and their own families. In agriculture, some hired servants, but no slaves, are employed. The yearly wages for a labouring servant are from four to five Ikeri Pagodas, one blanket, one pair of shoes, and a handkerchief, amounting in all to about two guineas. He finds his house and victuals. In weeding time, women are hired, at four Seers of rough rice a day. A man, when hired by the day, gets five Seers. These wages are very high, when it is considered that no servant works

here more than six hours. The labourers gave me the following account of the manner in which they pass their time. About eight o'clock of our day they rise from bed, and smoke tobacco they perform their evacuations, and ablutions; and having been purified, they worship the gods. They then eat, an operation in which two hours are expended. They then rest themselves half an hour, when they proceed to the field, and work six hours. On their return, they again pray, and take a little of any cold victuals that they have ready. They then look after the cattle, and give them water and fodder. The labour of the day is now over; and the workman, having again washed and prayed, takes his supper, and about seven o'clock goes to bed, where he remains thirteen hours. This is their employment during the six months of toil. In the remaining half of the year, little cultivation being carried on, they repair their houses, lay in a stock of firewood, carry out dung, and do other little jobs about the farm. Masters, of course, work still less.[37]

In such conditions, it would have taken a great deal of collective effort for the Indian artisans to generate any incentive for making radical changes in their processes. But we cannot say that Indian artisans lacked innovation.

Poor Market Intelligence and Limited Demand help Determine Response to Innovation

A study of artisans in late nineteenth and early twenteth centuries in India found that there were many innovators among the master artisans in industries like weaving textiles, brassware, and woodwork. Which of them did succeed depended on several factors.[38] In situations where market demand was limited or information about market opportunities was poor and communication inadequate, the members of the community saw the innovation as a threat to their means of livelihood and a deviation from the norm. In such cases, there was a hostile reaction and the innovator was destroyed. A remarkable case cited in the study was of Ramaneswaram, a weaver located in the textile town of Parmakudi in Tamil Nadu. Ramaneswaram invented a loom in which three weavers could weave a cloth at the same time. He tried to sell this loom to other members of his community. But his peers were hostile to the idea; they felt that this loom might cause a glut in the market and cause a crash in prices. So, one day they invaded his house, burnt it down including the loom he had built of which there was only one model. Ramaneswaram died a broken man.[39]

In other situations where market demand had increased, members of the community tried to appropriate the innovation and to use it to make greater profits. There is the story of another weaver who had worked in the Rajahmundry silk mills in the region of Andhra Pradesh where he had learnt how the dobby was used. Later he went to the village of Mori and set-up his loom to produce the same kind of saris as were produced in the mills; the saris were a hit in the market. But he did not share his secret; one day when he was out of the house the other weavers broke into his house to study his loom. Soon after there were many others copying his loom and trying to produce saris that looked similar to those he had made.[40]

In many cases, irrespective of demand, the innovator tried to keep his innovation secret from others, apparently out of fear that someone else by copying his method, would eat into his market and profits. In one extreme case, the master artisan did not even pass on information about his methods to his family. The crucial factor then seems to be the extent of demand for any product. In the case of the village of Mori, community members knew well there was a larger profit to be made so instead of destroying the loom of a rival, they tried to learn from it. In the case of Ramaneswaram, where the artisans never perceived that there could be higher demand or profits, their response was to destroy the innovation.

In Other Countries, State Supported Business Initiatives

One feature that set the artisans of other countries apart from those in India, was the role of the state. In Britain, it was the demand for large iron cannon that fuelled the rise in productivity of the blacksmiths. In Sweden, an early leader in iron and steel production, the Crown took active steps to organize production. Swedish blacksmiths used to produce in the fifteenth century, a product called osmund iron which was midway between ore and iron (iron was sold in bars); but it was easy to produce in a small furnace. So, for centuries blacksmiths not only produced it, they believed that osmund was a superior product even though it fetched a lesser price. It was only in 1604 that the parliament banned all export of osmund from the country and the government began to directly invest in bar iron forges. Not only this, the Swedish Crown invited a Dutch entrepreneur to make weapons in the country, so much so that they gave him a monopoly of weapons factories in Sweden. Swedish iron production never looked back.

The fact remains that any large-scale industrial organization required much support from the state. The English East India Company was one of the earliest and most successful corporations of this variety and state support had a crucial role to play in the well-being of the Company. Countries with governments that supported and initiated such organization, gained a lead in industrial production. India did not.

Innovation Dies Out for Lack of Documentation: Rockets of Tipu

The other feature that has been missing from Indian technological endeavours, has been documentation of knowledge and systematic working to produce better outcomes. Here we take a brief look at one famous innovation in the use of Indian iron in warfare, namely the case of the rockets used so effectively by Tipu Sultan, the last independent ruler of Mysore state.

Rockets had been in use in warfare since the twelfth to thirteenth centuries CE in China and sometime later in Europe. However, they do not seem to have been especially effective. The change that was brought about in eighteenth-century Mysore was to provide an iron casing for the solid propellant, namely gunpowder.

How it worked was like this. The rocket consisted of (1) a cylindrical iron casing, 7-10 inches long containing gunpowder and (2) it was tied to either a bamboo rod or a steel blade 3-6 ft long. By lighting the gunpowder inside the casing, the rocket generated gases that gave it forward motion so it could work like a projectile much like the rockets we see at Diwali. The rod acted as a primitive guidance mechanism. The iron casing allowed far more gunpowder to be packed inside so that the rocket emitted gases at higher temperature and speed and acquired greater range and power. Tipu Sultan's army had an entire Rocket corps that was put to extensive use in wartime.[41]

The impact of the rockets on the English army was reported by some of the English officers who participated in the Anglo-Mysore wars. Their reactions ranged from awe at the hail of rockets that caused death, injuries and lacerations to observations that the rockets were easily avoided and did not have much impact.

Whatever the individual reactions of army officers, the English army did preserve some of these rockets and carried them for display to England at the Royal Artillery Museum, Woolwich Arsenal. Here they were seen by the younger William Congreve, who worked at Woolwich Arsenal. He was so much impressed that he devoted a great part of his life to refining the mechanism of the rockets and persuading the British military to using these in war. He standardized construction details, improved techniques, increased the size of the rocket to carry still more gunpowder and nearly tripled the range. Later the British navy improvised on his suggestions and effectively used the rockets against the French fleet and in other wars as well.

An Indian scholar and former professor of Aerospace Engineering at the Indian Institute of Science Bangalore, R. Narasimha points out that to begin with, the Indian technology of the rockets was superior to anything the British had. However, over time, British efforts to master and improve the technology, involved an application of scientific principles about which contemporary Indians had no clue.[42]

Indian businessmen might have had money, but they never used it to systematize Indian production and move from artisanal workshops to a larger setting. The result was that when world demand did explode, Indian artisans got left behind. With little incentive to egg them on, and no knowledge management system to suggest ways of improving productivity, the Indian artisan, even with a winning product and a brand known the world over, faltered. By the time the British banned wootz production in 1860 in India, the death knell for the industry had already been rung.

NOTES

1. Ministry of Steel, 2018-19: 148.
2. Marshall, 1951, vol. 2: 536.
3. Reibold, 2009.
4. The grid was covered by an amorphous carbon layer. It was analysed with the help of optical microscopy, High Resolution Transmission Electron Microscopy (HRTEM) and X-ray diffraction.
5. Cementite is an iron carbide, an intermetallic compound of iron and carbon.
6. Prakash and Igaki, 1984.
7. Ibid.
8. The measure referred was librae, an ancient unit of weight, approx. 327 g.
9. Gilmour, 2015.
10. Ibid.
11. Varahamihira, 1981.
12. Juice of *arka* plant is *Calotropis gigantea.*
13. B. Prakash, 1991
14. *Kala ayasa* is an ancient Sanskrit name for a kind of iron with properties similar to those reported for wootz steel in later times.
15. Biswas, 1994.
16. Kautilya, 2.17.14.
17. Biswas, 1994.
18. Daryaee, 2014: 146.
19. Goitein, 2011: pt. 1: 55-6.
20. Goitein, 2011: pt. 1: 19, 320-1.
21. Al-Idrisi, 1960: 23.
22. Buchanan, 1807, vol. II: 16-18.
23. Dry black sand, of weight 42.5 pounds, would produce so Buchanan says, 11 wedges of finished iron. Each wedge weighed 1.82 pounds and was sufficient to make one ploughshare. A total of roughly 20 pounds of finished iron comes to 47 per cent.
24. The iron made from the sand sold at 0.25 fanam/1.4 annas per piece of 0.82 kg. This works out to 1.7 annas for 1 kg. of iron. Buchanan gives earning figures in fanams. Assuming these are gold fanams, we have calculated the equivalent earning in rupees, using benchmark: 1 gold pagoda = 10 gold fanams = 3.5 silver rupees. So 1 fanam equals 0.35 rupees or 5.6 annas (Buchanan, 1807, v. II: 13, 18).
25. Buchanan reports that the seer used here was equivalent to 24 rupees in weight. This would mean at a rate of 179 troy grains (11.6 g) to the rupee

(old rupee standard prevalent at the time), a weight of 278 g to the seer. For Mysore seer, see *Useful Tables forming an Appendix to the Journal of the Asiatic Society, Part the First, Coins, Weights and Measures of British India*, 1834: 84.

26. Voysey, 1832.
27. Ibid.
28. Biswas, 1994.
29. Dharampal, 1971: 23.
30. Buchanan, 2: 16-23. Also see endnote 24.
31. de Thevenot, 1687, 3: 43.
32. Jaikishan & Balasubramaniam, 2007b.
33. Parrish, 1956.
34. Jaikishan, 2007.
35. Ibid.
36. Sivramkrishna, 2009.
37. Buchanan, 1807, 3: 298.
38. Roy, 2007.
39. Ibid.
40. Ibid.
41. Narasimha, 1985.
42. Ibid.

CHAPTER 5

The Land of the Lotus Eaters

India had plenty of talented individuals, much artisanal skill and capital too. What was lacking seemed to be organization and knowledge systems and a desire to improve productivity. Indians never seemed to feel the need to improve productivity or to set-up large-scale organizations, whether it be governance systems, banks, or monetary systems. Uniformity, standardization, regulation and control; all these seem to have been anathema to Indians. Even the rupee, which remained India's currency for a good 500 years from Mughal times onwards, had so many different names and standards, that merely exchanging different kinds of coins was big business. Why should this be so?

Some people have argued that India never developed the methods of modern science which might have helped them along in improving productivity. Did India really lack in science and technology? The now popular notion of 'scientific temper', whatever that might be? The ability to scale up? If we look at arithmetic and mathematics for instance—arithmetic is to mathematics what spelling is to writing say the wags—we find that there was no shortage of discovery and creativity among Indian scholars.

From Aryabhata to Bhaskaracharya, the numerous mathematicians who flourished in ancient India, figured out many complex problems, in some cases centuries before the Europeans did, whether it was the idea of zero, solutions to indeterminate equations or even a solution to the infinite series.

Without this knowledge, it would not have been possible to build the immense temples with towering *shikharas*, which date to early medieval times. Yet after the fifteenth century, mathematics in India simply stagnated; Europe forged ahead.

THE PRACTICAL MATHEMATICIANS OF INDIA: BUILDING FIRE ALTARS

One of the earliest examples of the use of mathematics in India comes from the *Shulbasutras* of Baudhayana which were penned by roughly the eighth to seventh centuries BCE. Maharishi Baudhayana in these texts, describes how to use bricks to make different kinds of fire altars which are both aesthetically pleasing and ritually correct. The word *shulba* means 'rope' or 'cord'. A rope is used to show how to draw different kinds of figures in these *sutras* by tying the rope between two opposite ends, by dividing the rope into equal segments and so on. In the process the readers are also told, often in brief, terse sentences, how to make right angle squares, how to draw rectangles, how to transform rectangles into squares or vice versa and many other conversions of geometric shape. A knowledge of the geometry of shapes revealed in these *sutras*, is repeated in the other *Shulbasutras* of Apastamba and Katyayana.

A familiar-to-some-today sutra is the one in which Maharishi Baudhayana tells us that the diagonal of a square would create a square of double the area as compared to the square created by any of the sides of the square.[1] In another *sutra* we are told, that the square of the hypotenuse of a right angle triangle is equal to the sum of the squares of the two sides.[2]

The description given by Baudhayana in itself is so brief that it requires a very close reading to figure out what he is saying. Also noteworthy is that no attempt is made to tell us how he arrived at this result. In these and subsequent descriptions, his complete focus is on the aesthetics of the exercise, not its method or rationale.

Fire Altars Needed Knowledge of Basic Mathematics

Different types of *vedis* (fire altars), were prescribed in the Shastras, nearly all designed to create, inter alia, heightened visual appeal. One of the more complicated types of fire altar was that constructed in the shape of a falcon with spread wings, ready to take flight. Four different sizes of bricks were used in the construction of this kind of altar. Dr. George Gheverghese Joseph, while telling us of the contribution of Indian mathematics re-created the base layer of a Vedic fire-altar according to the information from the *sutras* (Figure 5.1). This showed how the repeated use of four kinds of simple shapes could create the complex shape of the fire altar.

One thing clear from the design above was that in order to construct all these figures, the local artisans needed the ability to draw precise mathematical shapes like squares, rectangles, trapeziums, and circles, if only to name the most basic units.

In order to construct the *vedis*, the artisans also needed to know how to divide a line into a number of equal parts, and how to construct a square and rectangle with a specific measure of side. The texts laid great emphasis on different parts of the altar being of equivalent area to each other. They needed to know how to draw a square equivalent in area to two squares or a square equivalent in area to a circle. This was the kind of information in which the *sutras* were helpful. The *Katyayana Shulbasutra* says that the cord stretched along the length of the diagonal of a rectangle, gives an area which the horizontal and vertical sides make together. Using

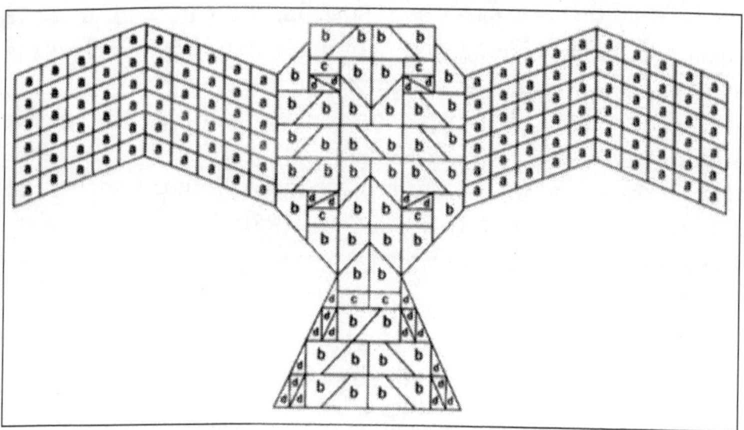

Source: Joseph, 2011: 325.

Note: Figure shows the first layer of a Vedic sacrificial altar in the shape of a falcon. The wings are each made from 60 bricks of type a, and the body from 46 of type b, 6 of type c, and 24 of type d.

Figure 5.1: Vedic sacrificial altar in the shape of a falcon

this idea, the *sutras* showed how to construct a square equal to the sum of two squares or equal to the difference of two squares.

For drawing these figures, the artisans of the times used material like the rope or *rajju*, bamboo rods and pegs driven into the ground.

Archaeologists found a falcon-shaped Vedic fire altar at Purola in Uttarkashi district of what is now Uttarakhand, in north India (Figure 5.2). Located on the left bank of the river Kamal, in a valley of terraced rice fields, this altar seems to have been used at least since the first century BCE to the second century CE.[3]

Made out of five different layers of brick, it was the creation of bricks that conform to a precise dimension. Bricklayers, masons, carpenters, and other workers, all would have had to work in considerable coordination with each other and with working knowledge of mathematics and/or the ability to communicate this knowledge. Where precision was lost, a crisis could happen.

There is an episode in the Adiparvan of the *Mahabharata* where an altar was to be constructed for the snake sacrifice by King Janmejaya. The king asked the brahmanas to tell him how the sacrifice was to be conducted. Now, no one knew how to construct

Source: Archaeological Survey of India, Dehradun circle.
Note: Picture of falcon shaped Vedic fire altar excavated at Purola.

Figure 5.2: Vedic fire altar at Purola

the sacrificial platform. So, the brahmanas researched all previous knowledge and came up with a design. The platform was being made according to the instructions of the brahmanas. When the sacrificial platform was being constructed, a professional builder of great intelligence and well-versed in the knowledge of laying foundations, a Suta by caste, said, that the soil upon which and the time at which the measurement for the sacrificial platform had been made, indicated that the sacrifice would not be completed; that it would be interrupted by a brahmana.[4] That is just what happened. The *Mahabharata* tells us that a brahmana interrupted the sacrifice and it could not be completed. Perhaps the sacrificial fire simply could not accommodate all that was being put into it. The *Suta's* judgement, based on practical knowledge, proved to be correct.

Segmentation of Priestly and Artisanal Knowledge

What we routinely see in India is that professional knowledge often ran separately from Brahmanic or theological learning; it was recorded in literature which ran in parallel to the Brahmanic school of learning. Architectural texts like the *Manasara* and *Mayamata* or chemistry books like the *Rasa-Ratna-Samuccaya* (रस-रत्न-समुच्चय) were not produced in any college or university. One can only speculate that these volumes were written by practising professionals and were most probably meant for others who practised the profession. That may be the reason why these texts are written with such little technical detail being given; the text was being written for colleagues who were well conversant with the craft. Little explanation was needed.

These are features that remain true of Indian streams of knowledge through the centuries. The verses are very terse.

- They give no proofs of whatever axioms they were using.
- They begin from a very practical point of departure; an application that had immediate use.
- Above all they focus on the aesthetics.
- Recording of reasons is almost irrelevant.

All involved, sage or artisan, were strongly focused on creating an aesthetically pleasing shape; almost as if whatever discoveries they might have made in the process were incidental.

A HEADSTART WITH NUMERALS

The immensity of the discoveries that were made as part of this kind of mental exuberance was quite amazing.

The most significant discovery without doubt was the idea of zero, the place value of numbers and the decimal method of notation. Before numerals were discovered, people used the concept of number names. Basically different philosophical concepts were used to express different numbers. But this was a complicated and tortuous process.

Thus the number, zero, was expressed in terms meaning void or sky like *shunya*, *ambar*, *vyoma*, *akasha*, *kha*; the number, one, was expressed by different terms for the earth which is one, such as *prithvi*, *dharti*, *dhara*, *vasundhara*; the number, two, was expressed by anything denoting a pair like Asvin, eye or *netra* or *lochana* or *akshi*; the number, three, was expressed by *triguna*, *trijagata*, *loka*, *trinetra*, *trikala*, etc.; the number, four, was expressed by *veda*, *shruti*, *ashrama*, *krta* (*yuga*) and so on.

Numbers written in this kind of notation could be complicated. Bhattotpala in a commentary on the *Brihat Samhita*, writes the number 1,582,237,800, quoting from the *Pulisa Siddhanta* which was written in about 400 CE. The numbers are read from right to left: '*kha* (0), *kha* (0), *ashta* (8), *muni* (7), *rama* (3), *asvi* (2), *netra* (2), *ashta* (8), *sara* (5), *ratripah* (1) = 1,582,237,800'.[5]

Looks like, in the ancient math book, just one problem which tried to do a simple mathematical operation, could run into several pages. It must have been quite an exercise in patience. The concept of zero and the decimal notation changed all this at one stroke. With the number system, the arrangement of letters also changed to the left-to-right convention familiar to us currently.

To appreciate the difference all this made, we only need to try to multiply 102 by 2 using roman numbers CII and II to see the huge advantage which the concept of zero and the place value system offered.

Arrival of Place Value Makes Mathematics Much Easier

For our present purpose the point to notice is that Indians had figured this one out soon after the Christian era began. The Hindu number system which became known to the world initially as the Arabic number system after those who carried this knowledge to Europe, became known in the Islamic world only from roughly the ninth century CE. It became popular in Europe much later.

We find one of the first instances of the use of Hindu numbers in the Bakhshali manuscript, a Buddhist text that was written on birch bark, and discovered in a cave in Central Asia. This specific manuscript seems to be a copy of a document. While the copy was produced somewhere roughly in the eighth century CE, the original text itself is attributed to the early centuries of the Christian era and in no case later than 400 CE.

It was the number system, which expanded the possibilities of mathematics infinitely. You could now use ten numbers to represent an infinite variety of values.

In a cave at Nashik dating to the second century CE, some of the numbers used in inscriptions, are shown below in Brahmi script along with their modern day equivalent:

1 2 3 4 5 6 7 8

9 10 20 40 70 100 200 500

1,000 2,000 3,000 4,000 8,000 70,000

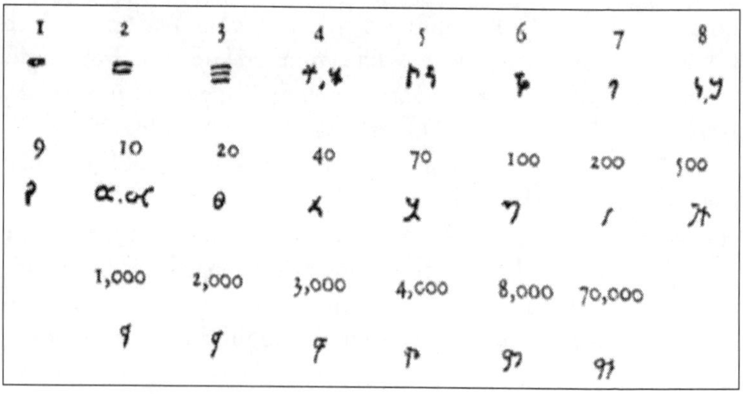

Source: Datta & Singh, 1962: 26.

Figure 5.3: Numbers used in inscriptions, shown in Brahmi script along with their modern-day equivalent

Till the place value system developed, people were simply adding *matras*, glyphs or diacritical signs, to the basic notation to denote the formation of hundreds and thousands. This will be clearer from the notation below:

= 100, = 200, = 300
= 1,000, = 2,000, = 3,000.

Source: Datta & Singh, 1962, p. 31.

Figure 5.4: Diacritical signs added to notations to show hundreds and thousands

The development of Nagari numerals over the centuries and a comparison of the Semitic and Brahmi numerals is given below:

It is difficult to say exactly when the ideas about place value system stabilized but the clearest indication of the place value system is found in the commentary named *Vyasa-Bhasya* on Patanjali's *Yogasutra*, which dates to the sixth century CE: 'Thus the same stroke is termed one in the units place, ten in the tens place, and hundreds in the hundreds place'.[6]

	Hieroglyphic	Phoenician	Hieratic	Demotic	Aśoka Inscriptions	Nānāghāt Inscriptions	Kuṣāna Inscriptions	Kṣatrapa & Andhra Inscriptions
1								
2								
3								
4								
5								
6								
7								
8								
9								
10								

Source: Datta & Singh, 1962, p. 106.

Figure 5.5: Semitic and Brahmi numerals

The Ahar inscription, found a few miles from Bulandshahr in Uttar Pradesh, uses both the old and the new systems. This inscription records gifts over many years from 864 CE onwards, the last entry dating to 904 CE. It has 28 lines recording various gifts made by donors to temples. The first few lines use the old notation while the lines after that, use the place value system.[7]

With the coming in of the number system with place value, there seems to have been a tremendous spurt in creativity with the unknown author of the *Surya Siddhanta*, Aryabhata, the first Bhaskara, Brahmagupta, Mahavira following upon each other quickly. Brahmagupta, an astronomer of the seventh century, was perhaps the first to use the zero as a definite number and not merely a placeholder unit.

COMMERCIAL PROBLEMS

These concepts expanded the mathematical frontier immensely. What Indian thinkers seem to have done was to to use the innovations to solve commercial problems extensively.

For instance they were deeply interested in commercial problems relating to accrual of interest on a specific principal in a given period of time. India was one of the few societies in the world where there was no taboo on charging of interest, so much so that some religious texts actually use the term *dharma vriddhi* to denote a legal rate of interest. Many of the problems we find in the Indian texts have to do with interest on different sums of money accumulating during different periods of time. Working out the fineness of gold was another theme that attracted attention of the learned ones of yore. Many such examples seem to have been used by sages in their hermitages to teach mathematics.

The focus of Aryabhata was astronomy but, he does give one rule relating to the problem of interest.

STRONG FOCUS ON PRACTICAL PROBLEMS

He states the problem of finding the unknown rate of interest per month, i.e. x, on a certain sum of money (p) which is lent for one month. After one month, the interest on p is lent for another six months (t). (A) is the sum of the interest on the principal and the interest on the interest. This is written as a quadratic equation. Aryabhata describes the solution thus:

> Multiply the sum of the interest on the principal and the interest on this interest (A) by the time (t) and by the principal (p). Add to this result the square of half the principal [$\{p/2\}^2$]. Take the square root of this. Subtract half the principal ($p/2$) and divide the remainder by the time (t). The result will be the (unknown) interest on the principal.[8]

Prthudakasvami, a scholar of the ninth century CE and a commentator on the *Brahma-Sphuta-Siddhanta*, gives many similar examples to illustrate rules of arithmetic. One such problem is: 'A horse was purchased by (nine) dealers in partnership whose contributions were one etc. up to nine; and was sold by them for five less than five hundred. Tell me what was each man's share of the sale proceed.'[9]

Once again, we note two things. One is that the underlying principle of the work that was done, was rarely stated in explicit terms, although they could hardly have reached their results without knowing it. Method, rationale seemed irrelevant.

Second and more importantly, Indian thinkers seemed to think mostly of practical matters. Commercial issues of profit and loss must have been important in the society of those times for them to devote so much time to such problems.

Other possible applications of quadratic equations which might have improved productivity, do not seem to have been thought of. Is it possible that Indian society in the past was so comfortable in its own skin that increasing productivity was unimportant?

SACRED GEOMETRY OF TEMPLE ARCHITECTURE

This engagement with the practical and the immediate, did produce some magnificent results. Towering temples from the sixth-seventh century CE onwards were one such result.

These Indian temples are extremely stable structures despite all their massive construction and towering *shikharas*. We do not of course know what principles of design were followed since little was stated by way of design principle. But one feature that is visible is great attention to ratio and proportion.

The basic grid on which the temple was built was a square of either 4×4 square design or 8×8 square design or rectangles of 4×6 or variations of these. Where the base grid was an 8×8 square grid that equalled 64 squares, the sanctum sanctorum normally equalled 4×4 squares. We give in Figure 5.6 below such a sample plan from a Shiva temple in central India:

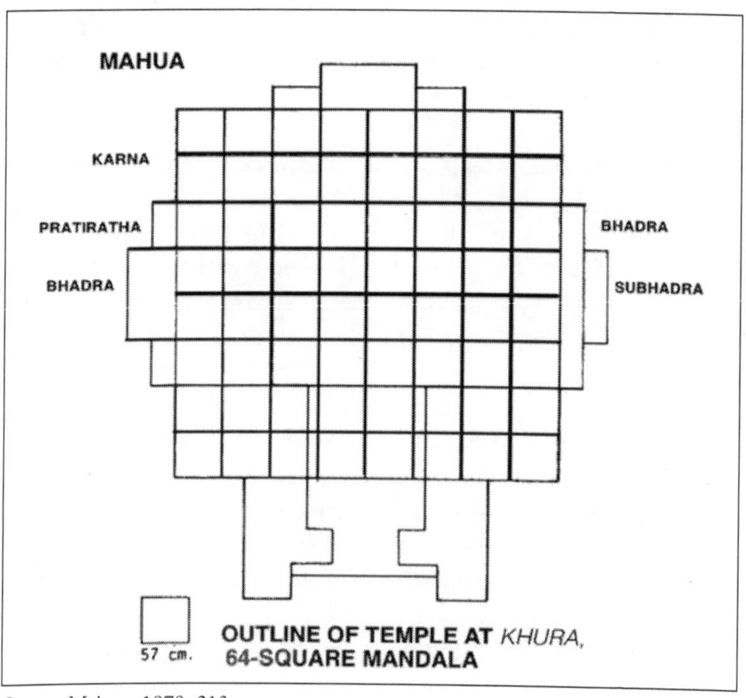

Source: Meister, 1979: 213.

Figure 5.6: Outline of Temple at Mahua, Central India*

* Figure 5.6 describes a temple at Mahua, district Shivpuri, Madhya Pradesh. The term *khura* used in the figure refers to an architectural portion of the base of the temple or the *vedibandha*. The base or *vedibandha* has several parts—plinth or *adhishthana*, next is *khura* which is in turn the base of the *kumbha*. This figure demonstrates what the plan of the *khura* portion would be for a horizontal section of the temple—rather as if you were to slice off the layers from the base.

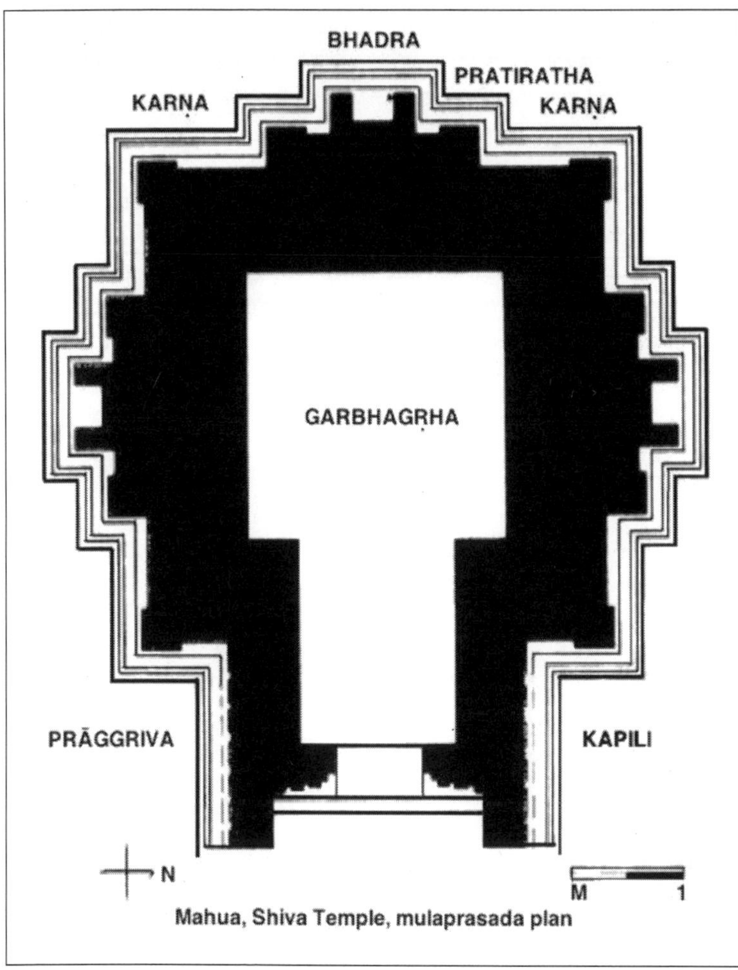

Source: Meister, 1979: 213.

Figure 5.7: Shiva Temple, central India

The *garbhagriha* or inner sanctum is made of 16 squares, and the adjoining squares at the four sides are then projected outwards on each of the other three walls. One of the projections is the entry to the sanctum and the other three projections serve as symbolic entries.[10] Sometimes these symbolic entries contain a niche with images.

There is a similar attention to proportion in the relation that the sides of the structure bear to each other. The linear measurements of the faces labelled as *bhadra*, *pratiratha* and *karna* on each of the sides, bear a certain ratio; in this particular case, the ratio is 2: 1: 2: 1: 2, that is karna (2): *pratiratha* (1): *bhadra* (2): *pratiratha* (1): *karna* (2). This ratio is common to the sanctum sanctorum of many temples in central India though there are variations too.

A scholar who has studied the temple of Ranakdevi at Wadhwan in Surendranagar district of Gujarat, pointed out a slightly more complex ratio of the sides in the structure here in Figure 5.8:[11]

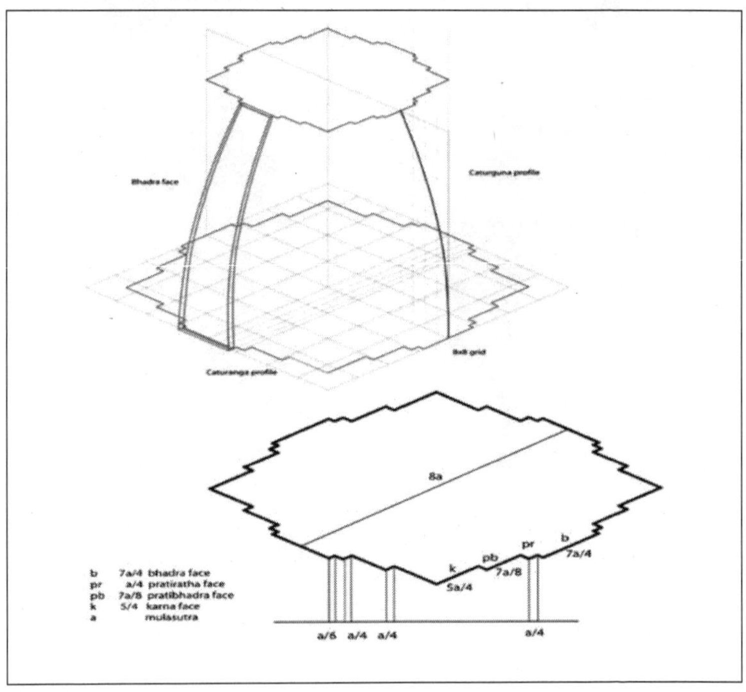

Source: Datta, 2010.

Figure 5.8: Temple at Rankadevi

Since the ritual grid is of 64 squares, the side of the square is 8a. As shown in the illustration the width of the projections on each of the four sides are 7a/4, a/4, 7a/8, 5a/4.[12] The *pratibhadra* face here is half the length of the *bhadra* face while the ratio between *pratiratha* and *bhadra* is 1: 7. The combination of these numbers which is slightly more complex than the first, produces a ratio of 5: 3.5: 1: 7: 1: 3.5: 5.

The curvilinear profile of the *shikhara* that distinguishes a large number of Hindu temples too is derived from the principles of geometrical progression. The *shikhara* consists of a number of horizontal rows which are placed in receding order on top of each other to arrive at the final shape. Several texts like the *Agni Purana* and the *Hayasirsa-Pancaratra* give the *sutras* which describe how the profile is to be drawn. Thus the *triguna sutra* gives the geometrical progression based on the number three. The *chaturguna sutra* gives the geometrical progression based on four and the *shadguna sutra* gives the geometrical progression based on six.[13]

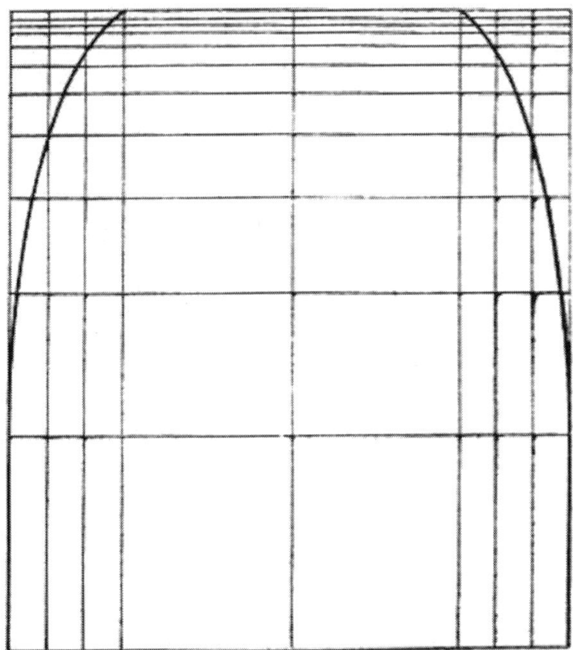

Source: Kramrisch, 1946, vol. I: 209.

Figure 5.9: Curve of *shikhara* drawn by means of *trigunasutra*

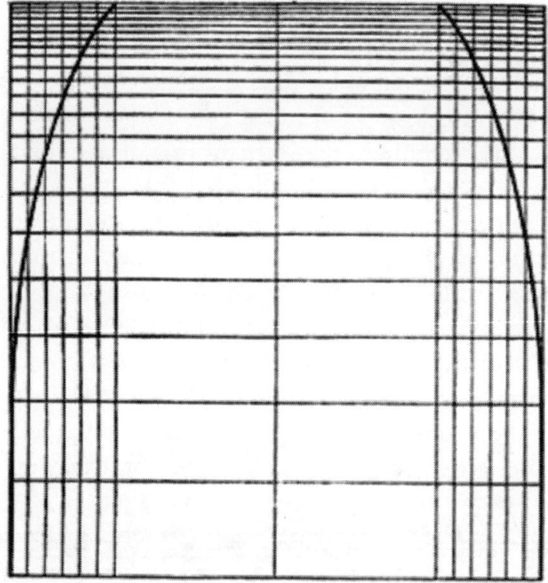

Source: Kramrisch, 1946, vol. I: 210.

Figure 5.10: Curve of *shikhara* drawn by means of *sadgunasutra*

The builders seem to have drawn a grid to mark out the line of the *shikhara*. The height of the temple *shikhara* was the height of the rectangle and the flat platform on which the *shikhara* would stand, was the base of the rectangle. Using the topmost portion of the *shikhara*, two parallel lines were drawn on either side of it, dividing the base of the rectangle into three portions. The texts reportedly say that the top of the *shikhara* was to be assigned six parts of the base while ten parts are allocated to the entire base.[14]

The rectangle at the base was in this way divided into two narrow rectangles at the sides and a larger one in the middle. The two narrow rectangles at the sides were further divided by drawing a series of vertical lines parallel to the height. The number of the divisions of the narrow rectangles varied from three divisions (using the *triguna sutra* in Figure 5.9) or six divisions (*shadguna sutra* in Figure 5.10) or any other set of divisions depending on the sutra to be followed.

Once the vertical lines were drawn, horizontal lines were drawn parallel to each other which represent a geometrical progression. In a *triguna sutra* for instance, for a given height H of the *shikhara*, the first horizontal line would be drawn at H/3. The remaining portion of the height of the rectangle would then be 2H/3. The second parallel would be drawn at (1/3)(2H/3) and the parallels would continue to be drawn at one-third of the height of the remaining portion and so on.

Once the grid was ready, the intersections of the horizontal and vertical lines were joined to get the curvilinear line of the shikhara.[15]

Magnificent Equations of Madhavacharya

This kind of computation based on the sum of an infinite series, was used by a brahmana from Kerala named Madhavacharya in the fourteenth century CE, for finding the value of trigonometrical functions. He began by using the arc of a circle equal to one-eighth of its circumference, inscribed in a square. Here is how David Pingree, one of the leading historians of mathematics and other 'exact' sciences of the olden world has translated the method to arrive at a value of π: 'Multiply the diameter (of a circle) by 4 and divide by 1. Then apply to this separately with negative and positive signs alternately the product of the diameter and 4 divided by the odd numbers 3, 5 and so on. . . . The result is the accurate circumference; it is extremely accurate if the division is carried out many times.'[16]

This, he says, gives us the infinite series:

$$C = 4D/1 - 4D/3 + 4D/5 - 4D/7 + 4D/9 \ldots$$

Which is also equivalent to the infinite series for π:

$$\pi/4 = 1 - 1/3 + 1/5 - 1/7 + 1/9 \ldots$$

The result of this formula is given using number names. It gives the value of π quite correctly to the eleventh decimal place.

Madhavacharya also found the infinite power series for the sine, cosine and the tangent by a combination of geometry and algebra, and not by using calculus.

He was doing brilliant mathematics. But he was just as much interested that the verses should be aesthetic.

He devised the *katapayadi* system in which each of the numbers 1, 2, 3, 4, 5, 6, 7, 8, 9, 0 were represented by a consonant followed immediately by a vowel. The result was that he wrote a verse which had a clear word meaning. At the same time, the numbers that the words reflected, suggested a sophisticated mathematical operation.[17]

Here is a translation of the Sanskrit verse: 'The ruler whose army has been struck down gathers together the best of advisors and remains firm in his conduct in all matters; then he shatters the (rival) king whose army has not been destroyed'. The numbers that the Sanskrit verse suggests are actually transformations of the first few terms in the infinite power series for sin θ![18]

We wonder if Indian mathematicians had achieved such a degree of sophistication, how is it that science did not progress much further; for, Madhavacharya was among the last great mathematicians produced in this country before modern times. Is it that they were interested in the aesthetics so much that any by-products that might have improved efficiency, were of little interest?

KNOWLEDGE AS A MEANS TO AN END

One possible clue could be that so much emphasis on practicality and instrumental knowledge, had reached its limits. For the one thing that is visible throughout these texts is that the results described above are rarely stated in explicit terms; rather they are assumed. Whether it is the height of the temple *shikhara* which appears to have been derived from an infinite series or it is the use of the Pythagorean Theorem to construct temple altars or the applications of indeterminate equations in commercial arithmetic, we are left to infer these axioms from the texts. Partly this may be because the *sutras* are given in verse form which imposes limitations on word usage. But nothing prohibited these scholars, great minds all, from providing prose commentaries on whatever it be that they had found.

Re-inventing the Wheel

One direct consequence of this method was that successive scholars had to work out these assumptions for themselves, making their job all the more difficult. No doubt there were schools which taught these texts and there was a school in Kerala which taught the texts of Madhavacharya for nearly 400 years after he passed away, but the emphasis was far more on rote learning and memorization of the *sutras* than proceeding further in the direction indicated by them.

The second Bhaskaracharya did write the *Lilavati* and *Bijaganita* which were basic mathematical texts but the emphasis throughout is on applications, not on the axioms themselves which were rarely stated. Students were actually expected to memorize specific problems to make it easier to solve a new one.

We wonder then whether knowledge was prized for its own sake or as the means towards achieving a limited end? The ends were achieved as we can see in Hindu architecture, but there things seemed to have stopped.

AN EXCESS OF THE GOOD LIFE?

Let us now return to the problem of productivity from where we began. Indians did have knowledge of science, so absence of knowledge could not be the reason for little effort to improve the productivity of systems.

It is entirely possible that India was so well supplied in terms of fertile land, plentiful food and plenty of space that there was little motivation to improve earnings beyond a point. We have seen that it did not take much effort to forge a rather comfortable life. Travellers for thousands of years noted with some wonder the low prices of food in India. Indian texts beginning from the Vedas onwards, are full of the availability of food and the need to give *anna-dana* or to donate food. The most heinous sin of all was not to give food to the needy one or to the guest. Among the many stories of the *Mahabharata*, the story of the 'Golden Mongoose' makes this point very well. A mongoose, whose body is half golden narrates on the occasion of the Ashwamedha Yajna conducted by Yudhishthira, the eldest Pandava prince, how he came to reach such a condition. He had been to the house of a poor householder who during a terrible famine in the land, had given the last available food in the house to an unknown guest. All other members of his household including his wife, son and pregnant daughter-in-law, also gave the guest their portions of food. After this sacrifice, the unknown guest who was none other than Dharma himself, blessed the brahmana and his family so that they all went to heaven. Such was the merit of this act that the body of the mongoose, merely from rolling in the hearth of the householder, turned to gold wherever it touched the hearth. Since then, said the mongoose, he had been looking for a sacrifice with similar merit so that he could turn the other half to gold as well.[19]

Such stories, and there are many in Indian literature, can only emerge from a culture of plenty, not poverty, or not a poverty of food at any rate.

Great Science but a Reluctance to Dirty Hands Retards Technology

Did such plenitude have any significant results for science and technology in India? One result which it may well have had, was to enable mathematical theory to flourish in the early days. Mathematics is said to be an area of knowledge which requires a certain degree of serendipity; this was one attribute that India always had in plenty. Living seemed to have been rather easy as can be seen from the large number of householders who took to the life of the mendicant and then came back to being householders. It was easy to live off the land in India. It could be even suggested that there might be an upper-caste angle too to mathematics in India: in this area of knowledge, cogitation was often an end in itself; the cogitator need not dirty their hands in actual experimentations. That also set a limit to how much this area of knowledge would progress in India.

Since there was so little pressure to improve, somehow, we could not develop precisely those means and technologies which could have increased the scale of production in India. So when the world moved into a mode where an increase in scale and use of technology became important, India began to lag. Whether it was shipping, transport, or the use of mechanical power, it was technology which enabled a sudden increase in scale to happen in the West; not so in India.

For those technologies to develop, a learning system of some kind was needed which recorded advancements made in science for posterity. That way, students need not return to first principles all the time. Rather, they could, to use the famous words of a coeval thinker from England, stand on the shoulders of giants to look further. The institutional mechanisms that at this time might enable one to stand on the shoulders of giants, though, seem to be missing in India. Come to think of it, even today, practicality is above all the most prized value in India. Learning for its own sake, rarely excites much commitment or curiosity. Nor does any effort to preserve or disseminate it. In such circumstances, planning for the future gets little value. Learning above all is an investment in an unknown future. It does not need to be justified by any immediate use at all. Once we internalize this lesson, the rest follows.

NOTES

1. Thibaut, 1875: 233.
2. Ibid., 234.
3. Nautiyal and Khanduri, 1988-9: 68-9.
4. Sukthankar, Adiparva, 47: 14-15. Retrieved on 11 February 2017 from https://sanskritdocuments.org/mirrors/mahabharata/unic/mbh01_sa.html
5. Datta & Singh, 1962, 1st published 1935, pt. 1: 59.
6. Ibid.: 85.
7. Ibid., pt. 1: 52-3.
8. Ibid., pt. 1: 219-20.
9. Ibid., pt. 1: 227-8.
10. Meister, 1979.
11. Datta, 2010.
12. Ibid.
13. Kramrisch, 1946, vol. 1: 209-10.

14. Kramrisch, 1946.
15. Ibid.
16. Pingree, 2003.
17. Ibid.
18. Ibid.
19. Sukthankar, Ashwamedhika Parva, 93: 1-84. Retrieved on 11 February 2018 from https://sanskritdocuments.org/mirrors/mahabharata/unic/mbh14_sa.html

CHAPTER 6

Improving the Learning Curve

As we delve into India's past to see and understand the nature of our strengths and weaknesses, we notice that Indian society has had and continues to have many strengths. As we have seen in the previous chapters, throughout history there were enough skills in India and enough prosperity. At least before colonial times, this was not a casteist society or xenophobic. Abul Fazl writing at the time of Akbar in the sixteenth century noticed with some wonderment the freedom in which Indians lived. 'There are no slaves in India', he reported. Instances of oppressive governance were rare, if at all. Mostly it was the kings who were under pressure to be nice to their people so as to attract more settlers to their land and ensure that more merchants came to their marts. *Zamindars* constantly tried to woo settlers to their *zamindaris*, hoping that they would bring in more fields under cultivation. They set up markets and promised safety and security to traders so as to increase the volume of trade passing through their territories. Under such circumstances and a favourable land-man ratio, the use of force to cow down people was not something that was easily possible. Babur in his *Baburnama* wrote with great wonderment about the large number of free artisans and craftsmen that existed in India and the high level of skills with which they worked. European travellers to India would speculate that it was the availability of high quality cheap food which was responsible for the low cost of production in India. One of the consequences of everyone having enough for their needs, people not suffering from serious wants, was that there was little hankering for possessing more and more. On the whole one can imagine India as a welcoming and stable society where no one wanted for food.

This feature about India being a reasonably caring society, is something that comes up again and again, in local and also foreign accounts of India. It continues to be something that distinguishes Indian behaviour. Strangers in India more often than not, got a friendly reception, then and now. Local people did not seem to feel a sense of threat. But there was it seems a caveat attached.

Strangers were welcome so long as the different mores they brought with them, were kept in isolation and not allowed to influence the local way of life. If Indians seemed to feel strongly about anything, it was the need to segregate society into little bits. Each one was welcome to do whatever they wished so long as they did it in their own social space. That about sums up the attitude of the Indians. Each social group was distinct and different from each other.

This feature of life got reflected in many different ways. There are myriads of gods in India and thousands of languages. The Indian census, done during colonial times, took the idea of difference so seriously that they even recorded languages spoken only by about 10 people or less.

All this was part and parcel of being a small-scale society. In the space where you lived, you knew everyone and everyone was known to you. The social ecosystem that developed was appropriate to that kind of existence. Documentation was barely needed. After all, if you knew everyone, why write down when each one was born and when each one died. What good would it do except waste time and energy? So India continued to exist in small groups, relatively isolated from each other. Mechanisms for exchange of information between groups hardly existed even while people came up with oral means of maintaining some memories.

In the meanwhile, Europe had found means of sharing information across social groups. The use of the written word was an important component of that process. The working of the various East India companies shows that systematic collection of information, using that information to devise impersonal protocols for working; consciously collecting and using feedback for course correction, were key operating methods. Such methods enabled the companies to run trans-atlantic operations and to scale-up their working considerably. The English East India Company had found a way to combine a certain flexibility in local working with the benefits of large-scale organization. This combination enabled the English company to be far more successful than all the others.

So Europe forged ahead to use its collective knowledge, accumulated over generations, to bring in industrialization and associated efficiencies, reduction in the cost of production and enlargement of the scale of society. Systems evolved that enabled the running of governments across continents, keeping tabs on revenues generated and controlling local disaffections.

World Became More Information-based, India got Left Behind

Basically the world changed. India, as it existed traditionally, got left behind. Only memories remained of a once wealthy and great nation. Being wealthy is about having the ability to make money. The amount of capital invested, the amount of wealth generated; all these are outcomes and not causes of growth. Economic growth in the modern world requires a different kind of sensibility. One important feature of that sensibility is to be able to move beyond face-to-face interactions and to function with impersonal rules and protocols. A related feature of the modern sensibility is to make a conscious effort to gather more and more information about any given situation, so as to be able to take a more consciously evidence-based decision. Both are features of large-scale societies.

Indian society found it difficult to generate means, whether formal or informal, of exchanging information across groups. Many innovations that developed in different parts of the country, simply died out. Whether it was in banking, iron and steel production, or pure science, what was developed, did not go to add to a general pool of learning. Inability to establish systematic networks of information and trust was, we saw, a major reason why India succumbed to colonialism.

In India there was a major transformation that happened since colonial times: the scale of operations for everything, increased dramatically. Many more people began travelling from one region to another; towns began to have larger concentrations of population, industries increased in size. Above all, the population increased manifold. In the three centuries since Akbar, from the sevententh century to the mid-twentieth century the population of India doubled from about 170 million to over 330 million at the time of Independence. In the seven decades since Independence, it more than tripled to 1,250 million. This meant that the entire eco-system in which Indians worked, changed. In India, those who wanted to forge ahead were becoming a part of this new system. Others were merely getting left behind. Unable to cope with the changes, Indians rapidly became distraught at the increase in poverty. Over the decades of colonial rule things had gone from bad to worse. Independence in 1947, brought some hope. But, even this hope could not cope with the rapidly increasing number of poor people in India. Most Indians simply found that their abilities to work effectively in this ever-changing eco-system, were wanting.

They still preferred to work as if working on a small scale, making adjustments and innovating only when a crisis forced them to.

FROM CRISIS TO CRISIS

Prime Minister Manmohan Singh, had a ring side view of things. For over two decades he worked in government departments that were tasked with improving the financial health of India. For five years, he had been Finance Minister and credited for having liberalized the Indian economy at the instance of the then Prime Minister P.V. Narasimha Rao. Then for ten years he was the prime minister of the country. On one memorable occasion, he let out what he thought was the secret of changing India: let a crisis develop and only then will Indians be ready for a change. Going from one crisis to another may be a most inefficient way of going about life, but this is what Indians seemed to be doing even while paying heavy social costs in the form of poverty, frequent riots and internal dissensions based on caste, religion and region.

In such a vitiated environment, it was all too easy for a recently independent nation to lose confidence. It is rather difficult to believe that as late as 1844, here is what a British magazine had to say about India:

Hindustan has been celebrated, in ancient and modern history, as one of the most favoured countries of the earth, abounding in the riches of nature, and teeming with the mostly costly productions of art. This remote country was partially known to the Greeks, and other nations of the West; they imported its diamonds, its spices, silks and costly manufactures. A land which contributed such expensive luxuries was readily supposed to contain inexhaustible wealth. . . . Hindustan, the seat of industry, of commerce and of the arts, when Europe was sunk in barbarism, the scene of many eventful revolutions from the Mahomedan invasions till its conquest by the armies of Britain, and inhabited by a people of peculiar manners, laws, institutions and religion, still presents a wide field for interesting inquiry and speculation'. ('Historical Sketch of the Origin, Rise, and Progress of the East India Company', 1844)

The journey from such an image of India to a point where people wonder how such a poor country could think of sending a mission to Mars, has been a traumatic one indeed.

In the past seventy odd years since Independence, Indians have not been much given to thinking big about themselves and their aspirations. So much so that considerable mirth emanated when once Prime Minister Narendra Modi mentioned the existence of plastic surgery in pre-modern times. Those folding up in mirth, including many historians of repute, did not even care to find out whether the prime minister was correct in his claim or not.

Rhinoplasty, one of the techniques of plastic surgery, was a rather common procedure in India; it had been in use for many centuries but, we forgot all that during colonial times. A failure to keep records over the centuries in effect meant that an entire civilization, and quite a bit of civilizational knowledge, had vanished. With it, went much of our self-esteem.

INDIA THINKS BIG AGAIN

However, as luck would have it, a new opportunity came by for Indians to follow at the turn of the twenty-first century. This happened because of the belief that significant computer systems of the world would not be able to cope with the change in date for the new century.

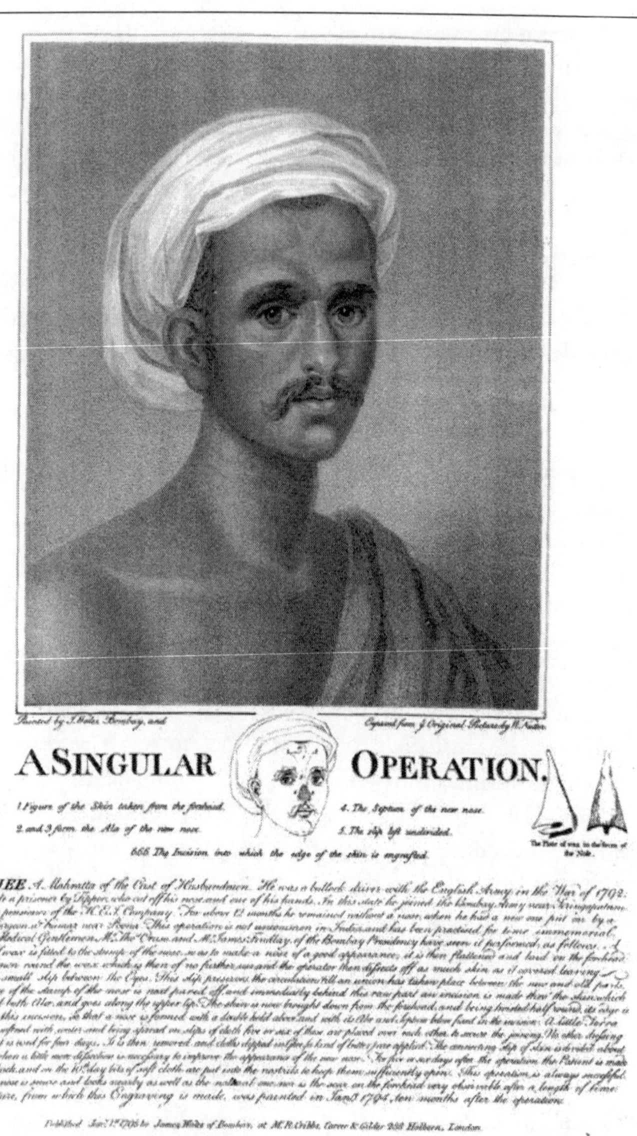

Source: The reconstruction of Cowasjee's nose was first reported in the *Hirrcarah or The Madras Gazette* on 4 August 1794 (Madras). This plate was created in 1795. Copies are also with the British Museum and the Welcome Museum.

Figure 6.1: Cowasjee gets a new nose

This was an opportunity that made Indians think big once again. As the story goes, the Western world was caught up in a hysteria about Y2K, believing that at the turn of the century the computer programmes of old would collapse because they would not be able to calculate dates properly. As it happened, India was one of the countries where, thanks to an archaic system of education, a lot of manpower existed that had skills in the use of legacy computer languages that the rest of the world had given up on long ago. Moreover, this was a set of people who were quite familiar with the English language. This archaic knowledge was put to good use in the context of proofing the world against Y2K. Whether the efforts paid off or not is a matter of speculation. What is not is that the opportunity provided Indians to think of themselves as global leaders in at least one field, that of computers. The world also began to see India not as a land of fake *gurus* and spurious *yogis* but as a modern nation of people who knew about computers. Since then the Indian computer industry has provided jobs to millions, made thousands of millionaires, a few billionaires and not looked back.

Indians have always been good with their hands and their brains; this is something of which there never was any doubt. However, the most important thing today for being on top of the world is to have a robust learning eco-system that underpins society. Learning docs not just mean formal knowledge taught in college but something much more.

Learning Eco-system Distinguishes Information from Opinion

A learning eco-system recognizes a fundamental difference between information and opinion, and tries to use that information for decision-making. This is not to say that Indians in the past have not been used to making evidence-based decisions; merely that the evidence used tended to be very local and personalized in nature. After all that is how society was organized in those days. But with fast changing technology and ever-larger and varied communities, it is no longer possible to know many people personally and uncertainty in decision-making increases. Decisions also become complicated. It is no longer possible to take good decisions on the basis of what one person knows, or what his friend knows or of what the entire neighbourhood knows. Decisions need to move beyond face-to-face interactions. The average of a thousand opinions will still remain inferior to an insight based on a systematic information set based on small samples.

So how do we encourage decision-making in India that is based on conscious efforts to collect evidence from multiple sources? That would involve at least two elements—one is the availability of information recorded systematically for years and second is the ability to make sense of that information. Both elements are equally critical to building a learning eco-system.

BUILDING A STEEP LEARNING CURVE

We began this volume by asking a question: what is it that obstructs India from being rich? We suggested earlier that perhaps the systematization of information to improve efficiencies and to improve decision-making, might well be the way forward. There is no lack of entrepreneurial skill or innovation in India. But for innovation to succeed, systematized networks of information and trust are needed to improve the learning curve. For everyone to learn the same lesson in their own individual ways and through different means, is not a very efficient method. It is very time consuming too. Systematic documentation in all walks of life so that we can learn from each other, can certainly improve the pace of growth.

In the course of this narrative, we have seen that right up to the colonial period, India possessed considerable skills in banking, in technology and in pure science. Entrepreneurial skill and a great ability to work constructively and productively with all kinds of social differences, we always had. There were few restrictions imposed on the economy; state intervention was hardly visible. Free enterprise, capital, technology and entrepreneurship are widely deemed to be key elements in any successful economy. Yet the one key element missing in all these stories has been the ability to keep systematic records of information and to use those records to learn from each other and from others.

Manikchand and Fatehchand of the house of Jagat Seth never did leave behind any diaries or record that might have helped their successor to understand a little bit of what they had achieved and how they had done it. There was no guide map to help the next Jagat Seth make a better decision when choosing between the East India Company and the *nawab* of Bengal.

For Innovation to Survive, Documentation is Critical

When we move to the story of wootz steel, again we find that while our artisans produced a kind of steel famous in the ancient world, they did not record how they achieved it. It remains a mystery till today. Clues to the mystery have been found by German researchers in a German university and by an American professor and American blacksmith working together; not by Indians in an Indian laboratory. It is truly wondrous that our ancestors achieved such things. But it is sad that with that kind of head-start in technology, India was unable to move to the industrial age much earlier.

In mathematics we see a similar story. Indian businessmen used basic mathematics for applications in commercial arithmetic. The formulations of Aryabhata and of Madhavacharya were scholastically brilliant. These were especially useful in astronomy. Our mathematicians found the infinite series. They even used it to build magnificent temples. But there they stopped. Knowledge did not jump across disciplines to act as a force multiplier for science and technology in general in India. Comparatively, mathematics and astronomy were key to the European Enlightenment.

Whatever be the sector, learning curves in India remained rather stagnant. For learning curves to be steeper, documentation and sharing of information across disciplines, certainly helps. Availability of systematic information sets can certainly help improve decision-making.

To recapitulate, the one feature that the English East India Company showed time and again was a great sensitivity to information and the ability to systematize that information to set-up protocols for decision-making. That enabled them to defeat Indian businessmen who had centuries of experience, skills, enterprise and access to a large variety of natural resources and marketable commodities of India. But then the English came from a tradition where keeping records of information was the norm. So why is it then that in Indian tradition, record-keeping was the exception rather than the rule?

THE BELIEF THAT INFORMATION SHOULD BE KEPT SECRET

In India, there could be a certain belief at work that says that learning must be kept secret. A *shloka* in an ancient chemistry text, the *Rasa-Ratna-Samuccaya* says that *rasavidya* remains powerful so long as it is secret. The verse compares shared knowledge with medicine which loses its power once it is disclosed to others. So a physician should not do anything by which the patients could learn about his medicine.[1] If keeping information secret was the norm, then passing on learning to the next generation, becomes impossible.

We Must Learn to Share Information

Whatever the origins of this idea, keeping knowledge secret has only meant that our society finds it difficult to retain any historical memories. Modern science and the modern world are so complex that we need society wide learning systems—individual workarounds are of little use. Sharing of information; documentation of ideas, it is these that are key to the learning curve.

India has always had a strong oral tradition of working. That kind of working tradition simply is not robust enough to enable efficiencies to evolve, or for learnings to be made across generations and innovations to happen.

One trouble with the oral and personalised way of working has been that memories, whether about one's life, family or nation, or about one's work, do die if not recorded systematically for posterity. We saw how the knowledge about wootz vanished in quick time even though it was something that people had been creating for centuries.

Similarly, when the diwan and subedar of Bengal, Murshid Quli Khan and Seth Manikchand, the rich banker, collaborated with each other to make the province of Bengal one of the richest *subahs* in the Mughal empire, it was probably a matter of chance. Similar collaborations had happened in other parts of India at other times. From our point of view what is pertinent is, that the learning that this kind of collaboration between state and banking could bring positive results, was quickly forgotten.

Systematic record-keeping requires the working of institutions across decades and even centuries. Institutional record-keeping in turn makes self-reflexivity possible. Such record-keeping and reflexivity provide the bedrock of an ecosystem that can inspire innovation.

The inability to keep systematic records or memories is compounded by a certain weakness in building institutions. It is institutions that help retain memories pertaining to work and public life. Documentation, memories, self-reflexivity, all these are complex tasks that need to transcend individuals and go beyond the lives of people to make a society capable of dealing with the enlargement of scales that has happened in modern times. By performing these tasks, it is institutions that outlive individuals; they enable societies to construct a certain vision of the future and to look for strategies to maximize the strengths of that society. Today it is that vision which is severely lacking as is our ability to nurture institutions. We simply go from crisis to crisis. To pre-empt crises, what we need is systematic information across the spectrum, to be used consciously for decision-making.

DOCUMENTATION IN ALL WALKS OF LIFE

The availability of systematic information requires documentation in normal, everyday work. Documentation should be built into the most routine of activities. Today we require special research-based studies to find out answers to the most routine questions—what is the disease burden in India, what is the average wage rate of a person with a diploma in business management or of an electrician, what is the average cost per ton kilometre incurred on transport of goods. This kind of information is available in millions of forms—maintained in dispensaries, factories, transport company offices, the railway yard, small businesses. We simply have not cared to systematize any of it. We are simply un-used to maintaining basic data on the parameters of normal existence.

Whichever sector we look at, we find that recording of observations not just by one person but a series of persons over time and across space, sometimes across generations, produced major innovations.

When the typhus hit the world in the early twenty-first century, doctors in England had little trouble in identifying it to be part of the strain which had devastated the world in 1918 since samples were still available in the repositories of England. Proper working of record-keeping, and information retrieval systems shortened the subsequent search for a solution.

One also recalls the story of Florence Nightingale who changed the way that hospitals worked and patients were cared for. When Florence Nightingale, widely regarded as the founder of the profession of nursing, reached the British base hospital at Scutari in Constantinople, during the Crimean War (1858), she found a dirty hospital sitting on a cesspool with filth in the corridors. Most of the patients dying in the hospital were dying not of their wounds but of typhoid and cholera. So, the first thing she did was to get scrubbing brushes and put everyone on duty at scrubbing the hospital clean. Even patients were put on the job. The hospital soon got cleaned up. The linen got washed. The emphasis on sanitation and hygiene soon paid off. The mortality rate of patients at that hospital came down by two thirds.

After returning to England, Nightingale wrote a treatise 'Notes on Hospitals'. She wrote that the sanitary condition of any hospital had an important bearing on patient wellness and mortality. More importantly, she pointed out the importance of hospital statistics like 'the proportion of recoveries, the proportion of deaths, and the average time in hospital' as important indicators of the efficiency of any hospital facility.[2] She insisted that hospitals where the patient recovered in six months could only said to be bad hospitals in comparison with hospitals where the patient recovered in six weeks. Florence Nightingale went on to make detailed observations about the manner in which hospital statistics should be maintained to ensure that the hospitals knew that they were actually curing patients rather than prolonging their agony. These ideas were accepted and implemented in the United Kingdom and adopted by the International Statistical Congress. Those practices, improved over time, still form the basis of considerable innovation in the field of healthcare.

Here was a case in which record-keeping helped to save lives and still helps to save lives everyday.

Florence Nightingale wrote all this in the year 1863 and what she wrote is now considered conventional wisdom the world over. India, though, is different. In India, even a century and a half later there is still no accepted country-wide convention or regulatory requirement either to record or collate such hospital statistics which might tell us about the efficiency of any particular hospital facility. Only a few hundred accredited hospital facilities, of their own volition, even care to record such data in the first place. Under the circumstances, learning through collective experience accumulated across the nation, over decades, simply does not happen.

Such facilities that do take care to master these learnings, achieve considerable success. A McKinsey report pointed out that Aravind Eye Care, one of the largest eye care facilities in the world 'performed cataract surgeries at one-sixth of the cost and with fewer infections than the National Health Service in the United Kingdom achieves'.[3]

What we need to do is to document and generalize these learnings so that every hospital does not need to learn about effective and efficient patient care from first principles.

Let us turn to a different sector-industry.

Most people know Henry Ford for having introduced the assembly line for production. What they may not know is its pre-history. For the assembly line to happen, what was needed first was the production of standardized interchangeable parts of machines; only such interchangeable parts could allow an assembly line to happen.

It was French gunsmith Honore LeBlanc who first seems to have conceived the idea of using standardized gun parts for the making of weapons. Such an innovation would have affected the business of other gunsmiths so his idea was not widely accepted. Meantime in England, Samuel Bentham used this idea to produce interchangeable parts for wooden pulleys in ships. Eli Whitney introduced these ideas in USA where he used them for making standardized weapon parts. It was after this that Ransom T Olds patented the idea of using an assembly line for his car manufacturing company in 1901. The result was that his production went up by 500 per cent in one year. At this point, Henry Ford innovated to generate the idea of a moving assembly line on a conveyor belt to make his Model T and revolutionized industrial production.

Ideas have long lives and innovation mostly happens in increments.

Let us go back to the stories we narrated earlier. Indian mathematicians of yore were operating in an oral tradition. By the fourteenth century they had exhausted the limits of what an oral tradition could possibly do. Innovations involving the evolution of mathematics and its use for society now shifted westwards where there were more efficient systems of learning and transmission of knowledge. In India, though, scholarship remained at a rather primitive vocational level with each generation of scholars re-inventing the wheel. An extreme example of this was the creation of the famed Jantar Mantar in the eighteenth century. These astronomical devices, much flaunted in India for their cunning in construction, were based on the *romak siddhanta*, the knowledge of astronomy from Greco-Roman times some two thousand years ago. Europe in the meanwhile, unbeknown to the makers of the Jantar Mantar, had moved far far ahead. To say the least, the Indian way of going back to first principles all the time simply because there was no process of accumulation of knowledge and its transmission was mostly through face to face interactions, was debilitating to innovation and learning.

A habit of documentation and written transmission of learning, are important since these shorten the lifespan of innovation and increase the efficiency of production.

Does this mean that only scientists, lab workers, clinics and hospitals should record the data they routinely deal with and not others? What for instance is the role of records in any social policy?

A path-breaking use of social data to overturn dearly held theories on suicide, was made by the sociologist Emile Durkheim. Till Durkheim, it was mostly believed that suicide was a matter of individual choice and often the result of a weak moral fibre. The French Criminal Justice Ministry published suicide data by age and sex for many years. Durkheim studied suicide data spread over decades to show that suicide was more a social fact than an individual decision. His seminal study of suicide published in 1897, showed that different social groups show different propensities to commit suicide. Catholics for instance, he suggested, were far less prone to commit suicide than were Protestants. He went on to show differing suicide mortality rates for different countries and groups and provided one of the earliest systematic understandings, laying the basis for those who hoped to intervene and stop such wastage of life.

Back home in India, there is hardly this kind of data available to study anything. Given limited data and poor abilities to use what is available, many researchers latch onto the easiest possible, popular explanations, howsoever incomplete. The widely-propounded expert view that farmers of India were committing suicide due to debt was one such, frequently echoing the quick wisdom of hundreds of journalists who had made, sometimes patently coloured, observations on agrarian distress in India. Those propounding this kind of facile argumentation, never stopped to ask that if the Indian farmer had been in debt for hundreds of years, how was it that indebtedness in the twentieth century had begun to drive him to suicide. They did not notice the strangeness of the fact that most of the suicides were happening not in the poorest areas of the country but in the upwardly mobile and newly prosperous regions. Actually the suicides had far more to do with a wholesale withdrawal of government from agrarian support systems, the cessation of agrarian extension services, a lack of health care and a complete absence of a risk cushion than with institutional credit.[4]

Documentation is the handmaiden of the desire to know. It is a way of life. If organized systematically and preserved long enough, it provides valuable impetus to research and innovation. The availability of documented information makes it possible for a society to use that information for more effective and efficient problem solving. It is in this area that we in India need to strengthen our efforts.

DOCUMENTATION INTEGRAL TO LARGE-SCALE SOCIETIES

We also need to remember that documentation is essential to the running of all large-scale systems. India as we have seen, has traditionally been a small-scale society. Now that things have changed, we also need to change the way in which we think and mould ourselves to meet new requirements.

Large-scale systems create a requirement that you interact frequently with people you may not know previously, with people from diverse social, ethnic and racial backgrounds. The easiest way to facilitate such interaction is through a set of widely shared and accepted rules or protocols. It is this that makes documentation an essential element of these systems. Banking for instance, needs a Know Your Customer protocol to make sure that the customer for whom a bank account is being opened is traceable. In an earlier age, these things were done based on trust and references from known persons. Reputation was therefore the most valuable attribute of any merchant. You could transfer huge sums of money through so and so banking house because of the reputation of that house. Once reputation was lost, that person would find it almost impossible to do business.

Given the scale of operations these days, all such activities tend to be anonymous. Balance sheets and PAN cards have replaced the comfort zone of knowing that this person was from your village, your city, your family, your friend circle. It also frees people from being tied to a place or a set of persons.

Documentation then becomes essential to the construction of individual identity in a way that it never was in the past. Documentation also allows all kinds of patterns to be discovered. When the State Bank of India for instance acquired data mining software around 2015, they ran it to discover all sorts of information. Newspaper reports quote the Chief General Manager SBI Kajal Ghose as saying, 'In the past, the branch managers would know the customers personally. Now with customers switching to alternate channels like online, mobile and ATMs, that level of familiarity is not there. This is where data analytics is of help.'[5]

Documentation is a crucial component of any learning ecosystem. Documentation is a tool used in large-scale societies to manage the growing complexity of daily life. It is no longer possible to take decisions only on the basis of personal knowledge. Learning curves improve and documentation happens with increasing formalization of the society and of economy. It is increasing interaction with formal institutions that leads to paperwork. A young middle-class couple two decades ago who wanted to build a house for themselves, would have had two options: (1) To save assiduously and ask their parents for a loan or (2) To approach a bank with their salary statements and some collateral. Given high interest rates of the 1990s, many people would have opted for the first choice. In which case they would not need to write a cash flow statement, get an appraisal of the property in question or get a home loan protection plan. Relatives and parents do not demand formal agreements and salary statements.

Or take the case of an employee in a *kirana* shop. Till today most such people have no provident fund, no group insurance scheme. They are all part of the informal economy and have no risk cover at all—no paperwork is needed to exist. Or take the case of a small enterprise working out of a slum colony in a metropolis. Without a *patta* of his or her land, the option of a bank loan for working capital would be ruled out. Then the owner would have to depend on moneylenders and pay usurious rates of interest. The offside is that formal financial institutions demand paperwork and guarantees.

By far the most important institution that generates paperwork is of course the state. When governments give money, they demand a paper trail. Even without giving money, every individual and every enterprise exists inside some government record. Governments do not collect data as a special effort. That is the nature of government. When an enterprise applies for a plot of land, when a household applies for an electricity connection, when an individual applies for a birth certificate, when a farmer applies for a tube well, data is automatically generated. When you pay tax, you generate data.

By definition states operate on very large scales. Managing those scales efficiently means systematization of information—this is something that Indian governments in the past have been very weak at. Where we have been able to create dedicated institutions for data collection, we have been able to generate systematic and reliable data sets like the census and various NSSO surveys. However, data collection that is part and parcel of routine government functioning is rarely systematized or even seen as being of value. We do not know the average time taken to decide a court case, the average time taken to process an application for an electricity connection. Most of these indicators refer to economic or social costs. So the average cost of cargo per tonne-kilometre is an important business cost. The average time taken to decide a trade dispute is an important business cost. The average time taken to decide a police case has a social cost. The examples go on and on. For a transition to a large-scale society, it is this kind of information that is needed. Nor is this a role that states can abdicate without heavy social costs.

TAKING FEEDBACK OR DATA AND ITS USES

A learning ecosystem also implies a society that is self-aware and that is constantly taking feedback about whatever it does. Being self-reflexive and taking feedback is the only way in which one could introduce a mid-course correction or locate a possible problem. This is what enables a society to adapt to a change in circumstances.

Indians have generally been slow to put in self-correctives in place. One way of eliciting feedback is simply to evaluate courses of action all the time. That is one of the principal uses to which data is put. Rarely so in India.

There are, however, exceptions that prove the rule. One such exception has been the success story scripted by the Indian Space Research Organization (ISRO). In the recent past, one of the more spectacular successes achieved by ISRO was the Mars Mission, known as the Mangalyaan. Prime Minister Narendra Modi reportedly applauded the project and said that in this mission, success was achieved at a low cost of 73 million US dollars, which was about the same as the per kilometre fare for an auto-rickshaw to Mars.

What we should be looking at is the method of ISRO. And that method is revealed far more in how they take their failures than how they take their successes.

In 2010-11, in the aftermath of the failure of the launch of the GSLV-F06, the seventh mission of the GSLV (Geosynchronous Satellite Launch Vehicle) on 25 December 2010, ISRO set-up a preliminary Failure Analysis Committee which reported that 'the primary cause of the failure is the untimely and inadvertent snapping of a group of 10 connectors located at the bottom portion of the Russian Cryogenic Stage'.[6] ISRO then set-up a detailed Failure Analysis Committee to go into the reasons why this happened and how to ensure that such an event would not recur. Within three years of this, ISRO successfully launched the eighth flight of the GSLV, the GSLV-D5 on 5 January 2014.

In ISRO, scientific research, discussion and taking feedback have been part of a long tradition of learning from failures. The results have been rather consistently spectacular.

It is not that other institutions in India do not learn from feedback. They do. The only difference is that the process is lethargic and uneven; takes years, if not decades. That is a loss of time, energy and money that India can ill-afford.

The government, for example, ran a rural poverty alleviation programme called the Integrated Rural Development Programme (IRDP) for over twenty years from 1978-9 till 1999. The programme was aimed at providing soft loans to poor people for buying assets with the objective that such people cross the poverty line. It became clear by 1996-7, as revealed in the Ninth Five Year Plan document, that an amount of Rs. 28,047.65 crore had been invested in the scheme and that 15.96 per cent of the people so assisted, had crossed the current poverty line. After two decades of desultory results it dawned that poor people preferred consumption loans rather than the loans that the IRDP offered. It was then that the IRDP was restructured. What is important here is that it took twenty years for any learning to happen. This is far too flat a learning curve to be acceptable.

Taking feedback is about having steeper learning curves. Setting up effective and efficient feedback systems is a good way to be self-reflexive.

It is a historical fact that we Indians were so sure of ourselves and of our achievements that we never cared to set-up feedback systems or even to be curious. Khafi Khan, the historian who lived during Mughal times, was busy extolling the wealth of his emperor and about the power of the Mughals when the English East India Company was busy changing the way manufacturing and trade was done in India. The Mughals never even cared to learn about these changes. Their indifference to the major transformations being initiated in India by the English, would in the end cost them their empire.

The triumph of Western liberal democracy is about the ability to constantly take feedback about whatever it is doing, good or bad. And to craft policies based on that feedback. The taking of feedback is what would give new life to every institution. This is what allows for course correction as and when correction is needed. Policies that are tuned to ground reality, help achieve better outcomes.

THE ROLE OF KNOWLEDGE INSTITUTIONS

To assist societies in becoming self-aware, to provide feedback about social policies, to preserve institutional memories, knowledge institutions play a critical role. Given their unique location—of being there in society and yet outside it; they have the capacity to maintain a certain distance from a given situation and to provide feedback. They also serve as the site of information exchange between different groups of people. They are important in that they determine the level of skills in any society.

In history, India has had a rich tradition of learning. The Indian system of learning was a decentralized system. Students might go to live with their guru, to be a part of his household and learn new skills. Alternatively, in the small towns and villages, parents often got together to hire a teacher to teach their children. Numeracy, basic skills in arithmetic and language, these were commonly taught in local schools. A seventeenth-century biography, the *Ardhakathanaka* written by a Jain merchant in the Agra-Jaunpur region, tells us that the merchant Banarasidas joined a local school at the age of eight. There he was taught the basics of reading and writing by a brahmana pandit. He learned for a period of one year; after that he learned about business with his uncle. Later at age fourteen, Banarasi-das went to stay with Pandit Devdutt where he learnt various Sanskrit texts, about *jyotisha* and languages.[7]

A Chinese traveller to India in the seventh century CE also said that children in India were instructed from age seven onwards. The five *vidyas* of instruction that he mentioned are: (1) Sabdavidya (Grammar and Philology); (2) Silpasthanavidya (of Arts and Mechanics), (3) Chikitsavidya (Medicine), (4) Hetuvidya (Logic), (5) Adhyatmavidya (Theology/Philosophy).[8]

Most such education however seems to have been at the initiative and cost of local people. The learning system consisted of small independent units whether *gurukula* or university or artisanal workshop, that operated entirely independently of each other. These units received patronage from kings, nobles, the rich and even the poor but were largely autonomous. Relative freedom from want and independence of operation, were their strengths.

Some famous institutions of learning like Nalanda and Vikramashila that survived over hundreds of years, were associated with the Buddhist *sangha*. In their heyday, these were rich institutions, patronized by the ruler of the day and often by the laity too. They were often given grants of land by the ruler. Sometimes uncultivated land was granted, the expectation being that the *sangha* would take a lead in cultivating it. As a considerable employer of labour, the *sangha* played an important role in the economic life of the community. But the wealth of these institutions also made them susceptible to attack. With the Turkish raids on India in the eleventh and twelfth centuries, these formal institutions were destroyed. While they existed, the monasteries of the *sangha* had sufficient resources at their disposal to be more or less autonomous—that was their strength.

One major weakness of education in the *sangha* was isolation from other streams of learning in society. Books on chemistry, architecture, medicine, among others were written by scholars and practitioners in isolation from formal institutions of learning. This feature of segmentation of knowledge, has continued to trouble the Indian system of education.

The colonial government was indifferent to education in India. It allowed the school system, such as it existed, to shrivel up for want of funds. Before the English company established rule in India, school education was mostly funded by families themselves. In the 1820s when some revenue officials in south India, conducted a survey of schools and colleges in Oriya, Kannada, Malayalam and Tamil-speaking areas, they found 1,62,626 students studying in 11,575 schools and 1,094 colleges.[9] These institutions were mostly subsidized by the parents of students. Assuming that half the population of 1.28 crore (recorded for the areas surveyed by the officials) was of school-going age, this meant that 2.5 per cent of the population was studying in these institutions. Remarkably, 49.5 per cent of all these students belonged to the Shudra caste.[10] And yet, under English rule, education was systematically neglected.

If there are any continuities to be seen in this respect in modern-day India, surely that is a matter of some concern. What a modern state system could have done was, to retain the strength the Indian system already had of relative autonomy and helped it by providing more funds, ensured an inclusive admission policy and built networks to facilitate the exchange of information.

In retrospect, the only thing the Indian state did do was to encourage an inclusive admission policy. For the rest, it destroyed the autonomy of educational institutions, starved them of funds, stopped competition between them and did little to build networks for knowledge exchange. And in the days of privatization, the refrain is that universities and colleges should generate their own funding and that research and innovation is the job of the private sector alone.

A great advantage that the Indian education system had in pre-colonial times was that it gave the teacher freedom to teach what he or she wanted. That is one advantage we gave away in the desire to bureaucratize everything. Knowledge institutions are very different creatures from bureaucracies. Bureaucracies are about power, resources and hierarchy. Bureaucratic rules are meant to put checks on the use of power and the discretion that goes with it. Government bureaucracies are obsessively concerned with processes and rules—outcomes are almost irrelevant.

Academic institutions are comparatively powerless—their strength comes from their local roots and their connection with students. Students merely by existing and by entering the job market, connect teaching institutions to the real world. Outcomes are real and are made public every placement season. Strengthening those connections would improve accountability of the institutions. If the NAAC accreditation framework for teaching institutions has become so robust in the last three decades, it is because institutions need to attract students by providing information and because students want to know which college to choose.

And yet with excessive centralization, it is this connection of the institution with the market that has been harmed in India in the decades since Independence. The affiliating university system that characterizes Indian universities, exists in no other country in the world. Pakistan is the other exception. It is a system that subordinates the college teacher entirely to the affiliating university. Syllabi are to be decided in the affiliating university system by a lengthy decision making process at university level. Some large universities even have over 800 colleges affiliated to them. We are told that centralization of this variety has been done in the name of quality of education. However, were any feedback to be taken about the actual results of the affiliating university system, they would show that the results are quite the opposite. Once college teachers have neither any authority, neither any stake in deciding what they can teach or the freedom to examine their students, they lose interest in the matter. In many public universities, syllabi have not been changed for decades. Neither have the fees been increased. Colleges in many states have found workarounds—they upgrade syllabi where it is possible to charge more fees to students and therefore students demand better services. To teach such courses, colleges hire better teachers; other students are left to fend for themselves.

If knowledge institutions are to be strengthened and these weaknesses addressed, governance reforms to work towards autonomy of all colleges are critical. Equally importantly, cross-fertilization of ideas needs to be encouraged by providing mechanisms for exchange of personnel between academia and industry, between academia and government.

Ironically, academic institutions are the one resource that Indian governments have failed to use for systematizing the enormous amounts of data generated on a daily basis. Traffic data can be used for transportation systems modelling. Data on the supplementary nutrition programme can be used to generate significant insights. For that kind of data exchange, what we need are formal mechanisms.

OF INFORMATION AND OPINION: A BELIEF THAT COST AN EMPIRE

In the absence of formal mechanisms and of institutions, it becomes easy to confuse information and opinion in small-scale societies. A manifestation of this confusion is the idea that as you think, so must all others. In the eighteenth and nineteenth centuries in India, we see again and again, Indian rulers acting on the belief that all soldiers, irrespective of nationality, race, caste and class, must behave the same way. They believed that if they paid the soldiers enough, they would serve in their armies. The armies of Indian rulers were a polyglot of different nationalities. The armies of the Maratha chiefs employed Arabs, Abyssinians, soldiers from Awadh, Sikhs, Sindhis and European officers of different nationalities. No Maratha chief had ever cared to set up any institution for formal training of their officers—they relied exclusively on the military labour market in India. Surely the English East India Company relied on this labour market too but not exclusively so. From the 1750s onwards, the English government had been sending regular army troops to fight in India. The East India Company paid the government for the use of all these services but the value of military training and even more importantly, the belief that these soldiers were serving their king and country, had no price. In this sense, English commanders could depend on their officers and troops in a way that no Indian ruler could. Surely there were any number of English and European adventurers who took service in the armies of the Indian rulers to make their fortunes but they were essentially mercenaries.

It is popularly believed that the English company won various wars in India due to superior technology. Were this opinion to be tested against the records of those times, it would not stand the test. The Marathas had been using artillery since the late seventeenth century. Initially the artillery was not especially effective but they, like other Indian rulers, learnt a great deal from the European companies. The cannon and small arms they manufactured eventually were not only good, often they surpassed the firearms of the Europeans. After the critical battle of Assaye in September 1803 at which the English East India Company defeated the forces of Daulat Rao Sindhia and other chieftains, Major General Arthur Wellesley, the commander-in-chief from the English side, remarked, 'Our loss has been very severe; but we have got more than 90 guns, 70 of which are the finest brass ordnance I have ever seen. . . '.[11]

A military historian has pointed out, 'The 1803 campaign showed that overwhelming firepower was not a guarantor of victory; if it was then the Marathas would have won the war'.[12]

The Marathas had more firepower and greater numbers (since the English were outnumbered at Assaye), yet a critical resource they were short of was, trained manpower to lead their armies.

In the aftermath of the Third Battle of Panipat in 1761 where the flower of Maratha cavalry wilted on the battlefield, the Maratha chiefs were severely short of officers. While they were heavily dependent on cavalry, they had observed the value of an infantry and of an artillery in the wars conducted by the European companies. Many Maratha chieftains started acquiring infantry units. They strengthened their artillery units and set-up factories for the manufacture of small arms and of cannon. For performing all these tasks, they needed officers and European adventurers were easily available. And these adventurers rose to the highest ranks of Indian armies. Two Frenchmen—first Benoit La Borgne (known better as Benoit de Boigne) and then Pierre Cuillier aka General Perron, became the commanders-in-chief of the army of the Sindhias. In turn de Boigne and Perron employed large number of French, English and Scottish soldiers of fortune in the army.

Both de Boigne and even Perron who eventually betrayed the Sindhias, were good soldiers. They consistently counselled their masters, first Mahadaji Sindhia and then his grand nephew Daulat Rao Sindhia, not to fight against the English company. Perhaps they realized that in a crunch, Englishmen, howsoever well-trained, could not be depended upon to fight people of their own nationality.

This went against the beliefs of the Maratha rulers—they seemed to believe that money would buy good services of a mercenary and that as values go, money topped the scale. These beliefs were very soon put to the test. The company was well aware of this weakness of the Sindhias. Once war seemed inevitable with Daulat Rao Sindhia, the English East India Company followed a strategy of stripping the Maratha army of its officer corps, by using any and all means.

Some months before the critical battle fought at Assaye, Governor-General Wellesley wrote to his brother Major General Arthur Wellesley the following missive: 'In the event of hostilities, you will take proper measures for withdrawing the European officers from the service of Scindiah, Holkar, and of every other chief opposed to you. You are at liberty to incur any expense requisite for this purpose, and to employ such emissaries as may appear most serviceable. . . .'[13]

More was to come. As per plan, on the eve of the Battle of Assaye, on 29 August 1803, the Governor-General in Council issued an open offer addressed to all British subjects in the military service of the Sindhias, the Raja of Berar or any other ruler allied to these rulers. It offered to all such British subjects who chose to retire from the armies of these chiefs, a provision in the employment of the East India Company equal to such pay and allowances that they had already been receiving from these rulers. Further it said that the provision would continue till such time as those officers chose to serve the company and even after quitting the service of the company, reasonable remuneration would be offered. Those who did not choose to avail of the offer would be deemed to have forfeited the right to protection of the British government. The proclamation extended the offer to the subjects of France or of any other foreign European or American state in the military employment of Daulat Rao Sindhia or the Raja of Berar or any other Maratha chief allied with them. The offer of equal pay was even extended to all non-commissioned officers and sepoys formerly in the service of the Company and to all other persons native of the British territories in India who were serving in the armies of these Maratha chieftains.[14] This proclamation was followed up on 16 September 1803 by yet another—this one held that all British subjects who still continued to serve in the armies of the enemy during a war, would be held guilty of high treason and that they had till 1 November to resign and seek the protection of the British government.[15]

Sindhia had already got wind of the discussions that would have preceded the proclamation. And in June-July of 1803, he had prescribed a new oath for his officers, requiring them to fight all enemies, irrespective of nationality. Dudrenec, an officer of Sindhia, refused to administer the oath to the officers of his brigade, fearing that most would rather quit than accept it; but it was administered in the other brigades, and the British officers almost without exception refused to take it. They were summarily dismissed.[16]

The results of the proclamation were catastrophic to the Marathas. After the proclamation of 29 August 1803, most of the officer corps of Sindhia resigned their commands and went over to the English. A study of the ex-Maratha pensioners of the company showed 110 persons who had served with Sindhia and Holkar before the Anglo-Maratha wars: this included 91 commissioned officers: 23 Frenchmen, 8 continentals and 60 British and British Eurasians.[17]

At one stroke, not only had the English company destroyed the command structure of the Marathas, they had secured access to all the critical inside information that these officers brought with them. If after all these blows, the Marathas still fought so valiantly as to cause severe losses to the English, it is ample tribute to the courage of the troops—1,500 English dead or wounded (of 4,500) against 1,200 Marathas. Wellington himself said that it took bayonets to force the Marathas away from their guns. The Marathas deserved better leaders. In later years, when asked which of his battles in Asia and Europe had been the toughest, Wellington replied 'Assaye'.

Indian rulers had for many centuries employed different nationalities in their armies with little distinction. They had believed that people would serve their paymasters for money alone. Those beliefs crumbled in the face of reality. Information beats opinion every time. The only way to distinguish one from the other is by way of reality testing.

BUILDING A LEARNING SOCIETY

We now return to the question that we had asked in the beginning of this book. How do we make India a wealthy nation once again? Our answer is that in order to do that, we need to build a learning society. It is a learning society that systematizes information, that consciously takes feedback, that uses systematic feedback for decision-making. It is a learning society that builds robust institutions for knowledge exchange, for innovation and to enable continuous increases in productivity. Every generation needs to add to the existing storehouse of knowledge in society.

Building a learning society, requires far more than an increase in the education budget. What we need to do is to build a supportive eco-system that would strengthen innovation and that would act as a force multiplier. Every aspect of modern life requires such an eco-system in which to flourish.

We would suggest that successful societies in the modern world are societies with a robust learning ecosystem that enables them to make systems work to the greater benefit of all. Equally they are about providing an opportunity to everyone to participate in economic growth. Above all, they are about being able to foresee threats and opportunities and adapt quickly. Such a society is a society that is self-reflexive; that constantly takes feedback. A learning ecosystem is one that prizes evidence over intuition.

It is the ability to generate new knowledge and to do innovative research which is the key to the making of wealth. It is this ability that needs to be fine-tuned. The best way to fine-tune that ability, is to build a culture of excellence and to build a learning eco-system, a suitable ecology of the mind, if you will.

It is a lazy habit of mind which subscribes to the general idea that the Western nations became prosperous mostly because of the colonies which they expropriated. Surely, they did do that. That the British looted Bengal and emptied its treasury within twenty years of the Battle of Plassey, is not at dispute. Nor is it disputed that the British connection was a drain of wealth. But to concentrate only on that is merely to befool ourselves.

We should stop looking for feel-good arguments which only see India as a victim. India is certainly not a victim any more. We have the ability and skills to do far better for ourselves and to regain our place in the world and we have no need of such arguments of victimhood.

The fact remains that the West possessed a deep vein of curiosity, a deep desire to learn and above all a tradition of documenting whatever they had learnt. This combined with natural aggression and the ability to organize their taxation system effectively, gave them competitive advantage. India may have been superior in intellect, skills, natural wealth and riches but it had no answer to this combination of systematized information for decision-taking and the ability to create organizations that worked on explicitly stated rules and standard operating protocols. The triumph of the West was the triumph of a knowledge society. As every school teacher knows, praise helps build self-esteem and the desire to do well but, the ability to do well, requires far more.

It is the building of a learning society then which is the task before us. For that we need to ensure that a culture of excellence takes deep root, not just in our institutions of learning but also in our institutions in general. The desire to excel is above all a state of mind.

To document what we do and build a storehouse of information to facilitate cutting-edge research; to use that information to build self-reflexivity about everything that we do; and to energize our educational institutions to build world-class human capital; these are the key tasks before us. It is these tasks that would give our society the resilience to adapt to changing circumstances and to constantly re-invent ourselves.

NOTES

1. Supplement *Rasa Ratna Samuccaya.* Chapter 6, verse 72.
2. Nightingale, 1863.
3. McKinsey Global Institute, 2015.
4. Rajivlochan, 2006.
5. Shetty, 2015, Retreived 25 January 2017, from http://timesofindia.indiatimes.com/business/india-business/SBI-uses-big-data-mining-to-check-defaults-biz-loss/articleshow/48397829.cms
6. Indian Space Research Organisation, 2010.
7. Banarasidas, 2007.
8. Hiuen Tsang, 1918: 78.
9. Dharampal, 2000: 18-19.
10. Dharampal, 2015: 213.
11. Wellington, 1859: vol. IV: 180. Letter to Major Malcolm, 26 September 1803.
12. Cooper, 2003: 210.
13. Martin, 1837, III: 156, 27 June 1803.
14. Proclamation of the Governor-General in Council, dated 29 August 1803. Bengal Papers 1803: 215.
15. Letter of Governor-General in Council to the Secret Committee, dated 24 December 1803. Bengal Papers 1803: 213.
16. Pemble, 1976: 394.
17. Ibid.: 393.

CHAPTER 7

The Way Forward

In the previous chapters we noticed that there is a direct relation between knowledge, governance and economic growth. It is in the interest of the state to help businesses grow. Governments that help businesses to prosper through the use of knowledge, reap huge returns. Societies where businesses prosper, are societies that grow rich and stable. What the state needs to do is to create the eco-system that allows all to grow rich in an equitable fashion. In India little thought has been given to the interconnections between knowledge, governance and economic growth even after the country, one of the richest and militarily most powerful societies in the world of those times, was enslaved to a small Western trading company that succeeded in controlling India precisely because of its superior access to knowledge and synergies between its businesses and the institutions of the state.

It hardly needs to be stated that higher business production can lead to more jobs, higher wages and a robust tax base. For countries to grow rich, business productivity needs to improve. A sustainable strategy to improve business capabilities would be, to provide resources that businessmen cannot generate for themselves without incurring extraordinary costs. Security, especially of property and, regulations that are stable, fair and implementable, are not things that businesses can create. Only the authorities of the state can. Similarly, providing an ever expanding pool of skilled manpower, which has skills to re-skill itself in harmony with changing needs and requirements too, is something that only the state can provide. The serendipity needed to pre-empt problems and needs too comes from robust knowledge institutions which depend substantially on the state. Following upon this we suggest the following points on which the state and people of India need to focus as they move forward in the twenty-first century.

SECURITY OF PROPERTY: USES OF DOCUMENTATION

A key component of any eco-system favourable to business is the availability of low-priced real estate, whether on sale or for rent. India is one of the few countries where the real estate sector has seen an almost continuous rise in prices for nearly a century. Much of the rise has to do with urbanization and to that extent it is positive. But much of the rise also has to do with a lack of transparency in the land market, with opaque and out-dated government procedures and a high level of black money. All these elements have led to the emergence of a massive land mafia.

One key to the opacity of the land market is a system of land records that is currently in shambles, especially in the urban sector. In India, it is the Department of Revenue in government that is vested with the charge of maintaining land record ownership data. There has been some effort to digitize ownership data but there has been little systematic effort to do ground proofing. Ground proofing in this case would mean matching the ownership data with the actual position on the ground. That in turn entails a systematic survey of land, updation of the survey numbers and seeding the land records with ownership data. Land mapping through satellite imagery, drones, all the technology that is needed for such a task is available; what we need is the will to execute it.

We have already seen that the Adhaar project has brought in considerable returns not just to the government but to the citizen by providing a secure identity to Indian citizens. Similarly, given technology available today, it is easily possible to devise a unique ID for lands. Plots of land could be assigned unique IDs based on any number of parameters; the easiest would be location of any piece of land on a given road. Once the roads are numbered for each municipal area, the properties could be numbered too. Then all that is needed is a satellite survey of the land to construct a basic map and a ground level survey to verify the map.

Satellite mapping of land in some areas been done in Andhra Pradesh, Delhi, Karnataka and Maharashtra in recent years. But unique IDs for land are yet to be allocated state-wide in any systematic fashion. Given the fact that government departments often function in silos, the same piece of land often is differently numbered in the records of the urban local body and the Department of Revenue. Cross-matching is rendered impossible. Very often even within the same local body, property numbers are changed over time. This makes it very difficult, if not impossible, to establish continuity in ownership of any piece of land.

Lack of ground proofing for decades now has led to a huge rise in land-related litigation. Lawyers benefit, the land mafia benefits, corrupt bureaucrats and politicians benefit from the resulting free-for-all. Yet land records is the one sector no government is willing to touch even though the lack of systematization is holding back India considerably.

Systematization of the land record database could result in substantial correction in land prices, reduction in land-related litigation, security to the landholders and more revenues to the government. Even when we look at history, systematic measurement of land is only associated with Sher Shah Sur, and with Akbar's administration, some 450 years ago. The British colonial administration did introduce some systematization. But since the ouster of the British the previous free for all has returned. One does wish that historical continuities of this variety could be avoided.

BUILDING KNOWLEDGE RESOURCES: FUNDING RESEARCH TO IMPROVE PRODUCTIVITY

Knowledge has been a key resource for any business to grow since times immemorial. Therefore, it seems somewhat amazing that the Indian state hesitates to fund research on a large-scale. After all, to say that research benefits businesses so they should make the requisite investment, presumes that businesses must look beyond mere profits. That is neither here nor there.

At the same time most discussions about research and innovation acknowledge that the success rate of ideas in the real world is low. For every idea that works, there are thousands that do not. That does not mean we should stop trying. To take just one example, the drug company Pfizer had been working on a promising heart drug for over a decade in 2006. They had pumped in nearly a billion US dollars into developing and testing the drug. And then they found out that the drug had led to 82 deaths and that the drug caused heart problems instead of solving them.[1] Pfizer pulled the plug on the drug immediately and all trials were stopped. It was a costly lesson in failed research. The public got to know about it, perhaps because of the scale of the matter and the number of deaths. The world is littered with such stories. But to ask industries to pay such high sunk costs, is an unrealistic expectation.

It is difficult to leave such calculations entirely to the market. Markets are a good guide to the immediate economic value of ideas but they can be a poor guide to intrinsic value. That is because markets have no long-term perspectives. Gestation periods of ideas are far too long for research and innovation to be left entirely to the mercies of the market.

We only need to remember all the illustrious people in the history of science and invention who died unsung. That is in the nature of research. Today every school child knows about the science of heredity and that Gregor Mendel, the Austrian monk, was the father of that science. Mendel did his experiments on pea plants for eight years and when he published his work in the 1860s, there was hardly any response. Historians of science have said that perhaps people at that time were looking for whether new species could be produced from existing ones, hence there was little market for the processes by which specific traits were transmitted within the same species. It was not till forty years after his death, that his ideas received wide recognition. Had Mendel been asked to seek funds from a private benefactor, he and many others like him, would have been unable to do that kind of research.

It is only governments that can have that kind of long-term perspective. Cutting edge research is too important to be left entirely to market mechanisms. It is here that we need the government to step in and provide real time support, financial and otherwise, for research into the sciences and society. It is governments that can best invest in building the wealth of the nation.

Given that Indian industry has been reluctant to pursue research goals, it is reasonable for governments to look towards funding research in government labs and in higher education institutions (whether government or private) and also to projects where industry is willing to pitch in some resources. Cutting down drastically on funding to higher education institutions has created a serious disconnect with industry which in turn has had serious negative consequences for the levels of learning among the student population. Figures for the year 2016-17 show that today the higher education sector gets about 3.8 per cent of India's annual expenditure on science research of an estimated Rs. 104,864 crore.[2] And yet all these universities and colleges put together account for nearly one-third share of India's annual output in terms of research papers and publications.

In respect of patents, the figures are even more telling.

For the year 2016-17, 45,444 applications were filed in India for patents. Only 29 per cent of these applications came from Indian applicants—the remaining patents were from foreign companies/nationals in India. When we look at the 13,195 Indian applicants, a break-up of the applications shows the following:

TABLE 7.1: BREAK-UP OF INDIAN APPLICANTS FOR PATENTS FOR THE YEAR 2016-17[3]

Category	Numbers Applied in this Category	Per cent of Applicants
Higher Education sector (Both private and government)	1,467	11
Organized private sector	4,738	36
Government Laboratories and Institutions	917	7
Individuals	6,073	46
Total	13,195	100

Source: See endnote 3.

No private institution in India even came close to the figure of 1840 patents filed by one single US major—Qualcomm. Indian industry does not seem to see much value in investing in research.

When we consider the minimal funding made available to institutions of higher education, their performance is indeed commendable. It is the nature of knowledge institutions to generate knowledge—however, much rules might emasculate them. If these institutions could be provided more research funds and set free of excessive controls, there is a fair chance that they will create great value for society.

While it is true that highly committed people continue to work on research despite low incentives, they deserve something more than the indifference that is offered currently. A one size fits all approach is only geared to the lowest common denominator; it can produce bureaucrats but, scientists are more difficult to make.

HELPING BUSINESSES WITH MARKET INTELLIGENCE AND KNOWLEDGE ARCHIVING

Quite apart from new knowledge, systematizing existing information sets can be very valuable to industry too. Market intelligence is an extremely valuable resource; it can be very costly too and is beyond the reach of most entrepreneurs. Much could be done to help businesses in this regard. A key player here is the Department of Commerce in India. Currently much of their efforts include providing various custom duty remissions to exporters. The department could easily be asked to specialize in different sectors and build-up some intelligence about international markets for different products. It could be an excellent helping hand. This is what the commercial and trade departments of other countries routinely do. If it so chooses, the Indian government could easily emulate them. There already exists a Commercial Officer attached to Indian Consulates in other countries—a knowledgeable officer could be valuable in such a role. If all these resources could coordinate with each other, generating actionable intelligence should not be difficult.

There already exists a Market Access Initiative for supporting participation in trade fairs, reverse buyer-seller meets for attracting foreign buyers, capacity building of exporters and various market surveys. More investment by way of financial and human resources in such initiatives could go a long way to help.

Market intelligence needs to be collected consistently for years and decades to be useful. Unfortunately, there is very little continuity in government policies regarding collecting information. Looked at from the perspective of the last seventy years, consistent support to business has hardly been a hallmark of Indian governments. Nor do businessmen demand more support.

Market intelligence can help in a large number of ways including brand-building. Lack of major Indian brands is a serious weakness in the Indian export scenario. Helping Indian businesses build their brands should be a key goal of state agencies.

Indian firms do not always realize the value of investing in market intelligence. We saw a recent example of this in how the Chinese successfully entered the Indian market for mobile phones. In the past decade or so, many Indian companies like Micromax and Karbonn had captured much of the Indian mobile phone market with their low-priced products. They were able to offer such low prices by getting the phones manufactured and even designed in China. Along with the outsourcing however, these companies were passing on key information about Indian consumer markets to their rivals. Very soon Chinese companies were in a position to access Indian markets themselves—at this point they no longer needed the Indian companies. In the last few years Chinese brands like Xiaomi, Vivo and Oppo have gained substantially in market share over their Indian rivals. Companies like Micromax are now shifting production back to India and focusing much more on product design than before. Long-term plans in business need to focus on market intelligence and on getting control over more and more of the value chain.

The basic activity of recording the experiences of various businessmen for use by their peers, could be helpful too. Without knowledge archiving, each businessman learns exactly the same lesson, makes the same mistake and pays the same price. Learning from first principles all the time keeps the learning curve rather flat. Programmes for writing case studies for use in various executive education and management courses could be a good way to address this issue. Management education in India today relies heavily on case studies from the West. Indigenous examples can certainly help to address that lacuna. Surely we can generate our own learning resources from the shared experience of our businesses. Information is the most valuable resource of all.

STREAMLINING GOVERNMENT DATA SETS

By far the largest information resources vest with the government. If the government in India were to systematize all the data they are sitting on, it is a knowledge goldmine—not only for planning public policy but for businesses as well. Census data is something that governments do make some effort to systematise and the pay-offs are considerable. Some decades ago, the then chairman of ITC (Indian Tobacco Company) used census data to recognize the youthfulness of the Indian population and its lack of wealth. Therefrom they devised the concept of packing their Charms brand cigrattes in small retail packs The concept of the small retail pack took the company to unexplored markets and brought huge profits. Today, when properly anonymized and used, information can generate all sorts of value.

A tool to get governments at different levels to dust off the data and get it out of record rooms could be to allocate 1 per cent of all budgets to programme evaluation and monitoring. After all, if 99 rupees out of 100 is used for implementation, surely 1 rupee could be used for evaluating whether the money spent has actually achieved anything. Different departments within government could cross verify each other and as an external check, 10 per cent of the data could always be validated by third parties. Colleges and universities would be happy to do the task. One advantage of using knowledge institutions for such tasks is that they add data to the public domain so shared knowledge resources get bumped up.

While these knowledge resources vary in each sector, broadly three kinds of data can be found in most sectors.

1. Data about households, classes of income and of expenditure; in case of farmers, some specific inputs that they purchase are also recorded to the extent that these are subsidised by government.
2. Data about skill sets among the working population and
3. Data about productivity.

All three kinds of data are important. Surely we do have dedicated organizations for data collection like the National Sample Survey Organisation or the Central Statistical Organization and the Registrar General of India for the decennial census. But quite apart from these periodic surveys, government departments routinely acquire a lot of data merely on account of the nature of their tasks—it is this that is neglected. For instance, transport departments collect information about driving licenses issued to vehicle owners and to that extent they have the profile of vehicle ownership and kinds of vehicles. The railways have information about freight costs by rail. Electronic way bills have information about freight rates for road transport. The list goes on and on.

Information in itself is a valuable resource, quite apart from its value in planning for the future.

A look at just one or two sectors is sufficient to tell us this. Increasingly many state governments use health insurance as a tool to purchase health services for their populations. The data generated on diseases and treatments, amounts to the health profile of the populations insured. Today the information is simply sitting in the servers either of insurance companies or the government. If properly captured and analysed, that data can tell us the health status of our population. Rather than selling off the data for a quick profit, it should be anonymized and made available to medical colleges, researchers and, public health departments for research purposes. Even more importantly, it should be analysed and given back to health facilities to improve patient care.

Throughout the developed world, patient related process and outcome measures are used to gather information to help improve delivery of health services. Door to needle time to measure the time taken to initiate therapy on patients suffering from heart attack; surgical site infection rates; numbers of repeat surgeries within 30 days—these are measures that can provide valuable feedback to caregivers.

An obsession with short-term outcomes and with money has led to the identification of expenditure as a key outcome. This can lead to perverse situations where a health care centre is declared complete; yet no operations can be conducted there because the operation theatre could not pass the swab test for maintaining a sterile environment. Such situations are routine in government. In the private sector, in the absence of any regulatory mechanisms, there is no information available.

However, the focus of any health care system should be patient-centric and the strategy best designed to ensure this would be to identify appropriate key performance indicators. Such indicators should be reported on regularly by the care provider to those who are paying for the programme. While expenditure can only be a minor performance indicator, morbidity and mortality rates, etc. certainly are major ones. Those doctors and hospitals that do not report data, should not be allowed to participate.

Here we encounter an important constraint—in many sectors, government alone has the legitimacy to demand data reporting. Private companies would be most reluctant to share information that has bearing on their business, with private agencies. Government alone can collect that information—provided it wishes to do so.

To say that such measures might be in the public interest but do not help businesses, only indicates an ostrich like mentality. India has always had a reputation for healing since ancient times. Today medical tourism presents a huge business opportunity. However, to take full advantage of the opportunity, we need to develop adequate quality assurance mechanisms to generate consumer confidence. This is where data can be of great help.

Countries like the Netherlands today, use information on the cost of treating different kinds of diseases to work out the risks of insuring different kinds of populations and compensate insurance companies accordingly. That way they can legally prohibit insurance companies from discriminating against patients with chronic diseases.

In an age of globalization, setting up protocols for data collection and quality assurance mechanisms, can be a big boost for business. In fact, the process of writing protocols to improve product quality has many unintended consequences. No doubt agencies like the USFDA (US Food and Drug Administration) were set-up to devise protocols in the interests of public safety. Today compliance with the USFDA norms and also with WHO Good Manufacturing Practices, is a minimum for pharma companies who wish to cater to the world market. Writing those protocols also means that these agencies tend to write about equipment and processes that they have seen and are familiar with. The spinoffs for equipment manufacturers in the West are considerable. A suitable response would be for India to improve its own indigenous norms to provide equivalent and even better solutions. The starting point of any such exercise is the routine collection of information that would enable feedback to improve productivity.

Each government department collects information as part of its routine activities. If done systematically and made available for public use, it can be very valuable.

MAKING IN INDIA: SYSTEMATIZING INFORMATION AND ITS USE

The information sets available with the state can be used to work out indicators of productivity. In order to make any plan to improve productivity, the figure of value added per worker needs to be drilled down to different industries by region and size of business. Currently there is no reliable time series data for industry specific productivity of this kind in India.

It is then left to specialised researches to fill up the gap. These are few and far between. An interesting study that looked at 487 firms for the period 1989-90 to 1996-7, said that the spill-over effects of foreign direct investment on productivity of firms in the neighbourhood was positive only for firms that already had some R&D capabilities and had the capacity to learn the new knowledge.[4]

Productivity studies would be useful feedback for building indigenous capabilities. R&D capabilities of firms in turn depend on the quality of skilled manpower churned out by the Indian system of education. Information about the skill profiles of working populations can provide key policy inputs. Surely the NSSO does conduct such surveys once every five years. Those can be supplemented with regional studies—information on the wage rates for specific skill sets in specific regions is an important input for anyone who wishes to set-up an industry over there. State Labour

Bureaus already collect much information that could be mined for data. Once this kind of information is systematized, it would also provide a suitable basis to work out policy initiatives for encouraging knowledge based industries.

Systematizing information in this fashion is not difficult to do. But the ability to generate a goal or even to see that a goal might be needed, is indeed difficult. For decades now, the Indian government has looked to the Ease of Doing Business indicators published by the World Bank as key benchmarks for improvement. Those surveys are conducted on the basis of rather limited data sets and the methodology used is completely opaque. Yet seldom has the government tried to conduct their own surveys or even to collect their own data. No one doubts the importance of making business easier to do but surely we could find our own ways for doing so and our own parameters. Slavery is an attribute of the mind as much as a physical condition.

A HIGH ORDER OF SKILLS: IMPROVING LABOUR PRODUCTIVITY

It is traditionally held that any investment in education is the most long-term of all investments. Education is a critical component of economic growth. Here we do not talk merely of the value of education to the learner. The value to the learner is given; it is the value of an education to society at large that is even more important. Improving education can directly improve the productivity of businesses. This in turn can lead to greater business profits and to much greater economic growth. Well trained labour is a serious asset to businesses.

Labour productivity as measured in terms of GDP at constant prices per worker, was reported to be 13,300 US dollars for India in 2013. This was only slightly above the South Asia average of 12,800 US dollars and it is one eighth of the US average of 107,600 US dollars.[5] Given that improvement in technical efficiency and skills can help raise labour productivity, there is certainly much to be done in India.

A very small percentage of the Indian workforce is exposed to any technical skills. The NSSO 66th round figures showed that less than 2 per cent of people of working age in India had received any formal education that provides vocational skills, whether diploma or degree.[6] And if we were to take into account all those who have non-formal vocational training of some kind which includes training acquired from hereditary sources or self-acquired or learnt on the job, we can only add another 5 per cent people.[7] This means that only about 7 per cent Indians of working age have exposure to any technical education, whether formal or non-formal.

The availability of recognizable skills is reflected in earning capabilities: those with a diploma or certificate earned on an average 31 per cent more in agriculture, 36 per cent more in trade, 64 per cent more in mining and quarrying, 80-95 per cent more in manufacturing and 98 per cent more in the construction sector, as compared to their peers who possessed only a secondary or higher secondary education.[8] This means that 93 per cent of the workforce in India today needs to be re-skilled.

An important constraint here is that Indian students till today prefer a more general education to a technical one. The figures in the table below provide ample testimony for this.

TABLE 7.2: TOTAL NUMBER OF STUDENTS IN HIGHER EDUCATION AND THEIR STREAMS 2015-16

Stream	Total Students who passed, reporting year 2015-16	Kind of Education (while classifying Science, Laws and Management as 'Technical')
Agriculture	51,222	Technical
Arts	39,37,577	General
Commerce	9,81,960	General
Engineering	12,61,118	Technical
Laws	82,637	Technical
Management	3,84,372	Technical
Medical	3,36,167	Technical
Science	14,91,479	Technical
Veterinary	7,009	Technical
Grand Total	85,33,541	

Source: All India Survey of Higher Education, 2015-16, Out Turn Report #55 A.

A strong preference for white collar jobs as opposed to blue collar jobs might be the reason why the services sector contributes a half share of the Gross Value Added for the country while manufacturing contributes only 18 per cent.

In the services sector too, what is troubling is that Indian service providers remain at the lower end of the value chain. In the field of software, they are good at writing code but examples of Indian software products are rather few. For that to happen, we need to change the way we look at technology and at higher education.

A general education can be of substantial value to a student, provided it is able to endow the student with the ability to think for himself or herself and to make sense of information. In order to improve the content of various educational programmes in the country, curricula need to be upgraded across the board. We also need to embrace wholeheartedly the technologies of the future.

The arrival of disruptive technologies like artificial intelligence and the internet of things have transformed the workplace. To get students, whatever their education, ready for the changes imminent, is a massive task. To essay that task, tools such as those provided by artificial intelligence and data analytics, need to be made available to students across the board. Currently such courses are confined to a small number of specialized courses in management and engineering institutions, creating an elite cadre. These are drops in the ocean. Societies show rapid economic growth when education is able to raise the average. Individual excellence and small elite cadres are no longer enough.

Future-oriented skills like data science, cyber security, machine learning need to be melded into the courses taught to students in the basic Arts, Science and Commerce programmes. Currently a very large number of students do not even know the basics of word processing and find it impossible to use spreadsheets. A specialized course in Artificial Intelligence or Data Science makes no sense. We should remember that artificial intelligence and data handling are merely tools and not an end. It is only when these tools are combined with a domain that value can be created.

To make optimal use of what information we have, we need to decide what kind of society we wish to build—a society that keeps on learning new skills and keeps pace with a changing world or a society that wishes to remain in a low-skill time warp.

WOULD LEARNING ADVANCED SKILLS LEAD TO JOB LOSSES?

Advanced automation and robotics are transforming industry—these are key strategic areas. To say that automation kills jobs can only lead to a dead-end. To put breaks on automation cannot create a productive high-growth economy. While automation does kill certain jobs in some sectors, others come up. It is only when we look across sectors rather than just a few occupations, that this becomes visible. An interesting study points out that robots tend to be used in industry only for repetitive tasks like material handling that involve very heavy labour.[9] To extrapolate from that to say that the adoption of robotics would lead to job losses across the board, is misconceived.

Interestingly, this fear about automation and machining skills leading to job losses is several hundred years old in India. In the late seventeenth century, English chaplain Ovington commented on how Indians tried to preserve the livelihood of scribes by avoiding the printing press and how they used foot messengers rather than the English system of using horse-riders for delivering the post:

> The Indians in sending their Letters abroad have not learnt the convenience of the quick Dispatches of our Posts: A Pattamar, i.e. a Foot Messenger, is generally employ'd to carry them to the remotest Bounds of the Empire. So that whenever the English are under a necessity of writing to Bengal, Maderas, or any other part of Indostan, a Person is sent on purpose upon the Errand.
>
> Neither have they endeavour'd to transcribe our Art of Printing; that would diminish the Repute and Livelihood of their Scrivans, who maintain numerous Families by the Pen.[10]

Again, in the early nineteenth century, Francis Buchanan while reporting on rice cultivation in south India observed much the same phenomenon: '. . . in India, it is seldom that an attempt is made to accomplish any thing by machinery, that can be performed by human labour'.[11]

The use of human labour to accomplish a task that machines can do, cannot in the modern world, postpone the use of technology. Technological advancement will happen come what may. All that avoidance of automation will achieve is, the continuance of low-paid, labour intensive jobs in India and eventually, serious job losses and a subsistence level economy. If we fail to use the opportunities available to us, markets would simply move to countries that follow more progressive policies. The faster we accept this, the sooner our industries can get ready for the change.

Industrial robots are poised to automate all kinds of tasks at the future workplace. From picking heavy materials on the shop-floor to assistance in conducting micro-surgeries and even giving you a shampoo, robots today have been developed for performing all kinds of tasks. Whether we wish to remain consumers of robot assisted services provided by Western companies or whether we would rather help Indian boys and girls develop and run those services, is a choice that only we can make.

India already has a vast population invested in agriculture. Rather than encouraging those farmers and farm-labourers to migrate to cities, what could be done is to increase the productivity of agriculture exponentially by using robotics. Today robots in agriculture can be used for a variety of operations including weed control, mowing, seeding, pruning, harvesting, sorting and packing food products, to name just a few activities. Robotic gardeners and harvesters can reduce the back-breaking labour involved in such operations and can add value. Many engineering departments in colleges throughout the country are already experimenting with building robots. All that energy can be usefully applied.

It is not a laughable idea. Industrial robots are already being produced in India though in a very small way. Given the costs involved, it might be expensive for farmers to purchase the robots themselves. But it is possible for village level entrepreneurs to buy the robots and to provide the services to farmers at a reasonable cost. Further, farmers need to make decisions that require a great deal of information all the time—when to sow their crop, what kind of fertilizer is best suited for their soil, what kind of disease has hit their crops and what pesticide to use, how much water to apply and so on. Using artificial intelligence can provide answers to such questions and create value both for businesses and farmers.

All these are tools that can lead to a massive increase in productivity. Skilling India is far more than merely teaching students how to be better fitters, car painters, nurses, doctors and engineers. It is about more than getting people into jobs. Skilling India is essentially about improving productivity in the workplace. Learning is a continuous process; it does not end with student-hood. What we need to do is to send out a direct message that the opportunity to improve and excel is always available and we need to make those opportunities available.

For inculcating high order skills and to improve the average skill-set across the board, we need to pay more attention to energizing our institutions of higher education.

ROBUST KNOWLEDGE INSTITUTIONS: THE VALUE OF A COLLEGE EDUCATION

With the introduction of the skilling programme in recent years, there has been a great deal of doubt expressed about the value of a college education. After all, some argue, a college education is not necessary to get into a job and there have been famous entrepreneurs who never went to college at all. Like many opinions, this one too is rarely tested against reality.

The abilities to succeed in the ongoing Fourth Industrial Revolution can't be had merely through hard work, native intelligence or by watching an *ustaad* work. That college education is irrelevant to success, is a myth. The myth has been around for at least three centuries. Its latest version features Bill Gates, a college dropout. Do notice, he did go to college and, one of the best ones, at that. Moreover, he drew upon that brief experience for creating goods that college graduates found useful. In contrast there is the case of the Thiel Fellows. Each fellow, under 23 years of age, was given seed money—a total of $100,000 over two years—to pursue business opportunities in preference to a college education. Each succeeded in their respective business. Yet, after their fellowship they chose to enroll for a college education to get the formal and structured learning that can only happen in a college.

Do not also forget that 200 years ago, it was the absence of formal and structured learning that brought the vibrant Indian economy down as soon as it came in contact with the First Industrial Revolution. The First Industrial Revolution was rooted in the scientific temper that Europe had nurtured for almost three hundred years then. At that time, till the eighteenth century, India was the monopoly supplier of saltpetre to the world, the substance needed to power military shells. India was also one of the major suppliers of zinc in the world. Indian technologists, as early as the fourth century BCE, had mastered the art of extracting zinc from its ore while the rest of the world struggled to find a way to stop the smelted zinc from evaporating. A study of the famed wootz steel of India was an important component of European researches that led to what we now know as steel. As late as 1795, the British were still trying to figure out how Indians made such high quality steel. English journals like the *Philosophical Transactions of the Royal Society of London* would carry articles with titles like, 'Experiments and Observations to Investigate the Nature of a Kind of Steel, Manufactured at Bombay, and There Called Wootz: With Remarks on the Properties and Composition of the Different States of Iron'. Within fifty years European researchers and experimenters, thanks to scientific research, had created superior ways of making steel. In the same time in the absence of formal and structured learning, Indians had lost all their prior skills and knowledge. In the absence of a sturdy system of learning and knowledge transmission, today we do not even know how our ancestors produced wootz for over a thousand years.

The Industrial Revolution was based on the scientific method and systematic learning. These are meta-skills, skills on the basis of which other skills can be developed. College is the site for acquiring such meta-skills. Whether it is the sciences or the social sciences and humanities, a grounding in the scientific method is essential for any further growth. It involves systematizing learning and transmission of knowledge and constant testing of ideas and beliefs against reality.

Even the IT boom of the 1990s, that happened by chance and benefitted by escaping the baleful eye of a lethargic government, was based on filling up the IT bodyshops with college graduates. As it turned out, in the absence of a robust culture of college education and research, the majority of the Indian IT industry continues to provide services of a lower order to international markets. Data entry, call centres, medical transcription, writing basic code; all these account for the bulk of the business processes outsourced to India.

Also, domestic markets account for a miniscule share of revenues of Indian IT companies. This indicates that most Indian businesses are still living in a pre-IT age. This is very different from the growth of say, the American IT sector, which is primarily driven by internal demand.

Each year about 85 lakh students graduate in India. Over half of them join the workforce every year. For these students to be part of the Fourth Industrial Revolution, what is needed is for the colleges to offer them programmes that are in tune with workplace requirements and that teach them to think.

Learning of this sort requires a stylized environment away from the daily routine of life. This is why colleges are needed. But learning and the scientific temper also require frequent reality testing of ideas. That connection with real life could be established, by simultaneously working on real life problems; by working on research projects; by doing internships.

KNOWLEDGE INSTITUTIONS: THE MISSING CONNECT WITH INDUSTRY

Currently it is this connection of colleges with the workplace that is almost non-existent in India. It is weak to the extent that colleges do not even systematically record placement data. Most colleges do not even have a placement cell. Some of this is changing in response to colleges competing with peers in the NIRF rankings. But, as yet there is almost no effort to consciously make graduates employable by providing them with higher order learning.

When the Confederation of Indian Industry collaborated with Wheebox to survey one lakh students in 2014, it discovered the dramatic absence of learning among college graduates. The survey tested students on their domain knowledge, communication skills, logical ability and aptitude only to discover that degree programmes that connected with industry, did much better. This meant that passable skills were available with only some 19 per cent of Arts students (those who constitute over 50 per cent of India's undergraduates). In contrast, programmes like B.Pharm and B.Tech that strongly encourage internships, had about 50 per cent students who were competent enough.[12]

Adding to the problem is the policy-policing to which colleges are subject to by the government. Colleges can float only government approved programmes that need to be transacted in only government approved ways. That hems in most college managements and teachers, disabling them from responding to the rapidly changing requirements of society and industry. Some private colleges do make efforts to stay in tune with the latest opportunities in the marketplace. They tend to convert all such demands into specialized courses that command higher fees in the marketplace. But these students are mere drops in the ocean. A few thousand students learning superior order skills are not sufficient to make the nation's economy grow by leaps and bounds.

THE ABILITY TO LEARN IS MORE IMPORTANT THAN LEARNING ITSELF

The ability to learn is a critical skill. Interestingly, the IIT graduates are valued as much as any management graduate for purely management jobs where no engineering skills are needed. Could it be that the IIT helps students to acquire a wide variety of skills, by the simple expedient of leaving the teacher free to teach and the student free to learn? Perhaps the most valuable skill of all is the ability to think logically and to use available information to optimise decision-making.

The ability to learn how to learn, in other words meta-learning, is needed in programmes across the board. For such skills to be honed, what is needed are colleges and universities where the widest possible selection of courses is available to students, both from the arts and sciences.

What top-level academic institutions offer is instruction in logic, analytical thinking, and the ability to build a reasoned argument. These are the skills that have the greatest value in everyday life. The debate about the commercialization of higher education does not matter to the economy of education in the least. Perhaps this is why we read in the newspapers everyday about which campuses saw the highest pay packages.

Students do not mind paying Rs. 15 to 19 lakh for a two-year MBA course in an IIM while they grudge paying even a miniscule sum of Rs. 7,000 per annum for a plain Master of Arts. Today, BA/MA degrees do not really teach how to run a business or how to communicate effectively. Many BCom degree holders are unable to analyse a balance sheet. Leland Stanford, the founder of Stanford University, famously said that before constructing anything, it is necessary to conceive it. He also said that often technically educated boys do not make the best businessmen; and that imagination and creativity were more important than mere technical skills.

The National Institution Ranking Framework provides valuable benchmarks for assessing the quality of teaching and learning and of curriculum reform across the country. It also allows colleges to learn about what their peers are doing. Sharing of knowledge has that advantage. While NIRF gives us a basic picture of the quality of higher education in the country, it also shows how much more is needed.

Fortunately, for the quality of teaching and learning to improve radically, the most important changes needed are non-monetary in nature. While money would certainly help, pumping in of more money is not the first priority. The first priority is a complete overthrow of the current pattern of governing higher education. It is when college teachers have the freedom to decide what they wish to teach, the freedom to interact more with business and industry that they have a much greater stake in the system. The numbers of autonomous colleges have certainly increased by leaps and bounds but they are yet to reach critical mass sufficient to make a difference. Of the 40,000 odd colleges in the country, less than 1000 are autonomous.

Recently, the government has gone out of its way to encourage college autonomy thereby removing the shackles imposed upon good colleges by the UGC and the affiliating universities. Such autonomy makes the college and teachers directly responsible for taking higher education forward, improving the skills of students, thereby making them more employable.

Government colleges that constitute 22 per cent of total college strength, are stymied by what can best be called the DPI-Syndrome wherein a bureaucrat uses antiquated rules and regulations of a colonial era to whip the faculty into submission. We need a policy that does away with the Director Public Instruction, and DPI analogues, and allows teachers to teach.

Freedom to teach would encourage more interaction with industry and help to dissolve the segmentation in learning systems that has been such an unfortunate part of Indian education for time immemorial. To identify any particular type of learning, whether theoretical or experiential as being intrinsically superior to the other, is a serious mistake. It is when both streams come together that the best learning happens.

Today the policy makers have created a weird Skill India programme that goes to the other end of the spectrum which insists on industry experience and specific skills in lieu of structured learning of generic subjects. The connect with industry can be built into college and university education through student internships. It could be strengthened by putting in place mechanisms for exchange of personnel between academia, industry and also government. But there is no escape from structured learning.

A study conducted by Scottish colleges calculated the real benefits of a college education in terms of earning to the student, greater earning to businesses and society at large and the value of taxes that the resulting increase in economic activity would generate. The study showed that as against an expenditure of £665.8 million on supporting the colleges of Scotland, the colleges contributed £14.9 billion and added 8.8 per cent to the total economic output of Scotland for the year 2013-14.[13] In India today, such benefits are not taken for granted. Regardless of whether higher education is treated as a public good or not, the positive externalities generated by higher education are so large that there is a definite case to subsidize higher education for those who cannot afford it.

The simple thing to understand is that in higher education, there are no short cuts. Moreover, investments in higher education are the equivalent of sunk costs. Profits don't happen immediately and, neither are they always tangible. Till now India was rich—in so far as it was—by default. The trick lies in being rich by design. College education is the essential basis for that.

A FUNCTIONAL LEGAL SYSTEM: CLEAR AND TRANSPARENT LAWS

An important element of a supportive eco-system for businesses is a functional legal system. The foundation of such a system is clarity in law. Currently however companies spend humungous amounts in trying to unravel what it is that the law actually means. Many of them also spend time and money in trying to game the system and to find loopholes to exploit. All this happens mostly because we make little attempt to rewrite and update laws from time to time. All legislation enacted by parliament and by the state governments, is supposed to be clarified by administrative rules and regulations. We need those provisions because it is not possible to go to the legislature constantly. In practice what has happened is that administrative departments continually issue new rules and regulations that refer to old rules sometimes issued decades in the past. The resultant maze allows fixers of all kinds to flourish. It is the government and businesses who are losers. What we need is for each administrative department of the government to write a master circular each year summing up the plethora of rules, public notices and clarifications that are issued on almost a daily basis. While issuing such annual master circulars, the departments must bite the bullet by specifying clearly that the circular would supersede all circulars issued previously on the subject. It is this call that departments hesitate to take. So ghost notifications and rules abound—again the only people who benefit from all the confusion are the fixers.

Poorly worded laws encourage fixers thereby creating the impression that this is being done deliberately to help specific interests. Whether or not this is true is irrelevant. The point is it creates mistrust. Even if it is a case of incompetent drafting, it allows people to exploit loopholes in the law. When people can see business rivals 'gaming' the system, they think they might as well do the same. So whether lawmakers are seen as corrupt or incompetent, the result is the same—people game the system. To avoid this, we need regular updation and scrapping of archaic laws.

REDUCING TIME FOR DISPUTE SETTLEMENT

The other lacuna in our legal system is the inordinate time taken to settle court cases. Today it is almost given that if anyone files a court case, he or she should be prepared that it might be decided only when one is dead and gone. Undertrials often expire in the currency of a court case. This continues to be the weakest point of Indian businesses and it makes the enforcement of contract impossible. To set-up special courts for urgent cases is only a stop-gap solution and yet another form of the Indian propensity for short-term thinking and *jugaad*. We need to find more long-term solutions.

The remedies have been pointed out by many commissions set-up from time to time. We need to increase judges at all levels and fill up vacancies, most especially vacancies in the lower courts where the pendency of cases is the highest. But this alone will not be sufficient. What we also need is a system of administrative management and backup for the judges consisting of support staff assisted by adequate automation. Many countries have set-up such modern systems.

A study points out that in 2004, the ratio of judges to disposals per year for the Delhi District courts was 654 against 1,336 for Australian judges. They recommended the creation of a dedicated administrative agency for the purpose of redesigning court procedures, bringing in best practices, administering courts and tribunals efficiently and advising the judiciary and legislature on legal reforms.[14]

These are common sense solutions that might take a little time to implement but the gains in terms of transaction costs reduced and the message to all those who wish to game the system, that such practices are unacceptable, would be enormous.

IMPROVING PRODUCTIVITY AND REMOVING PERVERSE INCENTIVES

Productive societies need fair laws that encourage a positive work ethic and penalize those who try to subuert the system. Today we have just the opposite—a dysfunctional legal system that allows those who game the system to get away with wrongdoing, thereby penalizing those who do work. To encourage a positive work ethic and to improve productivity across the board, government needs to remove perverse laws that incentivise inefficiency. Historically, India had a market where there was no state regulation of any kind. Today we have moved to the other extreme where government regulates practically everything that businesses do including investment decisions. Government regulations that purportedly guide business decisions about what to invest, how much to invest and where to invest only incentivise inefficiency. We have analogous laws in every sector.

One such example of such perverse laws is the definition of what constitutes 'small' in industry. Today the Ministry of Micro, Small and Medium Enterprises defines any manufacturing or service enterprise as being 'micro' where investment in plant and machinery does not exceed Rs. 25 lakh, as 'small', where such investment does not exceed five crore rupees and, as 'medium' where such investment does not exceed ten crore rupees. The word usage is indeed interesting—'does not exceed' is the operative term. India is unique in having such a definition of micro, small and medium—as though investing in equipment is a crime. Such criteria become the basis for state provided incentives to these units. That in turn ensures that there is an incentive to never grow up!

If any enterprise wishes to remain small, to run a 'mom and pop store', that is their privilege. But to offer them incentives to remain small not only distorts the market, it creates serious inefficiencies. A Global Manufacturing Scorecard for 2015 showed that India employs 57,244,000 people in the manufacturing sector to generate 298 billion USD which is 3 per cent of global output; China employs roughly double the number of people to generate more than six times as much or 2010 billion USD which is 20 per cent of global output; the United States employs 28 per cent of the population employed in India to produce more than six times as much or 1867 billion USD which is 18 per cent of global output.[15] No wonder then that India in 2017 with a GDP of 7.64 USD per person per hour has been ranked at the bottom in a listing of 63 countries where labour productivity is concerned.[16]

Studies of manufacturing productivity within India clearly show the large gap between the formal, read 'regulated' versus the informal, read 'unregulated' manufacturing sector.[17] For the period after 2003 in particular, overall the formal sector has shown twice the growth rate in productivity of the informal sector. When we look at the growth rate for specific groups of industries, we see that the informal sector in some industries does show higher growth rates. But that performance has more to do with the lack of regulation than anything else. Were the informal units to be asked to comply with environmental legislation and to pay minimum wages, a very large number would become simply uneconomical to run and would be forced to close down.

The social costs of preserving the informal units has been very high. The costs are of many kinds—social distress in the sense that the employees of these units live at subsistence level and have no social protection whatsoever; or environmental costs in the shape of pollution and unhealthy living conditions for the population where the unit is located. And we have the peculiar spectacle of 'small' businessmen running a large number of parallel units below the legal limit of five crores to avail of the incentives offered for remaining small. We even have the spectacle of businessmen erecting state of the art machinery and keeping it for display to the occasional visitor and foreign buyer, again to avail of these self-same incentives. As soon as the visitor departs, the machinery is closed down and put back into plastic wraps!

Such perverse laws abound in India. The only way to get out of the situation is to simply identify and abrogate laws of this kind.

We do not argue that there is any particular merit in largeness of scale where industry is concerned. Smallness or largeness may have little impact on the efficiency of a business. What we do argue against is incentivization of inefficiency. Size can be no excuse for that kind of perverse incentive.

The other thing to note is that times keep changing. To keep laws that might have had some use at some point of time in the past, without any course correction for years on end, can lead to serious inefficiencies. We need mechanisms to gather regular information, to read said information and to put in place correctives so that we can keep up with the times.

WORKING WITH THE WRITTEN WORD

It is these elements which put together, would enable India to make the transition from being small-scale to a large-scale society. Largeness of scale is not just about economies of scale. It is about the ability to interact with unknown people based on standard protocols. Anonymous protocols can set-up a framework for working and can facilitate exchange of information between socially and geographically disparate units. One of the first things that you get as soon as you land in any European city is a map with which to get around the city. It is assumed that the map frees you of the need to ask anyone about which way to go. Societies which have the ability to function on the basis of protocols and the written word, set the individual free of the need to depend exclusively on social and kinship networks.

A systematized information network is available to people irrespective of social or financial status. To that extent, information networks help to make societies inclusive.

By using the written word so extensively as guide maps to action, we enormously increase the range of our abilities. The East India Company governed an entire country from across the globe, using the written word. Right now, much of India is still caught in the loop of who-do-I-know, the assumption being that one can trust only someone that one knows.

Learning societies do not function so much on face-to-face interactions but on the written word and on protocols. That also means that there are serious sanctions against anyone who violates the protocol. If far too many people run red lights, the traffic system would fail to facilitate the smooth movement of vehicles on the road and it could even increase the costs for those who use the roads—paid in terms of human lives. We need to move beyond the stage where the only thing that works is our limited ability to trust other human beings who are known to us.

Surely the existence of social trust helps people. The human being is far more than a utility maximizing individual. But large-scale societies are underpinned by the assumption that there is a base network of institutions and rules that would help all people irrespective of who they might be. Such systems help to reduce risk. Above all they help to achieve inclusive growth and to provide a cushion to those who have nothing to begin with.

Taking the written word seriously is not about red tape or bureaucracy; it is what allows systems to function. It permeates everything that we do. That is why it is important to evaluate ourselves constantly and not to rest on our laurels. Excellence is something which needs to be constantly nurtured. It cannot be taken for granted and certainly not left dependent entirely on intuition. Intuition, howsoever powerful, is no substitute for the written word, nor is *jugaad* a replacement for protocol.

To make India great again, we need to do more than to invest more money; we need to change the way in which we think and plan and even the way we look at ourselves. That is something our history teaches us. We have always prized wealth. Individually, many of us possess the skills to make it too. But for societies to be affluent, they need to work on collective strategies to improve efficiency; they need to invest in the future. That is something India has lacked so far.

Most of all, to build a culture of excellence, Indians first need to believe that we can excel. Being a practical people, we give too much value to monetary incentives. Money is surely important but it is not the sole determinant of value. High achievers do not only work for money; they work because of their self-esteem, of the pleasure that creativity and achievement brings.

We are inadvertently blessed with a young and eager population. When the Americans complain that they must hire Indian engineers it is because they do not have enough Americans with those skills any more. A large number of Americans have already given up on learning science, technology, engineering and mathematics (STEM). They simply do not have enough American engineers any more. Moreover, they do not even have enough young people who could possibly study and fill up the gap. India could fruitfully use this opportunity. We could build an eco-system that allows for the incremental growth of knowledge. Make teachers answerable to the local community and their students. Allow freedom to create knowledge. Create institutions to systematize and share information.

Building a learning eco-system is above all an investment in an unknown future. The present century will likely be an Asian one. It is up to all of us to make it an Indian century.

MOVING TOWARDS A BETTER FUTURE

1. Ensure security of property: Security of landed property is fundamental to businesses. Systematization of the land record database could result in substantial correction in land prices, reduction in land-related litigation, security to the landholders and more revenues to the government. For such systematization, we need to:
   1.1. Create and implement systems of unique ID for plots of land
   1.2. Create and implement land titling systems.
2. Improve the learning curve: to do this, we need to build shared knowledge resources including data of all kinds across the spectrum. For that, we need to:
   2.1. Increase Public Investment in Research
   2.2. Support Market Intelligence and Knowledge Archiving in Businesses
   2.3. Systematize government datasets and make these available in public domain.
3. Create a high order of skills among the working population including encouragement to future oriented skills in machine learning, Internet of Things, data analytics, etc. Fears of job losses are misplaced and should not prevent investing in high order skills. We need these to go up the learning curve.
4. Build resilient Knowledge Institutions: Robust institutions have the capacity to generate new knowledge and to preserve know-

ledge of innovations. It is such institutions that can improve the learning curve. For that we need to:

4.1. Encourage college autonomy and remove checks on what educational institutions can teach

4.2. Frame clear rules for exchange of personnel between government, academia and business

4.3. Support undergraduate research projects.

4.4. Support student internships in industry.

5. Create a functional system of regulations: To achieve a functional system of regulation, we need to:

5.1. Frame clear and transparent laws and update regulations frequently to ensure that no cluttering of regulations happens, outdated ones are removed or incorporated into the existing ones

5.2. Reduce time taken to settle trade disputes.

6. Improve Productivity especially by removing perverse incentives that hamper productivity. To do this, we need to:

6.1. Scrap archaic laws that hamper productivity.

NOTES

1. Berenson, 2006.
2. Department of Science and Technology, Ministry of Science and Technology, Government of India, 2017.
3. Source of Data: Office of the Controller General of Patents, Designs and Trademarks, Department of Promotion of Industry and Internal Trade, Ministry of Commerce & Industry, Government of India. Government does not collect data according to these categories—data sorted out by us for the year 2016-17.
4. Kathuria, 2002.
5. Asian Productivity Organization, 2016: 62.
6. National Sample Survey Office, 2013: 26.
7. Ibid.
8. National Sample Survey Office, 2011: A-507.
9. Mani, 2019.
10. Ovington, 1929
11. Buchanan, 1807, III: 40-1.

12. PeopleStrong, Confederation of Indian Industry, Wheebox, 2014.
13. Economic Modelling Specialists International, 2015.
14. Dutta et al., 2019.
15. West & Lansang, 2018. Retrieved on 30 April 2019 from URL https://www.google.com/url?sa=t&rct=j&q=& esrc=s& source=web&cd=1& cad=rja&uact=8&ved=2ahUKEwiqn4bG9vjhAhUX3o8 KHQNo DUYQFjAAegQIAhAB&url=https%3A% 2F%2Fwww.brookings.edu%2Fresearch%2Fglobal-manufacturing-scorecard-how-the-us-compares-to-18-other-nations%2F&usg=AOvVaw2J0tj_cQUbsO38C1VYRoK-
16. Institute for Management Development, 2018: 404.
17. Krishna, Goldar, Aggarwal, Das, Erumban, & Das, 2018. Growth rate of total factor productivity in the Indian formal manufacturing sector has been twice that of the informal sector for the decade from 2003-4 till 2011-12. Total factor productivity is defined in economics as increases in productivity not explained either by investment in labour or capital.

Bibliography

Accounts Presented to the House of Commons from the East India Company Respecting their Annual Revenues and Disbursements (1801-8). London: East India Company.

Alavi, S. (1993). The Company Army and Rural Society: The Invalid Thanah 1780-1830. *Modern Asian Studies*, 27(1): 147-78.

Al-Idrisi (1960). *India and the Neighbouring Territories in the Kitāb etc.* (tr. Syed Maqbool Ahmad). Leiden: E.J. Brill.

All India Survey of Higher Education (2015-16). *Out Turn Report #55A.* New Delhi: MHRD.

Annadurai, K., K. Danasekharan and G. Mani (2017). 'Elimination of Maternal and Neonatal Tetanus in India: A Triumph Tale'. *International Journal of Preventive Medicine*, 8: 15.

Asian Productivity Organization (2016). *APO Productivity Databook.* Tokyo: Asian Productivity Organization.

Askari, S.H. (1961). 'Mughal Naval Weakness and Aurangzeb's Attitude Towards the Traders and Pirates on the Western Coast'. *Proceedings of the Indian History Congress*, 24: 162-70.

Banarasidas. (2007). *Ardhakathanaka* (tr. R. Chaudhury). New Delhi: Penguin.

Banerjee, R. (1998). 'A Wedding Feast or Political Arena?: Commercial Rivalry between the Ali Rajas and the English Factory in Northern Malabar in the 18th Century'. In R. Mukherjee and L. Subramaniam (eds.), *Politics and Trade in the Indian Ocean World: Essays in Honour of Ashin Das Gupta.* Delhi: Oxford University Press, pp. 83-112.

Basu, A.C. (1967). *Bengal in the Reign of Aurangzib: 1658-1707.* Calcutta: Progressive Publishers.

Bayly, W.B. (1816). 'Statistical View of the Population of Burdwan'. *Asiatick Researches on Transactions of the Society Instituted In Bengal, For Enquiring Into The History And Antiquities, The Arts, Sciences And Literature*, 12: 560.

Bengal Papers, 1803. Bengal also Fort St. George and Bombay Papers Presented to the House of Commons, on the Maratha War in 1803. London: House of Commons.

Berenson, A. (4 December 2006). Retrieved 19 January 2019, from www.nytimes.com: http://www.nytimes.com/2006/12/04/health/04pfizer.html

Bernier, F. (1916). *Travels in the Mogul Empire, AD 1656-68.* (ed. V.A. Smith, and tr. A. Constable). London: Humphrey Milford.

Bhadani, B.L. (1996). 'The Pastoral Sector in the Economy of Seventeenth Century Marwar'. In D. Tripathi and B.L. Bhadani (eds.), *Facets of a Marwar Historian: Aspects of India's Social and Economic History*. Jaipur: Publication Scheme, Jaipur, pp. 227-51.

Bhadani, B.L. (1999). *Peasants, Artisans and Entrepreneurs: Economy of Marwar in the Seventeenth century.* Jaipur: Rawat.

Bhagwati, J. and A. Pangariya (2013). *Why Growth Matters: How Economic Growth in India Reduced Poverty and the Lessons for Other Developing Countries.* New York: Public Affairs.

Bhandari, S.R. (1934). *Oswal Jati Ka Itihas.* Indore: Oswal History Publishing House.

Biswas, A.K. (1994). 'Iron and Steel in Pre-Modern India: A Critical Review'. *Indian Journal of History of Science*, 29(4): 579-610.

Biswas, P. (14 July 2014). http://indianexpress.com/article/cities/pune/pcmc-move-on-sarathi-under-fire-for-violating-law/. Retrieved 2 February 2018.

Bolts, W. (1772). *Considerations on India Affairs: Particularly Respecting the Present State of Bengal and Its Dependencies. To Which is Prefixed a Map of Those Countries, Chiefly from Actual Surveys.* London: J. Almon etc.

Broughton, T.D. (1892). *Letters Written in A Mahratta Camp, During the Year 1809 Descriptive of the Character, Manners Domestic Habits And Religious Ceremonies of the Mahrattas.* Westminster: Archibald Constable and Company.

Bruce, J. (1810). *Annals of the Honourable East India Company From their Establishment by the Charter of Queen Elizabeth 1600, to the Union of the London and English East-India Companies 1707-8.* London: Black, Parry and Kingsbury.

Buchanan, F. (1807). *A Journey from Madras through the Countries of Mysore, Canara, and Malabar, performed under the orders of the most noble the Marquis Wellesley, Governor General of India, for the Express Purpose of Investigating the State of Agriculture, Arts, and Commerce.* 3 vols., London: East India Company.

Calkins, P.B. (March 1972). 'Revenue Administration and the Formation of a Regionally Oriented Ruling Group in Bengal, 1700-40'. Chicago, unpublished thesis, University of Chicago.

Chatterjee, K. (1992). 'Trade and Darbar Politics in the Bengal Subah, 1733-57'. *Modern Asian Studies*, 26(2): 233-73.

Chaudhuri, K.N. (1978). *The Trading World of Asia and the East India Company: 1660-1760.* Cambridge: Cambridge University Press.

Chaudhuri, S. (1975). *Trade and Commercial Organisation in Bengal: 1650-1720.* Calcutta: Indian Council of Historical Research.

Chaudhury, S. (1995). *From Prosperity to Decline: Eighteenth Century Bengal.* New Delhi: Manohar.

Choudhary, S. et al. (2018). 'Tharparkar: The Pride of Desert'. *Journal of Entomology and Zoology Studies*, 6(2), 1915-19.

Confederation of Indian Industry (February 2014). https://www.mycii.in/KmResourceApplication/38613. LeveragingICTforMSME.pdf. Retrieved 22 November 2017.

Cooper, R.G. (2003). *The Anglo-Maratha Campaigns and the Contest for India: the Struggle for Control of the South Asian Military Economy.* Cambridge: Cambridge University Press.

Daryaee, T. (2014). *Sasanian Persia: the Rise and Fall of an Empire.* London: I.B. Tauris.

Datta, B. and A.N. Singh (1962, 1st pub. 1935 & 1938). *History of Hindu Mathematics: A Sourcebook.* Bombay: Asia Publishing House.

Datta, R. (1990). 'Rural Bengal: Social Structure and Agrarian Economy in the Late Eighteenth Century'. Kings College London: unpublished doctroral thesis.

—— (2000). *Society, Economy and the Market: Commercialization in Rural Bengal c. 1760-1800*, New Delhi: Manohar.

Datta, S. (October 2010). 'Infinite Sequences in the Constructive Geometry of Tenth-century Hindu Temple Superstructures. *Nexus Network Journal: Architecture and Mathematics*, 12(3): 471-83.

Department of Science and Technology, Ministry of Science and Technology, Government of India (December 2017). Retrieved 2 February 2019, from http://nstmis-dst.org/PDF2017/table1.pdf

Dharampal (1971, rpt. 1983). *Indian Science and Technology in the Eighteenth Century.* Goa: Other India Press.

—— (2000). *The Beautiful Tree, Indian Indigenous Education in the Eighteenth Century.* Mapusa, Goa: Other India Press.

—— (2015). *Essential Writings of Dharampal.* New Delhi: Publications Division, Ministry of Information and Broadcasting, Government of India.

Doogar, R. (2013). 'From Merchant-Banking to Zamindari: Jains in 18th and 19th Century Murshidabad'. In Rosie Llewellyn-Jones and Neeta Das, Llewellyn-Jones, *Murshidabad: Forgotten Capital of Bengal.* Marg Publishers.

Dutta, P. et al. (25 March 2019). How to Modernise the Working of Courts and Tribunals in India (NIPFP Working Paper No. 258) Retrieved 25 April 2019, from https://www.nipfp.org.in/media/medialibrary/2019/03/WP_2019_258.pdf

Economic Modelling Specialists International. (September 2015). Retrieved 29 January 2019, from https://collegesscotland.ac.uk/our-work/demonstrating the-economic-value/460-demonstrating-the-economic-value-of-scotlands-colleges-report-main-report

Elliot, H.M. (1877). *The History of India as Told by Its Own Historians.* London: Turner and Company.

Firminger, W.K. (ed.). (1812, rpt. 1984). *Affairs of the East India Company (Being the Fifth Report from the Select Committee of the House of Commons 28 July 1812).* Delhi: Neeraj Publishing House.

Foster, W. (1906). *The English Factories in India: 1618-21; A Calendar of Documents in the India office, British Museum and Public Record Office* (vol. 1). Oxford: Clarendon Press.

—— (1921). *Early Travels in India: 1583-1619.* (ed. W. Foster). London: Humphrey Milford; Oxford University Press.

Gilmour, B. (2015). 'New Evidence for the Early Making and Heat-treating of Crucible Steel: Kindi's Iron Treatise'. In S. Srinivasan, S. Ranganathan, and A. Guimlia-Mair (eds.), *Metals and Civilisations; Proceedings of the Seventh International Conference on the Beginnings of the Use of Metals and Alloys (BUMA VII).* Bangalore: National Institute of Advanced Studies, pp. 193-7.

Goitein, S.D. and M.A. Friedman (2011). *India Traders of the Middle Ages: Documents from the Cairo Geniza 'India Book'.* Boston, Leiden: Ben Zvi Institute Jerusalem and Brill.

Grose, J.H. (1772). 'A Voyage to the East Indies; containing Authentic Accounts of the Mogul Government'. London: S. Hooper.

Gupta, A.D. (1967). *Malabar in Asian Trade, 1740-1800.* London: Cambridge University Press.

—— (1994 rpt.). *Indian Merchants and the Decline of Surat c.1700-1750.* New Delhi: Manohar.

—— (1998). 'Trade and Politics in Eighteenth Century India'. In Muzaffar Alam and Sanjay Subrahmanyam (eds.). *The Mughal State, 1526-1750*, New Delhi: Oxford University Press, pp. 361-97.

Gupta, S.P. (1982). 'Prices and Rural Commerce in Seventeenth-Century Eastern Rajasthan . *Proceedings of Indian History Congress*, 270-82.

Habib, I. (1964). 'Usury in Medieval India'. *Comparative Studies in Society and History*, 6(4): 393-419.

Hamilton, F.B. (1833). *A Geographical, Statistical and Historical Description of the District, or Zila of Dinajpur in the Province or Soubah of Bengal.* Calcutta: Asiatic Society.

Hasan, N. and S.P. Gupta (1967). 'Prices of Food Grains in the Territories of

Amber (*c.* 1650-1750)'. *Proceedings of Indian History Congress*, 29(1): 345-68.

Hedges, W. (1887). *The Diary of William Hedges, Esq. (Afterwards Sir William Hedges), During His Agency in Bengal; As well as on his Voyage out and return Overland (1681-7)*, ed. R. Barlow & tr. R. Barlow. London: Hakluyt Society.

Herklots, G. (1829). Table shewing the market price of Grain &c. in lower Bengal from the year 1700 to 1813, extracted from authentic documents of one month in each year, for which, generally, the month of August was selected. *Gleanings in Science*, v. 1: 368-9.

'Historical Sketch of the Origin, Rise, and Progress of the East India Company'. (1844, July Supplement). *The Saturday Magazine*, 775, London: John W. Parker, pp. 33-40.

Hiuen Tsang (1918). *Si-yu-ki: Records of the Western World* (tr. S. Beal). London: Kegan Paul, Trench, Trubner and Co. Ltd.

Hoffman, P.T. (September 2012). 'Why was it Europeans Who Conquered the World?' *The Journal of Economic History*, 72(3): 601-33.

House of Commons, Parliamentary Papers Online. (n.d.).

Indian Council of Medical Research (2010). *Nutrient Requirements and Recommended Dietary Allowances for Indians; A Report of the Expert Group of the Indian Council of Medical Research 2009.* Hyderabad: National Institute of Nutrition, Indian Council of Medical Research.

Indian Records Series: Bengal in 1756-7, A Selection of Public and Private Papers Dealing with the Affairs of the British in Bengal During the Reign of Siraj-uddaula, ed. S.C. Hill, 1905. London: Government of India.

Indian Space Research Organisation. (December 2010). http://www.isro.gov.in. Retrieved 25 January 2017, from http://www.isro.gov.in/update/31-dec-2010/gslv-f06-failure-preliminary-findings-and-further-steps

Institute for Management Development (2018). *IMD World Competitiveness Yearbook 2018*. Lausanne: Institute for Management Development.

Jaikishan, S. (2007). 'Survey of Iron and Wootz Steel Production Sites in Northern Telangana'. *Indian Journal of the History of Science*, 42(3): 445-60.

Jaikishan, S. and R. Balasubramaniam, (2007a). 'Social Aspects of Wootz Steel Manufacture in Northern Telangana'. *Indian Journal of the History of Science*, 42(3): 481-91.

—— (2007b). 'Material Evidences for Wootz Steel Production in Northern Telangana'. *Indian Journal of History of Science*, 42(3): 461-80.

Joseph, G.G. (2011). *The Crest of the Peacock: Non-European Roots of Mathematics.* Princeton & Oxford: Princeton University Press.

Kathuria, V. (2002). 'Liberalisation, FDI, and Productivity Spillovers—An

Analysis of Indian Manufacturing Firms'. *Oxford Economic Papers*, 54(4): 688-718.

Kautilya (1995). *Arthashastra* (tr. R.P. Kangale). Mumbai: Maharashtra Rajya Sahitya Sanskruti Mandal.

Khan, A.M. (1969, digital version 2008). *The Transition in Bengal, 1756-75: A Study of Saiyid Muhammad Reza Khan.* Cambridge: Cambridge University Press.

Khan, I.A. (August 1976). 'The Middle Classes in the Mughal Empire'. *Social Scientist*, 5(1): 28-49.

KPMG. (2017). Retrieved 28 January 2019, from https://assets.kpmg/content/dam/kpmg/ch/pdf/cost-of-capital-study-2017-en.pdf

Kramrisch, S. (1946). *The Hindu Temple.* Calcutta: University of Calcutta.

Krishna, K.L., B. Goldar, S.C. Aggarwal, D.K. Das, A.A. Erumban and P.C. Das (September 2018). (Centre for Development Economics, Working Paper No. 291) Retrieved 30 April 2019, from http://www.cdedse.org/pdf/work291.pdf

Kumar, M. (2013). 'Peasants, Pastoralists and Rulers: Aspects of Ecology and Polity in Seventeenth and Eighteenth century Rajasthan'. *History and Society*, New Series.

—— (2017). 'Money, Market and Merchants: A Study of Trade and Commerce in Eighteenth Century Western Rajasthan'. MDU Rohtak: unpublished thesis.

Lala, R.M. (2004). *The Creation of Wealth: The Tatas from the Nineteenth to the Twenty First Century.* New Delhi: Penguin Books.

Lauriston, J.L. (2014). *A Memoir of the Mughal Empire, Events of 1757-61.* (tr. G.S. Cheema). Delhi: Manohar.

Little, J.H. (1960). *The House of Jagat Seth.* Calcutta: Calcutta Historical Society.

Malcolm, M.G. (1823). *Memoir of Central India including Malwa, and Adjoining Provinces with the History, and Copious Illustrations, of the Past and Present Condition of that Country.* London: Kingsbury Parbury and Allen, Leadenhall Street.

Malekandathil, P. (2010, revd. edn. 2013). *Maritime India: Trade, Religion and Polity in the Indian Ocean.* New Delhi: Primus Books.

Mani, S. (February 2019). 'Robot Apocalypse: How Will Automation Affect India's Manufacturing Industry?' *Economic and Political Weekly*, 54(8): 40-8.

Marshall, S.J. (1951). *Taxila.* Cambridge: Cambridge University Press.

Martin, M. (ed.). (1837). *The Despatches, Minutes, and Correspondence of the Marquess Wellesley, K.G., During His Administration in India.* London: W.H. Allen & Co.

McKinsey Global Institute (2015). *Global Growth: Can Productivity Save the Day in an Aging World.* McKinsey & Company.

Meister, M.W. (1979). 'Mandala and Practice in Nagara Architecture in North India'. *Journal of the American Oriental Society*, 99(2): 204-19.

Ministry of Finance, Government of India (2017). *Economic Survey 2016-17.* New Delhi: Government of India.

—— (2018). *Economic Survey: 2017-18.* New Delhi: Government of India.

Ministry of Steel (2019). *Annual Report, 2018-19.* Ministry of Steel, Government of India. New Delhi: Ministry of Steel, Government of India.

Moosvi, S. (2008, rpt. 2010). *People, Taxation and Trade in Mughal India.* New Delhi: Oxford University Press.

Mukerji, N.G. (1903). *A Monograph on the Silk Fabrics of Bengal.* Calcutta: Government Secretariat Press.

Mukherjee, T. (2009). 'The Co-Ordinating State and the Economy: The Nizamat in Eighteenth-Century'. *Modern Asian Studies*, 43(2): 389-436.

Mun, T. (1895). *England's Treasure by Forraign Trade, or, The Ballance of Our Forraign Trade is the Rule of Our Treasure written by Thomas Mun; and Now Published for the Common Good by his son John Mun.* London: Macmillan.

Narasimha, R. (1985). *Rockets in Mysore and Britain, 1750-1850 AD.* Retrieved 23 June 2018, from Institutional Repository@NAL: http://nal-ir.nal.res.in/id/eprint/2382

Nautiyal, K.P. and B.M. Khanduri (1988-9). 'Excavations of a Vedic Brick Altar At Purola, District Uttarkashi, Central Himalaya'. *Puratattva*, 19: 68-9.

Nightingale, F. (1863). *Notes on Hospitals.* London: Longman, Green, Longman, Roberts and Green.

NSSO (2011). *NSS Report No. 537: Employment and Unemployment Situation in India. NSS 66th Round. July 2009-June 2010.* New Delhi: Ministry of Statistics and Program Implementation, Government of India.

—— (2013). *NSS Report No. 551: Status of Education and Vocational Training in India; NSS 66th Round; July 2009-June 2010.* New Delhi: Ministry of Statistics and Program Implmentation, Government of India.

Oaten, E.F. (1909). *European Tavellers in India.* London: Kegan Paul and Trubner.

O'Brien, P.K. and P.A. Hunt (10 December 1992). *English State Taxes and Other Revenues, 1559-1603.* Retrieved 4 November 2017, from http://www.esfdb.org/table.aspx?resourceid=11227

Ovington, J. (1929). *A Voyage to Surat in the Year 1689*, ed. H.G. Rawlinson. London: Humphrey Milford.

Parrish, J.B. (1956). 'Iron and Steel in the Balance of World Power'. *Journal of Political Economy*, 64(5): 369-88.

Pemble, J. (1976). 'Resources and Techniques in the Second Maratha War'. *The Historical Journal*, 19(2), 375-404.

PeopleStrong, Confederation of Indian Industry, Wheebox (2014). *The India Skills Report 2014*. Retrieved 21 February 2016, from https://www.google.com/url?sa=t&rct=j&q=&esrc=s&source=web&cd=4 &cad=rja&uact=8&ved=2ahUKEwiDv8z7lv7hAhXLbSsKHY 6eDSwQFjADegQIBRAC&url=https%3A%2F%2Fwheebox.com% 2Fwheebox%2Fresources%2FIndiaSkillsReport.pdf& usg=AOvVaw3W3XVPBS1694NLuH59RtmI

Pingree, D. (Fall 2003). 'The logic of non-Western Science: Mathematical Discoveries in Medieval India'. *Daedalus*, 132(4): 45-53.

Prakash, B. (1991). 'Metallurgy of Iron and Steel Making and Blacksmithy in Ancient India'. *Indian Journal of History of Science*, 26(4): 351-71.

Prakash, B. and K. Igaki (1984). 'Ancient Iron Making in Bastar District'. *Indian Journal of History of Science*, 19(2): 172-85.

Prakash, O. (1985). *The Dutch East India Company and the Economy of Bengal, 1630-1720*. Princeton, New Jersey: Princeton University Press.

Raj, G. (2000). *Reach for the Stars: The Evolution of India's Rocket Programme*. New Delhi: Penguin Books India.

Rajivlochan, M. and M. Rajivlochan (2006). *Farmers Suicides: Facts and Possible Policy Interventions*. Pune: YASHADA.

RBSA (2018). Retrieved 26 January 2019, from https://rbsa.in/archives_of_research_reports/RBSA_Advisors_ Reward_of_The_Rupee.pdf

Reibold, M.P. (2009). 'Discovery of Nanotubes in Ancient Damascus Steel'. In D. T. Cat (ed.), *Physics and Engineering of New Materials* (pp. 305-10). Berlin, Germany: Springer-Verlag Berlin and Heidelberg GmbH & Co.

Roy, T. (2007). 'Out of Tradition: Master Artisans and Economic Change in Colonial India'. *The Journal of Asian Studies*, 66(6): 963-91.

Salim, G.H. (1902). *Riyaz-us-Salatin, a History of Bengal*. (tr. M.A. Salam) Calcutta: Asiatic Society.

Sato, M. and B. Bhadani (1987). *Economy and Polity of Rajasthan: Study of Kota and Marwar*. Jaipur: Jaipur Publication Scheme.

Scott, W.R. (1910). *The Constitution and Finance of English, Scottish and Irish Joint-Stock Companies to 1720*. Cambridge: Cambridge University Press.

Sen, A., P. Ghosh, K. Gupta and H.C. Bohra (1981). *Sheep in Rajasthan*. Jodhpur: Central Arid Zone Research Institute.

Shetty, M. (8 August 2015). *SBI Uses Big Data*. Retrieved 25 January 2017, from *Times of India*: http://timesofindia.indiatimes.com/business/india-business/SBI-uses-big-data-mining-to-check-defaults-biz-loss/articleshow/48397829.cms

Singh, Dilbagh (1990). *The State, Landlords and Peasants: Rajasthan in the 18th Century*. New Delhi: Manohar.

Sinha, N.K. (1956). *The Economic History of Bengal: From Plassey to the Permanent Settlement.* Calcutta: Firma K.L. Mukhopadhyay.

Sivramkrishna, S. (2009). 'Ascertaining Living Standards in Erstwhile Mysore, Southern India, from Francis Buchanan's Journey of 1800-01: An Empirical Contribution to the Great Divergence Debate'. *Journal of the Social and Economic History of the Orient*, 52(4/5): 695-733.

Sixth Report from the Select Committee, Appointed to take into Consideration the State of the Administration of Justice in the provinces of Bengal, Bahar and Orissa. House of Commons Parliamentary Papers. London: House of Commons Parliamentary Papers (1782).

Sukthankar, V.S. (ed.). (n.d.). http://sanskritdocuments.org/mirrors/mahabharata/mahabharata-bori.html. Retrieved January 2017.

Supplement Rasaratnasamuccaya (n.d.). *Indian Journal of History of Science*, 24(1).

Sykes, W.H. (1847). 'Vital Statistics of the East India Company's Armies in India, European and Native'. *Journal of the Statistical Society of London*, 10(2), 100-31.

Taknet, D.K. (2015). *The Marwari Heritage* (ed. V. Baswani). Jaipur: International Institute of Management and Entrepreneurship.

Temple, R.C. (ed.). (1911). *The Diaries of Streynsham Master, 1675-80.* London: Government of India.

Terry, E. (1707). *A Voyage to East-India: Wherein Some things are Taken Notice of, In Our Passage Thither, But Many More in Our Abode There, Within That Rich and Most Spacious Empire of the Great Mogul.* London: J. Wilkie and Co.

de Thevenot, J. (1687). *The Travels of Monsieur de Thevenot into the Levant* (in three parts). (tr. A. Lovell) London: H. Faithorne, J. Adamforn, C. Skegnes and T. Newborough.

Thibaut, D.G. (1875). 'On the Sulvasutras'. *Journal of the Asiatic Society of Bengal*, III: 227-75.

Tone, W.H. (1800). 'An Illustration of Some Institutions of the Mahratta People'. *The Asiatic Annual Register, A View of The History of Hindustan, and of the Politics, Commerce and Literature of Asia, for the Year 1799.* London: J. Debrett, Piccadilly.

Tyagi, M. (2014). 'The Role of "Hundis" in the Jaipur Kingdom in Pre-Colonial India'. *Social Scientist*, 42(3/4): 25-44.

U.S. Bureau of Economic Analysis (n.d.). *https://fred.stlouisfed.org/series/GNPA*. Retrieved 4 January 2018.

Useful Tables forming an Appendix to the Journal of the Asiatic Society, Part the

First, Coins, Weights and Measures of British India (1834). Calcutta: Baptist Mission Press.

Varahamihira (1981, rpt. 1986). *Brhat Samhita.* (tr. M.R. Bhat). Delhi: Motilal Banarsidass.

Voysey, D. (1832). 'Description of the Native Manufacture of Steel in Southern India (Extracted from the manuscript journals of the late Dr. Voysey)', ed. J. Prinsep. *Journal of the Asiatic Society of Bengal*, vol. I, no. 6: 245-7.

Watt, S.G. (1899). *Dictionary of the Economic Products of India.* Calcutta: Government of India.

Wellington, A.D. (1859). *Supplementary Despatches and Memoranda of Field Marshal Arthur Duke of Wellington, K.G.: India, 1797-1805*, ed. D. Arthur Richard Wellesley. London: John Allen.

West, M.D. and C. Lansang (2018). *Global Manufacturing Scorecard: How the US Compares to 18 Other Nations.* Brookings Institution. Retricved from https://www.brookings.edu/research/global-manufacturing-scorecard-how-the-us-compares-to-18-other-nations

White, D.L. (1995). *Competition and Collaboration, Parsi Merchants and the English East India Company in 18th Century India.* New Delhi: Munshiram Manoharlal.

World Bank. (1990). *World Development Report 1990: Poverty.* Oxford: Oxford University Press.

—— (2017). *Data: GDP (current US$).* Retrieved 4 January 2018, from https://data.worldbank.org/indicator/NY.GDP.MKTP. CD?locations=US-IN

—— (April 2018). *Poverty and Equity Brief, South Asia: India.* Retrieved November 14, 2018, from https://databank.worldbank.org/data/download/poverty/33EF03BB-9722-4AE2-ABC7-AA2972D68AFE/Archives-2018/Global_POVEQ_ IND.pdf

Index